The Letters of Hildegard of Bingen

The Letters of Hildegard of Bingen

VOLUME I

Translated by

Joseph L. Baird
Radd K. Ehrman

New York   Oxford
OXFORD UNIVERSITY PRESS

Oxford University Press

Oxford New York
Athens Auckland Bangkok Bogotá Bombay
Buenos Aires Calcutta Cape Town Dar es Salaam
Delhi Florence Hong Kong Istanbul Karachi
Kuala Lumpur Madras Madrid Melbourne
Mexico City Nairobi Paris Singapore
Taipei Tokyo Toronto Warsaw

and associated companies in
Berlin Ibadan

Copyright © 1994 by Oxford University Press

First published in 1994 by Oxford University Press, Inc.
198 Madison Avenue, New York, New York 10016

First issued as an Oxford University Press paperback, 1998.

Oxford is a registered trademark of Oxford University Press, Inc.

All rights reserved. No part of this publication may be reproduced,
stored in a retrieval system, or transmitted, in any form or by any means,
electronic, mechanical, photocopying, recording, or otherwise,
without the prior permission of Oxford University Press.

Library of Congress Cataloging-in-Publication Data
Hildegard, Saint, 1098-1179.
[Correspondence. English]
The letters of Hildegard of Bingen / translated by
Joseph L. Baird, Radd K. Ehrman.
p. cm. Includes bibliographical references and index.
ISBN 0-19-508937-5 (v. 1); ISBN 0-19-512117-1 (pbk.)
1. Hildegard, Saint, 1098-1179—Correspondence. 2. Christian
saints—Germany—Bingen (Rhineland-Palatinate)—Correspondence.
3. Bingen (Rhineland-Palatinate, Germany)—Biography. I. Baird,
Joseph L. II. Ehrman, Radd K. III. Title.
BX4700.H5A3 1994
282'.092—dc20
[B]   93-33715

1 3 5 7 9 8 6 4 2

Printed in the United States of America
on acid-free paper

*This book is severally dedicated,
to Four Extraordinary Women*

to my mother *in memoriam*
Bertis Lee Baird
1909–1989

to her granddaughter
Bertis Eve Baird
1966–

AND

to my mother, Leta Ehrman
and my wife, Cynthia Ehrman

Acknowledgments

As is usual for any work of this magnitude, debts have accumulated, and it is our pleasure here to acknowledge our gratitude. First and foremost, we owe our deepest appreciation to Professor Barbara Newman of Northwestern University, without whose learned criticism and creative insight this work would never have achieved its present form. From very early on when this book was still work in progress, Professor Newman answered our queries with courtesy and *humanitate*, and, later, she read the entire manuscript with meticulous attention. We are deeply endebted to her wisdom and experience. We would also like to thank Professor Monika Klaes for her quick response to our letter of enquiry about the letters not contained in Van Acker, and for her generous permission to use her edition of these important letters in our work. All Hildegard scholars are, of course, endebted to Lieven Van Acker for his excellent edition of the correspondence, but our debt is more specific, and we would like to express our appreciation here for his unfailing courtesy and helpfulness in all his contacts with us. Appreciation is due, too, to Timothy Reuter, who answered our electronic cry for help about a puzzling image in one of the letters with an E-mail message from Munich.

Thanks are due also to our friends and colleagues at Kent State University: to Kirk Freudenburg, who puzzled with us, on numerous occasions, over Hildegard's peculiar Latin constructions; to Harold Fry, Ron Crawford, and Emil Sattler, for their expert German assistance; to Rick Newton, for encouragement and support; to Marjorie Pagan, for photocopying, general helpfulness, and unfailing pleasantness; to Baird's informal Latin group—Andy Wilson, Filitsa and John Mullen, and Jeff Simcox—for their enthusiasm and interest in the project; and to Michael Nagy, for his Fridays.

Finally, we are grateful to the Kent State University Research Office for support in the form of photocopying funds.

Contents

Introduction, 3

Letter 1   Hildegard to Bernard, Abbot of Clairvaux, 27
Letter 1r   Abbot Bernard of Clairvaux to Hildegard, 31
Letter 2   Hildegard to Pope Eugenius, 32
Letter 3   Hildegard to Pope Eugenius, 33
Letter 4   Pope Eugenius to Hildegard, 34
Letter 5   Hildegard to Pope Eugenius, 36
Letter 6   Hildegard to Pope Eugenius, 37
Letter 7   Hildegard to Bernard and Gregory, Cardinals, 39
Letter 8   Hildegard to Pope Anastasius, 41
Letter 9   Hildegard to Pope Hadrian, 44
Letter 10   Hildegard to Pope Alexander III, 45
Letter 10r   Pope Alexander III to Wezelinus, 46
Letter 11   Hildegard to Hartwig, Archbishop of Bremen, 47
Letter 12   Hildegard to Hartwig, Archbishop of Bremen, 48
Letter 13   Hartwig, Archbishop of Bremen, to Hildegard, 49
Letter 13r   Hildegard to Hartwig, Archbishop of Bremen, 51
Letter 14   Arnold, Archbishop of Cologne, to Hildegard, 52
Letter 14r   Hildegard to Arnold, Archbishop of Cologne, 53
Letter 15   Dean Philip and the Clerics of Cologne to Hildegard, 53
Letter 15r   Hildegard to the Shepherds of the Church, 54

Letter 16   Philip, Archbishop of Cologne, to Hildegard, 65
Letter 16r Hildegard to Philip, Archbishop of Cologne, 66
Letter 17   Hildegard to Philip, Archbishop of Cologne, 68
Letter 18   Heinrich, Archbishop of Mainz, to Hildegard, 69
Letter 18r Hildegard to Heinrich, Archbishop of Mainz, 70
Letter 19   Hildegard to Heinrich, Archbishop of Mainz, 71
Letter 20   Arnold, Archbishop of Mainz, to Hildegard, 71
Letter 20r Hildegard to Arnold, Archbishop of Mainz, 72
Letter 21   Hildegard to Conrad, Archbishop of Mainz, 73
Letter 22   Conrad, Archbishop of Mainz, to Hildegard, 74
Letter 22r Hildegard to Conrad, Archbishop of Mainz, 75
Letter 23   Hildegard to the prelates at Mainz, 76
Letter 24   Hildegard to Christian, Archbishop of Mainz, 80
Letter 24r Christian, Archbishop of Mainz, to Hildegard, 82
Letter 25   Eberhard, Archbishop of Salzburg, to Hildegard, 84
Letter 25r Hildegard to Eberhard, Archbishop of Salzburg, 85
Letter 26   Hillinus, Archbishop of Trier, to Hildegard, 86
Letter 26r Hildegard to Hillinus, Archbishop of Trier, 88
Letter 27   Arnold, Archbishop of Trier, to Hildegard, 89
Letter 27r Hildegard to Arnold, Archbishop of Trier, 90
Letter 28   Hildegard to Arnold, Archbishop of Trier, 92
Letter 29   Arnold, Superior of St. Andrew in Cologne, to Hildegard, 93
Letter 30   Hildegard to Eberhard, Bishop of Bamberg, 93
Letter 31   Eberhard, Bishop of Bamberg, to Hildegard, 94
Letter 31r Hildegard to Eberhard, Bishop of Bamberg, 95
Letter 32   Henry, Bishop of Beauvais, to Hildegard, 99
Letter 32r Hildegard to Henry, Bishop of Beauvais, 100
Letter 33   Hildegard to Gero, Bishop of Halberstadt, 100
Letter 34   Amalricus, Bishop of Jerusalem, to Hildegard, 101
Letter 35   Hermann, Bishop of Constance, to Hildegard, 102
Letter 35r Hildegard to Hermann, Bishop of Constance, 103
Letter 36   Hildegard to Hermann, Bishop of Constance, 104
Letter 37   Heinrich, Bishop of Liège, to Hildegard, 104
Letter 37r Hildegard to Heinrich, Bishop of Liège, 105
Letter 38   Daniel, Bishop of Prague, to Hildegard, 106
Letter 38r Hildegard to Daniel, Bishop of Prague, 107
Letter 39   Odo of Soissons to Hildegard, 108

Letter 39r	Hildegard to Odo of Soissons, 109
Letter 40	Odo of Soissons to Hildegard, 109
Letter 40r	Hildegard to Odo of Paris, 111
Letter 41	Gunther, Bishop of Speyer, to Hildegard, 112
Letter 41r	Hildegard to Gunther, Bishop of Speyer, 113
Letter 42	Hildegard to Godfrey, Bishop of Utrecht, 114
Letter 43	Godfrey, Bishop of Utrecht, to Hildegard, 115
Letter 43r	Hildegard to Godfrey, Bishop of Utrecht, 116
Letter 44	Adelbert, Bishop of Verdun, to Hildegard, 117
Letter 45	Conrad, Bishop of Worms, to Hildegard, 117
Letter 45r	Hildegard to Conrad, Bishop of Worms, 118
Letter 46	Hildegard to Abbot Wolfard, 119
Letter 47	Hildegard to Prior Frederick, 120
Letter 48	Godfrey the Monk to Hildegard, 120
Letter 48r	Hildegard to the Monk Godfrey, 121
Letter 49	An Abbess to Hildegard, 122
Letter 49r	Hildegard to the Abbess, 123
Letter 50	Abbess Sophia to Hildegard, 123
Letter 50r	Hildegard to the Abbess Sophia, 124
Letter 51	Certain Monks to Hildegard, 125
Letter 52	Mistress Tengswich to Hildegard, 127
Letter 52r	Hildegard to the Congregation of Nuns, 128
Letter 53	Canon Udalric to Hildegard, 130
Letter 53r	Hildegard to Canon Udalric, 131
Letter 54	Hildegard to Provost Andrew, 131
Letter 55	An Abbot to Hildegard, 132
Letter 55r	Hildegard to the Abbot, 133
Letter 56	Hildegard to an Abbot, 134
Letter 57	Hildegard to an Abbot, 134
Letter 58	Hildegard to Prior Dimo, 136
Letter 59	Hildegard to the Congregation of Monks, 137
Letter 60	An Abbot to Hildegard, 139
Letter 61	An Abbess to Hildegard, 139
Letter 61r	Hildegard to the Abbess, 140
Letter 62	Gertrude, a Nun, to Hildegard, 141
Letter 62r	Hildegard to the Nun Gertrude, 142
Letter 63	Hildegard to the Congregation of Nuns, 143

Letter 64	Hildegard to Abbess Richardis, 143
Letter 65	Hildegard to a Certain Monk, 144
Letter 66	A Certain Superior to Hildegard, 145
Letter 66r	Hildegard to the Superior, 145
Letter 67	Hildegard to the Priest Berthold, 146
Letter 68	Abbot Gedolphus to Hildegard, 147
Letter 68r	Hildegard to Abbot Gedolphus, 148
Letter 69	Gedolphus to Hildegard, 151
Letter 70	Five Abbots to Hildegard, 152
Letter 70r	Hildegard to the Five Abbots, 153
Letter 71	Hildegard to an Abbot, 155
Letter 72	The Abbot to Hildegard, 156
Letter 72r	Hildegard to the Abbot, 157
Letter 73	Hildegard to the Congregation of Nuns, 157
Letter 74	Abbot Kuno to Hildegard, 158
Letter 74r	Hildegard to Abbot Kuno, 159
Letter 75	Hildegard to the Abbot, 162
Letter 76	Abbot Helengerus to Hildegard, 163
Letter 76r	Hildegard to Abbot Helengerus, 164
Letter 77	Abbot Helengerus to Hildegard, 165
Letter 77r	Hildegard to Abbot Helengerus, 166
Letter 78	Prior Adelbert to Hildegard, 172
Letter 78r	Hildegard to the Congregation of Monks, 173
Letter 79	Hildegard to a Certain Monk, 176
Letter 80	Morard, Monk, to Hildegard, 176
Letter 80r	Hildegard to the Monk Morard, 177
Letter 81	Hildegard to the Abbot Ruthard, 178
Letter 82	Abbot Eberhard to Hildegard, 179
Letter 83	The Congregation of Monks to Hildegard, 180
Letter 83r	Hildegard to the Congregation of Monks, 180
Letter 84	A Prior to Hildegard, 181
Letter 84r	Hildegard to the Prior, 183
Letter 85	Abbot Adam to Hildegard, 191
Letter 85r/a	Hildegard to Abbot Adam, 192
Letter 85r/b	Hildegard to Adam, the Abbot, 195
Letter 86	Hildegard to Adam, Abbot, 196
Letter 87	A Certain Monk to Hildegard, 197

Letter 87r/a Hildegard to the Secretary, 198
Letter 87r/b Hildegard to the Secretary, 199
Letter 88 Hildegard to a Hospitaler, 199
Letter 89 Hildegard to Rudeger, the Monk, 200
Letter 90 Hildegard to a Certain Monk, 201

Endnotes, 203
Bibliography, 217
Scripture Index, 221
General Index, 223

The Letters of Hildegard of Bingen

Introduction

It must have been an awe-inspiring sight, a truly lovely and captivating scene: On solemn feast days the ladies of Mount St. Rupert, all of noble lineage, gathered in procession and made their way slowly to the choir, walking in splendor, clad all in white, with silk veils so long they reached to their feet and lightly touched the floor. With the grace natural to their highborn estate, they walked, with unbound, free-flowing hair, and with elegant gold rings on their fingers. They sang as they walked, their melodious voices pouring forth psalms and hymns of praise to the Divine, and on their heads they wore crowns of gold filigree that at once affirmed and belied their earthly nobility, for, emphasizing spiritual other-ness, these resplendent circlets bore figures of the cross on the sides and back, and, on the front, the confirming image of the *Agnus Dei*. And all was graceful beauty, loveliness and melody, and unstinting praise, like a vision of paradise—a ceremony fit for the King, the outer splendor deliberately calculated to reflect the inward spirituality.

And yet, to some, it was a distasteful, even irreligious, ceremony, for we learn of the extraordinary activity of this extraordinary monastery under the governance of Hildegard of Bingen only from a hostile source (see Letter 52). These charges against her—of accepting only nobility into her community, of indulging feminine vanity—Hildegard answered, in part, by what must surely be the highest paean of praise to womankind to come down to us from the Middle Ages: "O woman, what a splendid being you are! For you have set your foundation in the sun, and you have conquered the world" (Letter 52r).

Although Hildegard continues her defense by asserting that the strictures against feminine decoration do not apply to virgins, who stand "in the unsullied purity of paradise," she does not, as might have been expected, elaborate the argument by recourse to the medieval commonplace of the monastery as the *hortus conclusus,* "the enclosed garden," the earthly paradise wherein the tranquillity and beauty of the supernal could, in part, be recaptured. Yet such an image, such a complex of ideas, must, surely, have been latent in her thought as she worked out the myriad details of this uncommon ceremony. Indeed, in another letter (23), she makes an argument of just that kind for the power and efficacy of music. Inspired by the Holy Spirit, the prophets, she asserts,

> were called for this purpose: not only to compose psalms and canticles (by which the hearts of listeners would be inflamed) but also to construct various kinds of musical instruments to enhance these songs of praise with melodic strains. Thereby, both through the form and quality of the instruments, as well as through the meaning of the words which accompany them, those who hear might be taught about inward things, since they have been admonished and aroused by outward things. In such a way, these holy prophets get beyond the music of this exile and recall to mind that divine melody of praise which Adam, in company with the angels, enjoyed in God before his fall.

It is fortunate that so large a collection of the correspondence—nearly 400 of Hildegard's own letters—has been preserved, for these epistles enlarge our view of Hildegard far beyond that of the near-unapproachable seer of the *Scivias* and the other visionary works. In these letters, instead, we find the practical abbess, as above, concerning herself with the pragmatic details of religious ceremony, a ritual modeled, to be sure, on her ethereal visions of the celestial virtues but worked out nonetheless on an earthly plane. In this instance, too, it is significant that we are privileged to see her through the eyes—the unawed eyes at that—of a contemporary. Or we find her, as in the other letter referred to above, working toward a still inchoate philosophy of music, a theory that, one has the sense, might well have been worked out in far more systematic detail in another visionary work if she had lived a few years longer.

None of this is to say, of course, that the seer is not present in the letters. Far from it. Here, too, as elsewhere, there is a continual oscillation between the almost abject humility of the "poor little form of a woman" and the commanding authority of the voice of the Living Light, so much so indeed that they often merge so completely that it is difficult to determine who is Who. Still, there is something far more personal here: the near hysteria of the woman who has recourse to the authority of the Living Light in a desperate—and futile—attempt to hold on to the beloved nun who has been taken from her; the sorrowful resignation, without recriminations, upon receiving word of the untimely death of that nun; the deep sorrow on the loss of music to her community through the edicts of excommunication; the care taken to respond to even the most trivial of requests from those who sought her out as the very oracle of God; the continuing devoted memory to those who cared for her, taught her, and loved her as a child; the stubborn refusal to compromise her principles, even in advanced old age, despite the threat and, eventually, the fact of interdict; the sheer audacity of the woman, who felt herself buoyed by the wings of the Divine, and called forth the strength to speak out to a weak, effeminate age; et cetera.

Hildegard of Bingen was born in 1098 in Bermersheim, a small town not far from Mainz, the tenth child of a local nobleman named Hildebert and his wife Mechthild. From earliest childhood she gave indications of unusual faculties, seeing, as she herself affirms, brilliant lights and strange visions. In her childish naivete, she thought that everybody "saw" as she did, and so she queried her nurse, but, receiving a negative, was abashed and resolved to keep her peace. It was as early as the age of three—or five, according to the prefatory remarks in the *Scivias*—that she began experiencing such paranormal phenomena when she saw a light so bright that *anima mea contremuit*, "my very soul shook."[1] Perhaps because she was such an unusual, other-worldly, child, or perhaps simply because, as the tenth child of her parents, she was offered up as a spiritual tithe, at the age of eight she was presented as an oblate to God. At this time she entered a small cell attached to the Benedictine monastery of Mount St. Disibod, where she was entrusted to the care of the anchoress Jutta of Sponheim. Here she was to stay—in relative obscurity—for some thirty years. The early years she spent alone with Jutta, but the little cell of two grew as, over the years, more and more noble, young girls placed themselves under Jutta's governance, and upon Jutta's death in 1136 Hildegard herself was elected to her position as head of the community.

From Jutta, Hildegard received a rudimentary education, or, as the *Vita* (I.i.2) puts it, she was taught the Psalter, that is, presumably, she was taught to read Latin. Beyond this early nurturing, the most significant service that Jutta performed was to put Hildegard in contact with the monk Volmar, who not only continued, and broadened, her education, but once she began her own writing career, served as her secretary, confidant, and friend for the rest of his life (and much of hers) until his death in 1173. It was Volmar who encouraged her to begin her first major work, the *Scivias*, exhorting her to put those things in writing "secretly," until he could determine what they were and from whence they came. And it was Volmar, who, once convinced of the divine inspiration, brought her writing to the attention of Kuno, abbot of St. Disibod. Kuno brought the matter to the attention of Heinrich, archbishop of Mainz; and Heinrich, to Pope Eugenius, who just happened to be presiding over the Synod of Trier in 1147–48, and from that happy coincidence the career—and fame—of Hildegard took wing. The pope himself read Hildegard's work to the assembled prelates. They were all duly impressed, and impelled by their urging (along with the specific support of Bernard of Clairvaux), Eugenius gave his sanction to her work, and commanded her to continue writing. The correspondence itself began in that same eventful year of 1147, when, only a short time before the reading in Trier, Hildegard wrote to Bernard seeking his advice and approval.

At this point Hildegard is forty-nine years old! She had received the call to put her visions into writing only some six years earlier, in 1141. Thus it is startling to realize, on reviewing the facts of her history, that she did not begin her lifework—at least her public lifework—until she was forty-three, and this despite the fact that she had been receiving visions from infancy. That long delay was doubtless the result of the accident of gender.[2] What one can say, most certainly, is that from the age of forty-three forward, until her death at eighty-one (even old age seeming powerless to slow her down), Hildegard—to use an image dear to her heart—tilled the Lord's garden with great diligence. She produced six major written works, she founded two flourishing monasteries, she wrote music, she gave birth to the earliest full-fledged morality play, she became the correspondent—and advisor—of popes, kings, emperor. It was a full life indeed.

The extent of Hildegard's education is a problem not likely ever to be solved. We know that Jutta supplied rudimentary instruction, and that Volmar built on that foundation. Beyond that, not very much. We know that her grasp of Latin syntax and structure is somewhat less than certain, and we know that she herself always claims, insists (and others insist for her), that she is *indocta*, "unlearned" and untaught. Concerning this matter, the author of the *Vita* (II.i.14) writes:

> It is a great and wondrous matter that she wrote with her own hand,[3] and uttered aloud with a pure, unsullied mind those things which she heard and saw in her spirit, using the same sense and the same words. She was content to rely on only one faithful man as her collaborator, who undertook to arrange the cases, tenses, and genders grammatically (since she herself was unschooled in grammar). He did not, however, take it upon himself to add or subtract anything whatsoever from the sense or meaning.

And Hildegard is even more determined to deny any mere earthly learning. She acknowledges her celestial knowledge, of course, is confident—even defiant—in her possession of it, but that knowledge came, as it were, despite her ignorance, or perhaps not *despite* but *because* of it:

> I saw a great splendor in which resounded a voice from Heaven, saying to me, "O fragile human, ashes of ashes, and filth of filth! Say and write what you see and hear. But since you are timid in speaking, and simple in expounding, and untaught in writing, speak and write these things not by human mouth, and not by the understanding of human invention, and not by the requirements of human composition, but as you see and hear them on high in the heavenly places in the wonders of God. . . . " And immediately I knew the meaning of the exposition of the Scriptures, namely, the Psalter, the Gospel and the other catholic volumes of both the Old and the New Testaments, though I did not have the interpretation of the words of their texts or the division of the syllables or the knowledge of cases or tenses.[4]

A part of this attitude is owing, of course, to pure convention, to the omnipresent humility formula, but in this case it seems to be that *and much more*. The more the *paupercula* "the poor little form of a woman" stresses her wretchedness, her humility, her ignorance of earthly learning, the more credence is given to her otherworldly illumination. How could one lacking the very basic instruments of grammar speak with such authority, such great confidence, unless inspired by the Divine? In this respect it is interesting to note Volmar's response on first learning of Hildegard's visions: he sought to discover what these visions were and whence they had come. For him, there was no question of the inspiration, only a matter of the direction from which that inspiration had come.

In any case, whatever weight we might feel compelled to give to her protestations of ignorance, it is certainly true that her learning and ability far exceed that of the acquisition of the mere rudiments of Latin, however shaky her grammar may be at times. On occasion she soars to real grandeur and eloquence, as in her learned disquisition on the wondrous properties of music (Letter 23), or in her majestic trumpeting forth of her own divine mission (*Scivias* "Protestificatio"), or in her use of humble, homey images to express a divine purpose (like, for instance, her vision of herself as a helpless feather conveyed by the wind of the Holy Spirit, used again and again in the letters and elsewhere), or in her (calculated?) shift between the extreme humility of the wretched woman and the thundering, commanding voice of the Living Light (used throughout). Moreover, she was far more widely read than her protestations would lead one to believe. Peter Dronke has argued for her acquaintance not only with the Scriptures but also with the writings of the Church Fathers (perhaps even including Origen), as well as with Classical texts such as Cicero's *De Natura Deorum*, Lucan's *Pharsalia*, and Seneca's *Quaestiones Naturales*.[5]

One of the greatest challenges in reading (and translating) Hildegard indeed comes not from her own difficulty with the scholarly language, but, as it were, from her very ease with it, her fecund and canny use of its creative possibilities. Perhaps the most notable example of this is her use of *viriditas*, a word never far from Hildegard's reach. This *viriditas*, this despair of translators, this "greenness" enters into the very fabric of the universe in Hildegard's cosmic scheme of things. In Hildegard's usage it is a profound, immense, dynamically energized term. The world in the height of the spring season is filled with *viriditas*, God breathed the breath of *viriditas* into the inhabitants of the garden of Eden, even the smallest twig on the most insignificant tree is animated with *viriditas*, the sun brings the life of *viriditas* into the world; and (in the spiritual realm) the prelate who is filled with *taedium* (weariness) is lacking in *viriditas*, the garden where the virtues grow is imbued with *viriditas*, the neophyte must strive for *viriditas*, and the holy Virgin is the *viridissima virga*. Hildegard can even speak with aplomb of a saint as the *viriditas digiti Dei*, "the *viriditas* of the finger of God," as she does of St. Disibod (Letter 74r).

For *viriditas* to flourish—in the natural world, in the spiritual realm—there must be moisture *(humor, humiditas)*, another concept Hildegard has taken over and made wholly her own. Even the very stones have *humor* (Letter 31r), and if earth did not have *humiditatem et viriditatem*, it would crumble like ashes. "For I"—so speaks the mystic voice through Hildegard—"formed rocks from fire and water like bones, and I established earth from *humiditate et viriditate* like marrow" (Letter 15r). And this, too, is spiritual, since *humiditas* and *viriditas* are, as manifestations of God's power, qualities of the human soul, for "the grace of God shines like the sun and sends its gifts in various ways: in wisdom *(sapientia)*, in viridity *(viriditate)*, in moisture *(humiditate)*" (Letter 85r/b). It is for such reasons that Hildegard continuously advises her correspondents to be on guard lest their virtues become as dry as the dust: "Watch carefully lest your God-given viridity dry up *(arescat)* because of the instability of your thought" (Letter 85r/a); or ends a letter with the devout reflection, "May your eye live in God, and may the viridity of your soul never dry up *(arescat)*" (Letter 20r). Thought of this sort leads naturally to the garden imagery in which Hildegard's works, including the letters, abound.

And this leads to an understanding of Hildegard's enigmatic *pigmentarius* as a designation for bishops or priests,[6] a usage that has never been satisfactorily explained. This word, which in its basic sense means "a dealer in paints or perfumes," still carries, for Hildegard, an aura of color and fragrance, for it has to do with gardens, and, as might be expected, gardens both physical and spiritual. A *pigmentarius* is apparently one who, by his industry, works to enhance the lovely colors and delightful odors of his flower or herb garden. In Letter 84r, for example, Hildegard exhorts a prior to rouse the members of his order "out of their ignorance, just as a good *pigmentarius* eradicates rank weeds from his garden." Thus the administrator or prelate, in Hildegard's special language, becomes the gardener, whose spiritual responsibility it is to dutifully tend his garden. It is for this reason that Hildegard uses the phrase *vivens odor* as a designation for "monk." None of this is, of course, mere frivolous quibbling or light word play. It is grounded firmly in *viriditas* and *humor/humiditas* and the thorough merging of the physical/spiritual so characteristic of Hildegard's thought.

That these ideas are habitual with Hildegard from her earliest writing can be seen in the peroration of her letter to St. Bernard, the opening missive of her correspondence, where one can also see something of the eloquence that she is sometimes capable of in her exalted mode:

> *Oro te per serenitatem Patris, et per eius Verbum admirabile, et per suauem humorem compunctionis, Spiritum veritatis, et per sanctum sonitum, per quem sonat omnis creatura, et per ipsum Verbum, de quo ortus est mundus, et per altitudinem Patris, qui in suaui uiriditate misit Verbum in Virginis uterum, unde suxit carnem sicut circumedificatur mel fauo.*

> And so I beseech your aid, through the serenity of the Father and through His wondrous Word and through the sweet moisture of compunction, the spirit of truth, and through that holy sound, which all creation echoes, and through that same Word which gave birth to the world, and through the sublimity of the Father, who sent the Word with sweet fruitfulness into the womb of the Virgin, from which He soaked up flesh, just as honey is surrounded by the honeycomb.

This present work is, of course, a collection of letters, but once that fact is acknowledged, qualifications are immediately in order. If, for example, readers bring to these letters the usual modern expectations of intimacy, self-revelation, relative brevity, or even notions of single-person-to-single-person communication, they are likely to be disappointed if not utterly mystified. Perhaps the most important factor to bear in mind with respect to medieval letter collections indeed is the general public-ness of the form, for the medieval letter was a far more public document than our modern predilections lead us to expect. Rarely, if ever, was an individual letter intended for a single recipient alone.[7] Modes of production (secretaries, copyists, etc.), modes of transmission (carriers, messengers), even modes of composition (copybooks containing model letters) made real privacy unlikely at best; and the mode, inevitably, helped to shape and mold the form. As a result, even in those instances where a letter addresses individual problems, it still tends to be cast in generalized, public form, laboriously working through its set formulas, agonizingly slow (from a modern perspective) to get to the main point at issue. And—though this is less the case with Hildegard's own letters than with letters addressed to her—those formulas tended to be very rigorous and complex, as prescribed by the popular *artes dictaminis*. This accounts for the elaborate salutations, for which there were very precise rules with respect to class, status, et cetera, as well as for the ostentatious (and, to modern ears, fulsome) praise directed to the intended recipient.[8] Yet perhaps the best evidence to confirm the public nature of the epistolary process lies in those instances where the letter that has come down to us consists wholly of formulas without any real substance at all. For sometimes the message was so private—or perhaps so dangerous—that to commit it to writing was, to say the least, impolitic. In such cases, the *nuncius* or carrier himself delivered the message orally, the "letter" serving simply as an introduction or as a token of respect and friendship to the recipient.[9] See, for example, Letters 11 and 45, where the point of the correspondence remains vaguely, maddeningly obscure.

The public nature of letters could also have disquieting consequences for what we like to think of as authenticity. The texts of letters, more perhaps than with other types of writing, were subject to various kinds of tampering, by recipient as well as original writer after the letter had been sent out. "The text of a letter," as Constable remarks (51),

> was liable to revision at any stage in its history from the original dictation up to its incorporation into the final collection or other form where it could rest secure from the hands of would-be improvers. These included not only the author but also scribes, secretaries, and even the recipients of letters, who were considered to own the texts of letters sent to them ... and were sometimes asked by the author to make changes in the text.

The correspondence between Hildegard and Tengswich of Andernach (Letters 53, 53r), for example, was subjected to substantial revision, the form in the later collection of the letters being an edited, "cleaned up" version of that in the earlier one.[10] Yet perhaps the greatest temptation for a copier or secretary was the addition of interesting, related, but non-authorial material to the text of a letter, or of merging two or even three different letters and presenting them as a single whole. A brief comparison of the *Patrologia* edition of the letters with Van Acker's will indicate how frequently the challenge of such temptations was taken up. Also, see Letter 15r in this collection, with its two long appendages of doubtfully authentic material, printed by Van Acker as appendices to the letter. This is, of course, a matter more pertinent to an edition than to a translation, but the reader ought to be aware of the problem.

A final factor that should be noted with respect to the medieval letter-form is the wide range of subject matter that was considered appropriate to the genre. Sometimes a letter, in its brevity and singularity of purpose, is little different from what we might expect from a modern writer, as, for example, Letter 68 in this collection, where Abbot Gedolphus of Brauweiler writes a simple request for help for a woman possessed of the devil—though even here it should be noted how delayed the request is by the necessities of form, a full paragraph of praise for the recipient of the letter. Yet this is scarcely the norm, for the medieval letter, and the letters collected here in particular, vary widely with respect to length, subject matter, and general mode of presentation. As Constable remarks (p. 14), "This concept of the letter as *sermo absentium* [word of the absent] opened the way to including within the epistolary genre many works—especially works like sermons and polemical treatises, in which the writer sought to appeal directly to the reader—that would not today commonly be written in the form of a letter." Thus the epistolary genre, with its openness of form, would appear to be the perfect medium for this twelfth-century seer, who had a great deal to say to the people of her time in all stations of life, and much of what she said was admonitory, edifying, and instructional. Herein, therefore, are to be found sermons and treatises, some of quite extensive length, and reports of visions and even a kind of prescribed exorcism ritual, as well as varied other subject matter. What one does not find here, at least not to speak of, is any kind of emotional self-revelation, even, for example, in those letters that deal with what we know was a great personal loss to Hildegard, the departure of her favorite nun, Richardis. This is the twelfth, not the nineteenth century.

Some knowledge of the political and religious climate of the time is also important for an understanding of the letters. The age into which Hildegard was born was a turbulent, disorderly age, a time of petty wars and fierce struggles, of unruly secular leaders and undisciplined Church officials, a time of popes and anti-popes, emperors and anti-emperors, a time, in short, of bloody conflict between Church and State. Henry IV, quixotic in disposition and thoroughly unprincipled in character, was king of Germany and putative ruler of the empire. This "worshipper of Baal," as Hildegard was later to call him, opposed the authority of the Church on all fronts, and, when he could not achieve his will through legitimate means, created his own anti-pope (Clement III), by whom he was crowned emperor some fourteen years before Hildegard's birth, in 1084. The history of Henry's reign is one of almost constant conflict and bloodshed, the balance of power shifting erratically back and forth between Empire and Church. When Henry sought a means to his coronation, he did not lack for bishops, and even cardinals, who were all too ready to fulfill his will by excommunicating and deposing the currently sitting pope. It was indeed against just this evil—a priesthood that owed its allegiance not to the mitre but to the crown—that the supreme office of the Church had rallied all its awesome powers in stubborn opposition.

By the late eleventh century, the Church had become thoroughly secularized. Church offices, from archbishoprics on down, were being bought and sold with impunity, real plums carrying with them massive power and influence going to the highest bidder without the slightest nod to the spiritual qualifications of the would-be incumbent. Specific examples of egregious abuses would be easy enough to cite (such as the case of one Godfrey, an ignorant and vicious man, who bought the archbishopric of Trier for a rumored 1,100 marks of silver), but the real problem lay in how commonplace the practice was, how generally accepted as the norm. Secular princes sold bishoprics and abbacies, and the dependent offices of these were sold in turn by the new, simoniacal incumbents. Simony,[11] with all its attendant grievances, had thoroughly infected the Church at all levels, from which scarcely any office, including the papal throne, was exempt. Compounding this problem of pure simony was the matter of lay investiture. With roots stretching as far back as the ninth century, lay investiture—the power by which a secular prince invested his own dependent with the full powers of a spiritual office without intervention by the Church—grew up slowly but, it must be acknowledged, quite naturally, for the temporalities attending such offices—lands and wealth—created, in effect, great feudal barons, little different from their secular counterparts; and, in time, kings had come to look upon these spiritual "barons" in much the same way as they did their own secular nobility. And little wonder, for these spiritual leaders reveled in worldly ambitions: they commanded immense power and influence, they were lords over vast estates, they led their own armies, they had wives and concubines.

Such was the state of things when Gregory VII became pope in 1073. And it was against such evils that Gregory, the great reforming pope, began directing all his energies. The principal target of Gregorian reform was the so-called triple threat to Christianity: clerical marriage, simony, and lay investiture. Of these three, the latter became the symbolic focus of the struggle between Church and Empire, a struggle which was destined to continue far beyond Gregory's lifetime. It was not until 1122, with the Concordat of Worms, nearly half a century after Gregory launched his campaign, that the investiture struggle was finally resolved. Still, the settlement was a compromise at best. The emperor retained the right to oversee elections and to invest the spiritual offices with the temporalities, and thus the power to overawe and to command the loyalties of the incumbents.

The struggles between the Empire and Church continued throughout Hildegard's lifetime. Most of her active life was spent under the reign of Frederick I, Barbarossa (1152–90), and, like Hildegard's own bête noir Henry IV, Barbarossa also created anti-popes—three successive ones: Victor IV, Paschal III, and Calixtus III—in his continual efforts to achieve his imperial aims. And unless it be thought that these were mere ideological struggles, the harsh, physical reality of the conflict must be stressed: these were cruel, bloody, slaughter-filled times.[12] Hildegard corresponded with prelates on both sides of the issue, as she did, for example, with Conrad, for a short time archbishop of Mainz, and Christian de Buch, usurper of that see. When Frederick held the Diet of Würzburg in order to secure recognition of his anti-pope Paschal III, Conrad fled the assemby in order to attach himself to the canonically elected Alexander III. Frederick immediately replaced him as archbishop with Christian de Buch, whom he soon afterward despatched into Italy with his anti-pope with orders to reduce the Italian cities and take over Rome. Christian, a ferocious but very able general, ensconced Paschal in Viterbo, ravaged the countryside around Rome, and would have fulfilled his command to the letter save for the timely arrival of a rescuing Sicilian army. Needless to say, these were trying, uncertain, and fearsome times for the German prelates. Some, like Christian de Buch, attached themselves fiercely to the imperial cause; some, like Conrad, held with the pope; others were forced to choose, willy-nilly, between the two according to their conscience—or their circumstances. It is little wonder that some of Hildegard's correspondents express the need for caution in their letters.

Given these facts, the question naturally arises about Hildegard's own attitude toward the empire and toward Barbarossa in particular. The answer to that question is far fuzzier and more ambiguous than might be hoped. When Frederick was first elected king of Germany, Hildegard wrote him a letter of congratulations and, as one would expect of Hildegard, of advice. We know, too, that she once visited him, some time probably in the mid-1150s, in the royal palace at Ingelheim, for Frederick writes to inform her that the predictions she made to him on that occasion had all come true. And despite the schism which began with the disputed papal election in 1159, a rupture that lasted for eighteen years, and despite the fact that he was excommunicated by Alexander III in 1160, Hildegard seems to have managed to maintain some kind of relationship with him. In 1163, for example—that is, after his excommunication—she accepted Frederick's charter of protection for Mount St. Rupert. And we know that she numbered among her friends many of the German prelates who favored the emperor, one of whom was the powerful Philip of Heinsberg, quondam imperial chancellor, who was a frequent visitor at Mount St. Rupert, and who, late in her life, came loyally to Hildegard's defense when her community had been placed under interdict over the disputed burial of a man within the monastery grounds. On the other hand, when, after the death of the anti-pope Victor IV, Frederick attempted to impose his new choice upon the Church, Hildegard took him to task in no uncertain terms, calling him a "madman" and an "infant." *And* we know that Hildegard came from an aristocratic background and that she continued to have aristocratic leanings.[13] But that is all we know, and we might well have expected more from the fearless seer on the upper Rhine.

In any case, it is this age—from the late eleventh century up to her own time (she is quite specific)—that Hildegard calls the "womanish time," not, of course, because "manly" things were not being done (violence, bloodshed, wars) but because, as she says, the justice of God has become weak. The letters make fairly clear what she means by this: the prelates of the Church, the representatives of God's justice on earth, have grown weak and effeminate from easy living; their love of luxury and bodily pleasures has sapped their manly fortitude; their zeal for the Lord's work has become tepid and feeble; their message to the world has become sterile and, worse, perverted and distorted. Hence this present age, as she writes (26r) to Hillinus, archbishop of Trier, is a "squalid, womanish time." And, hence, God has, paradoxically, called forth a woman to bring virility back into the Church.

This weakness of God's justice, the pre-eminent sign of the *tempus muliebre*, "the womanish age," is firmly linked in Hildegard's mind with schism and heresy. She traces its beginnings, after all, to Henry IV, that great schismatic maker of anti-popes, whom Hildegard is always reluctant to name but instead labels as that iniquitous "worshipper of Baal." Her age was certainly a time rife with heresies, a time when even vicious and ignorant leaders could rise up from the masses preaching outlandish doctrines and gain a following. In fact, fear of being counted among such schismatics was, at least in part, the motivating force behind her earliest extant letter, the letter to St. Bernard seeking approval of her strange visions. Hildegard was, of course, no schismatic, and it could be argued indeed that much of her work (not just the sermons so designated) was directed against the heretical notions of her age, for, in her view, a mighty female warrior *(bellatrix)* had arisen, whom God had called forth to bring virility back into the Church, and if Hildegard was not exactly that warrior herself, she was certainly her standard-bearer (see Letter 23).

Catharism was the most powerful heresy of the age, a stream of thought that the Church seemed powerless to bring under control, and which steadily gained influence over the minds of poor and powerful alike until Innocent III's Albigensian Crusade of the early thirteenth century.[14] Considering its gnostic origins, it is surprising that Catharism exerted such power over the popular mind, but that fact seems to owe more to the abuses within the orthodox Church itself than to the power of the doctrine. The arrogance, sloth, and general worldliness of the prelates of the Church prepared a rich field for the seeds of heresy, as Hildegard herself makes clear in her criticism of clerics for encouraging the Cathars (Letter 15r) by their moral laxity. The Cathars themselves, by contrast, were noted for the purity of their lives.[15]

As a dualist heresy, Catharism was especially repugnant to Hildegard. Holding that the universe is divided between two all-powerful, warring principles, the Cathars believed that the material world—the domain, even the creation, of the Evil One—is itself evil, and must be rejected absolutely. One could scarcely conceive of a doctrine more distasteful to the seer who taught the essential goodness, the sanctity of all creation. In pointed contradiction to the basic tenet of Catharism, Hildegard writes that all created things

> are the materials for the instruction of mankind, which he comprehends by touching, kissing, and embracing, since they serve him: by touching, because a man remains in them; by kissing, because he gains knowledge through them; by embracing, because he exercises his noble power through them. Thus mankind would have no freedom of possibility if they did not exist with him. So, they with mankind, and mankind with them [Letter 15r].

And whether directly addressing the Cathars or not, she soars to the heights of eloquence in expounding how the created world, the handiwork of God, declares the glory of the Lord:

> But the fire has a flame which the wind quickens, so that the flame becomes a blazing fire. Thus the word is in the voice and the word is heard, and the fire has a flame and it is praise to God, and the wind moves the flame and it is praise to God, and the word is in the voice and it is praise to God, and the word is heard and it is praise to God. Therefore, all of creation is praise to God[16] [Letter 77r].

But let us turn more directly to technique and style in the correspondence. The distinctive quality of the letters, as of her other visionary works, is the way in which Hildegard displaces her own self from the center. Typically, a letter opens with a voucher for the verity of the message to follow, and this is true whether or not the message that follows is particularly prophetic or divine: "The Living Light has said to me"; "In the inspiration of a true vision, I saw and heard these words"; "The Fountain of Waters cries out to you"; "He Who gives life to the living says"; "The one who was, and is, and is about to come speaks"; "In a vision I saw," et cetera. The words that follow such openings are the words of the Divine or the Living Light itself, whether quoted directly or reported indirectly from an earlier vision—though frequently mingled strangely, inextricably with Hildegard's own words. All of this is, of course, a means of gaining authenticity for her word, the bid of "the poor feminine creature" for authority in a very masculine world.[17] Whatever the case, it seems certainly to be true that Hildegard is more comfortable speaking through voices other than her own. For in addition to the voice of the Living Light, the letters have quite a large cast of characters, since frequently, even here, Hildegard strikes the chords of her other, more allegorical works by vivifying abstract concepts, giving life and voice to virtues and vices, and thereby gaining objective distance, as it were, for her own distinctive message by projecting it onto her own created beings. The method, it must be confessed, is a little odd, considering the context, and, at times, a little strained.

Sometimes, she simply personalizes the abstractions as helpers to be enlisted or as distracters to be avoided, as she does in Letter 12 with an admonition to "be zealous to build the tower of celestial Jerusalem, and may God give you that sweetest mother Mercy as your assistant." At other times, she brings them fully on stage to enact the message of God's will teaching the proper way of life.[18] Hildegard uses such scenic frameworks in a variety of ways. In some letters the personified virtues directly address the recipients in monologues, with a plea to amend their lives, or to hold firm in the way of the Lord. Thus in Letter 25r to Archbishop Eberhard, Hildegard brings on two abstractions, Divine Love *(Caritas)* and Obedience *(Obedientia)*, to perform a scene that includes costuming (for the two virtues are "clad in regal garments") and dramatic action (they knock at the archbishop's door). In a pattern found in the *Ordo Virtutum* and in *Scivias* III.xiii, Divine Love and Obedience speak their lines in succession, here addressing Eberhard directly, and although they enter together and knock at the door at the same time, there is no interplay between them, the recitation being more important than the stage action. Also participating in this little vignette is a third virtue, Wisdom *(Sapientia),* who, after the other two abstractions have played their parts, speaks a sort of epilogue, again addressed directly to Eberhard, echoing Divine Love's speech urging the archbishop to search and cleanse wounds. Although distanced in this way from the immediate voice of the writer, this miniature drama is a strikingly effective appeal to the senses, with the virtues not only heard speaking directly to the reader, but also "seen" in their sumptuous costumes, dramatically engaged in action, drawing Eberhard into an immediate relationship with the virtues. For rather than offering a detached theological discourse, they speak personally, lovingly, in their exhortation to proper action. Under the influence of the *Canticles,* for example, Hildegard has Divine Love use erotic language that one might associate more with *amor* than with *caritas,* beseeching Eberhard, as she does, to take her into his bed as his beloved. It is a very effective means to symbolize Eberhard's Christian responsibilities.

Elsewhere, Hildegard expands the dramatic action further, not just using simple monologues addressed to the recipient but staging a full miniature drama enacted by virtues and vices. In Letter 58 to Dimo of Bamberg, Divine Love and Obedience again appear, here joined on the stage by Humility *(Humilitas),* and a vice, Pride *(Superbia).* As Barbara Newman has pointed out, there are problems of gender in the working out of the dramatic conflict here.[19] Since abstractions are ordinarily feminine in Latin, Hildegard regularly portrays the personified virtues as female, in accordance with their grammatical gender. And yet here *Obedientia* is cast as the masculine figure of a *miles* "knight" and *Superbia,* also feminine in gender, as a male *vernaculus* "serf." One wonders why Hildegard does not here use the perfectly viable feminine noun *bellatrix,* which carries all the military aura while still maintaining the female-ness of the character, as she does in Letter 23, where *justitia* (feminine in gender) is described as a female warrior *(bellatrix)* "battling against injustice."[20] There are also problems of class or decorum, since the highborn Pride is presented as a servile character and Obedience, contrary to the nature of the virtue personified, has to be admonished to perform his duty. "Like many of Hildegard's visions," as Newman remarks (81), "the story on a literal plane is incoherent." Yet, to Hildegard, such minor inconsistencies are unimportant. What matters is the large sense behind the story when Pride is unmasked as Lucifer, and Divine Love is recognized as Christ. On that level the drama works very well indeed.

Sometimes the enactment of the illustrative drama and its relation to the recipient's situation is very complicated indeed. Letter 85r/b to an abbot named Adam, for example, opens up immediately with the allegorical drama: "He Who Is says: The sun shines and sends forth its rays. And a certain man, a friend of the sun, had a garden in which he desired to plant many herbs and flowers." Then there enter into that garden, from the north and east respectively, two representatives of the forces of nature, who also somehow, strangely, represent the virtues and vices (as we learn later from Hildegard's explication of the parable): a "contorted figure" with black hair and horrible face and a handsome young man with "bright, shining hair." The contorted figure confronts the young man, and threatens the destruction of the garden, a threat which he immediately counters, saying that he will cause a fountain to spring up and irrigate the garden and keep it fresh. "Ha!" retorts the old woman in a lively rejoinder, "That is as possible as if locusts would eat through hard rock." And indeed it is so, for, on one level at least, this is a parable of the year, of the course of the seasons, and so, despite his adamant assertion, the young man idly wanders off playing his harp while winter ravages the garden. When he does finally take notice, he calls the sun back into Taurus and brings the viridity of summer into the garden again.

Then Hildegard makes the application: "Now, you, O father, understand that these words are spoken to you," for "you have a garden of people, in which as the representative of Christ you seek to plant many wholesome desires and good works." And so we wind up with the curious situation where the figurative garden is real, that is, with real vegetation subject to the ravages of winter and the rejuvenation of springtime. But the real garden, that is, Adam's "garden," is figurative, where one plants "wholesome desires and good works." Hildegard's explication is quite lengthy, and she brings on stage the vices and virtues (corresponding to the two figures of the original parable) to work out the meanings dramatically. The scene becomes quite lively: when the virtues, in their turn, oppose the vices, maintaining that they will cause the fountain of living water to flow and preserve the garden, the vices laugh scornfully, countering that that is as possible as fragile flesh remaining forever unblemished and unwrinkled. And so the vices win, just as, in the orginal scene, winter inevitably comes with its destructive power. Then, at length, the realization is borne in on us that this simple little drama is an explanation of the reason for evil in the world, for "the virtues permit this thing to be done by the just judgment of God, so that men may understand what they are."

Thus does Hildegard make use of her gift for dramatic presentation to the fullest measure, employing many voices to present her message to the people.

A few words about the present translation are perhaps in order:

The translator of Hildegard's letters is faced with several imposing difficulties, not least of which is the manuscript tradition and the corollary issue of the authenticity of parts of the correspondence. Until very recently, a reader of the letters was obliged either to use the manuscripts themselves, if he had access to them, or to trust the *Patrologia* edition (vol. 197), a text based on the Riesencodex, a manuscript which, although compiled shortly after Hildegard's death, is highly unreliable.[21] The inadequacies of the *Patrologia* edition have been addressed by various scholars. As early as 1882, J. Pitra published 145 letters not found in the earlier edition,[22] and, quite recently, Peter Dronke has published text of twelve previously unedited letters.[23] Moreover, Monika Klaes has edited the text of three letters between Hildegard and Abbot Gedolphus of Brauweiler in her new critical edition of the *Vita Hildegardis*, shortly to be published as volume 126 of the *Corpus Christianorum* series.[24] Still, this comes rather short of a definitive edition of all the letters. This deficiency began to be addressed with the publication of two prolegomena toward a new text by Lieven Van Acker in 1988 and 1989, followed shortly by the first volume of his edition of the correspondence, based upon a reassessment of the complexities of the manuscript tradition.[25] When it is completed, this latest edition will be the first genuinely critical text of the entire corpus of the correspondence, the first volume of which forms the basis for the present work, which will be continued as the volumes appear.

The arrangement of the letters will immediately strike the reader as peculiar—if not absolutely wrong-headed. That is because that arrangement is medieval, not modern, hierarchical, not chronological. In order to systematize the material in a logical order, Van Acker adapted a practice, already found in the manuscript tradition, of arranging the letters according to the rank or status of the correspondent,[26] and for this purpose he established ten classifications for the 390 letters and responses. Class I (Letters 1–45r) comprises correspondence with popes (in chronological order), archbishops and bishops (in hierarchical order and alphabetically according to the modern names of their sees). There are certain exceptions to this classification: the letters between Bernard of Clairvaux and Hildegard take the primary position since, as the earliest extant, they mark the beginning of Hildegard's writing career; Letter 7, to the cardinals Bernard of St. Clement and Gregory of St. Angeli, comes immediately after the correspondence with Pope Eugenius on the grounds that they were acting on the pope's behalf.[27] The second class (Letters 56–250r) includes those letters to and from ecclesiastics associated with a specific locale; these have been arranged alphabetically by place. Class III (Letters 251–310) contains letters to clergy whose names are known but who cannot be identified geographically; as with Class I, these are also arranged by hierarchy. Class IV (Letters 311–31) includes correspondence with the noble laity, such as King Conrad III and Frederick Barbarossa. Here, too, a hierarchichal arrangement is followed. Class V (Letters 332–43) is correspondence to the laity of specific geographical sites arranged, as with Class II, in alphabetical order of place. Class VI (Letters 344–56) comprises correspondence with laity of uncertain geographical location. Class VII (Letters 357–73) includes letters in which there is no decisive evidence of the status, lay or clergy, of the correspondents. Class VIII (Letters 374–90) contains text found in the manuscripts of those letters of dubious epistolary character, such as Hildegard's sermon against the Cathars (Letter 381), and the greatest portion of *Ad praelatos Moguntinenses (To the Prelates of Mainz)*, some of which forms the basis for Letter 23 in Class I, but most of which is, as Van Acker calls it, "a fused writing."[28] Class IX is made up of those writings traditionally enumerated with the letters, but which are not of an epistolary nature at all; examples are the *Solutiones XXXVIII Quaestionum (Solutions to 38 Questions)*, which Hildegard sent in response to a request from Guibert of Gembloux, and the *Explanatio Regulae S. Benedicti (Explanation of the Rule of St. Benedict)*, written at the request of a monastery. Class X, the last, contains spurious material, such as falsified letters of Pope Eugenius III and Anastasius IV.[29]

The arrangement of the letters in descending order of importance of correspondents has a certain neatness about it, although it does, as Van Acker himself noted, present problems even for the textual editor.[30] It also causes, one must candidly admit, serious difficulties for the reader, since such a classification does not allow for a smooth flow of themes. With respect to those letters that concern the controversy about Hildegard's protégée Richardis von Stade, for example, the hierarchical arrangement leads to an awkwardly disjunctive account of the matter. Reference solely to the letters translated in the present volume makes the point abundantly clear, and the problem is exacerbated, of course, by the fact that some of the pieces in this complicated matter will appear only in subsequent volumes. We first hear of the case only obliquely in Letter 4 when Pope Eugenius agrees to hand the matter over to Archbishop Heinrich of Mainz. After a space of eight letters, in number 12 Hildegard makes an impassioned appeal for help in the matter to Richardis's brother, Hartwig. In 13, Hartwig informs Hildegard of his sister's death, and in 13r Hildegard expresses her magnanimous sentiments toward the deceased nun. Five letters later (Letter 18) Archbishop Heinrich of Mainz addresses Hildegard in no uncertain terms, ordering her to release Richardis (still alive at this point, of course) to her new position, and Hildegard's response, equally intransigent, is her stubborn refusal to do so. Then there is an interval of forty-six letters before, in Letter 64, Hildegard's lament is addressed directly to the yet-living Richardis.[31]

While the arrangement followed in the edition is not always conducive to a smoothly flowing exposition of the events in Hildegard's life, the reason that we have followed Van Acker's ordering of the text is not far to seek, since, again, his work represents the first reliable edition of the letters in modern times. The other factor to consider is that his text will appear in several volumes, of which only the first is now available.[32] Since the translator is, of course, obliged to make use of the best available edition, we cannot do otherwise than follow his arrangement until such time as the critical edition is published in its entirety and another disposition of the letters, chronological or thematic, becomes practicable.

Even after the establishment of a sound text, however, there remains for the reader—and the translator—the problem of Hildegard's language: her intricately coded vocabulary and her difficulties with the learned language.[33] For certainly, at times, Hildegard can be very obscure indeed, either in the content of a vision or in the way she describes it.[34] An image in Letter 5 will serve to illustrate the point. Here, Hildegard writes Pope Eugenius III in oblique reference to Archbishop Heinrich of Mainz, and she takes the occasion to address one of her favorite themes, the teaching and disciplining of subordinates in the Church: "The mountains, on the other hand, leap over the key to the way of truth, and they do not prepare the way so that they might fly to the mountain of myrrh." The mountains here, as frequently in the letters, apparently represent the ecclesiastical authorities, but Hildegard is content to let the pope dwell on his own on the imagery of their leaping over a key and flying to the mountain of myrrh.[35] Such obscurity, in the words of Gebeno of

Eberbach, is the very nature of the visionary experience, but, unlike the revelations in the *Scivias* and the *Liber Divinorum Operum*, the encoded visions are not, in the letters, uniformly supplied with exegeses to explain their enigmas. There are exceptions, of course, such as her detailed explanation to an abbot of the garden imagery of her vision (Letter 85r/b). Still, that is not the rule. In a letter to Pope Eugenius, for example, she gives the following advice to the pontiff in allegorical form:

> A jewel lies on the road, but a bear comes along and seeing that it is very fine stretches out his paw to pick it up and carry it off. But, suddenly, an eagle swoops down and snatches the jewel, wraps it in the covering of its wings, and carries it into the palace of the king. And this jewel shines so splendidly before the king that he sets great store by it, and because of his love of this jewel, he gives the eagle golden slippers, and praises it highly for its uprightness. Now, you who sit as Christ's representative on the throne of the Church, choose the better part so that you may be the eagle who overcomes the bear; in this way, you may adorn the halls of the Church with those souls entrusted to you. Thus you may snatch yourself from this world and enter the regions above in your golden slippers.

Sometimes she opens up a letter immediately with a vision, unexplained in itself, and then directly applies the personified image to the person addressed, as she does to a prior in Letter 47:

> He Who Is says: A king saw a ladder darkened by the changes in time of pestilence. But then the sun shone forth and dispelled the darkness. This delighted the king, and he said: This unstable ladder is tired out, because sometimes it reaches to lofty heights and sometimes is overshadowed by darkness.
> And your mind is just like this, o man.

With respect to Hildegard's Latinity, it should first of all be observed that there is still some question of just how much Volmar (or, late in her life, Guibert of Gembloux) contributed toward making her Latin as readable as it is.[36] Yet Newman has well observed that "although the seer was self-conscious about her 'unpolished' style, she seems to have cherished it as a mark that her inspiration must be divine because she herself scarcely knew how to write."[37] There we must simply let the matter rest, and, here, merely indicate some of the problems.

A marked feature of Hildegard's style is a general looseness of sentence structure, with phrase attracting phrase, and clause, clause, all strung rather adventitiously together on the thread of the thought. This fact, in and of itself, poses no real problem for the reader, and, in fact, has its own kind of simple charm. Still, at times, this accumulation of qualifying or merely additive elements without clear or unambiguous markers of the logical relationships among the ideas results in a passage of almost impenetrable opacity. Note, for example, the difficulty of threading one's way through the forest of clauses in the following:

Et quis est homo iste? Scilicet ille qui corpus suum habet sicut ancillam et animam suam sicut dilectissimam dominam. Nam qui etiam ferox est in impietate tamquam ursus, et ferocitatem illam recusat atque ad solem iustitie, qui pius et clemens est, anhelat, hic Deo placet, ita quod Deus illum super precepta sua constituit, dans uirgam ferream in manus ipsius ad erudiendum oues suas ad montem myrrhe. Nunc audi et disce, ut in gustu anime tue super his erubescas, qui aliquando mores ursi habes qui sepe in semetipso occulte murmurat, et etiam interdum mores asini, ita quod non es prouidus in causis tuis, sed tediosus, sed et etiam in aliis quibusdam rebus inutilis; et ideo malitiam ursi aliquando in impietate non perficis. Item mores etiam habes aliquorum uolatilium que nec de superioribus nec de infimis sunt, ita quod superiora ea uincunt et quod infima illa ledere non possunt.

Clearly, the problem here is that matter of the extreme grammatical looseness in the development of the ideas—loose even for Hildegard—with its large number of vague connectives *(nam, et, et etiam, item etiam)* and its non-logical (or logic-defying) use of logical conjunctions *(ita quod, et ideo)*. But see Letter 76r for the translation.

A similar problem occurs because Hildegard is sometimes rather vague in her use of pronouns. In her answer to Tengswich of Andernach (52r), for example, Hildegard writes, *Audi: Terra sudat uiriditatem graminis, usque dum eam hiems superat. Et hiems aufert pulchritudinem illius floris, et illa tegit uiriditatem sui floris, deinceps non ualens se reuelare quasi numquam aruerit, quia hiems illam abstulit.* In a passage of such importance for the working out of Hildegard's argument, this imprecise use of such a large number of pronouns in so short a passage—*eam, illius, illa, sui, se, illam*—does little, shall we say, to contribute to clarity.

The problem is vastly compounded, of course, when such negligence with respect to precise rules of grammar is used to express ideas which are themselves highly abstruse, as in the letter to Pope Hadrian (Letter 9), where either the imagery is so contorted as to be intelligible only to the recipient, if in fact even to him, or as to be deliberately indecipherable. In such cases, it has seemed best to translate quite literally, simply following, as faithfully as possible, the words on the page with the Latin text supplied in an endnote.

On a few occasions, on the other hand, when the nature of the material so demanded, we have followed a middle course and taken a phrase or sentence that could be made more presentable, and rendered it into more idiomatic English, where the reader would not have been well served by a literal translation. Such a case is found in Hildegard's response to Tengswich and her congregation in the passage from Letter 52r cited just above. In very literal translation the passage would read: "Hear: the earth sweats forth the viridity of the grass up until the time that winter overcomes it. And the winter takes away the beauty of that flower and it covers the viridity of its flower, not thereafter being able to reveal itself as if it never withered, because the winter has taken it away." In our rendering, we have, we feel, managed to dispel the awkwardness, while retaining the sense and flavor of the original: "Listen: The earth keeps the grass green and vital, until winter conquers it. Then winter takes away the beauty of that flower and covers over its vital force so that it is unable to manifest itself as if it had never withered up, because winter has ravaged it." Still, this was a relatively uncomplicated situation, and as long as the Latin text is supplied in an endnote (as we do), the translators can, one would think, do no great harm. But compare the following passage (Letter 15r) where an understanding of the complexity of Hildegard's thought processes in the letter as a whole is required in order to grasp the full sense of the passage:

> But you ought to steep them in the precepts of the law, and thereby restrain them, lest any of them, in his frailty (his marrow, as it were), do whatever he wishes, just as the earth is steeped and restrained by humidity and viridity, lest it turn to ashes. On account of you, however, they are scattered like ashes and always do whatever they wish.
>
> *Nam eos per precepta legis perfundere et constringere deberetis, ne ullus eorum per fragilitatem, quasi per medullam faceret quod sibi eligit, uelut terra humiditate et uiriditate perfusa et constricta est, ne cinis sit. Propter uos autem ut cinis sparguntur et in unaquaque causa que volunt faciunt.*

The surface meaning here seems clear enough; yet the cosmological sense of this dense passage—the interweaving of the spiritual and the natural—is nigh impossible to render. The general scheme of thought appears to be something like this: priests should so thoroughly soak *(perfundere)* their flocks in the precepts of the law that their very marrow (i.e., their fragility) would be penetrated and strengthened, just as the earth is soaked and strengthened by humidity and viridity, those qualities in the macrocosm—the earth's marrow, as it were, as she had explained earlier—which correspond to marrow in the little world of man.

It is this complexity of the thought process or the loss of a logical step in that process that frequently causes problems in reading Hildegard. In Letter 77r, for example, she writes, "And just as the secret Son of God came secretly into the world, so, too, He gathered to Himself a foreign nature, that is, those who give up the world and the pomp of the world." The conception here is quite breathtaking when one fully grasps the movement of the thought. Hildegard begins with a medieval commonplace and enlarges upon it in a strikingly imaginative way: at the incarnation, Christ gathered to Himself a "foreign nature," that is, the flesh of humanity, but an integral part of this divine taking on of a foreign nature is a gathering to Himself of those holy men and women who have rejected the world and the pomp of the world as foreign nature to themselves—or perhaps it is that in rejecting the world, they, like Christ, have taken on a nature (that is, a heavenly nature) foreign to themselves. The missing logical step here can be supplied by reference to the beginning of the paragraph where the Son of God is described as "gathering to Himself" at His incarnation "two planets," that is virgins and monks.

With respect to matters of style it should also be noted that Hildegard feels enough at ease with the language to engage in light wordplay and punning, as she does with *auxilium/exsilium* in Letter 20r, *prelatus* ("prelate," "chosen") in Letter 5, and *uisceribus* ("bowels" of mercy, "maw" of the devil)-

in Letter 78r. And note the elaborate kind of wordplay in the following passage from Letter 52r:

> Let a woman remain within her chamber so that she may preserve her modesty, for the serpent breathed the fiery danger of horrible lust into her. Why should she do this? Because the beauty of woman radiated and blazed forth in the primordial root, and in her was formed that chamber in which every creature lies hidden. Why is she so resplendent? For two reasons: on the one hand, because she was created by the finger of God and, on the other, because she was endowed with wondrous beauty.
>
> *Mulier intra cubiculum lateat, ita quod magnam uerecundiam habeat, quia magna pericula horribilis lasciuie serpens in illam sufflauit. Quomodo? Forma mulieris fulminauit et radiauit in prima radice, in qua formatum est hoc, in quo omnis creatura latet. Quomodo? In duabus partibus, scilicet in altera experte facture digiti Dei, et in altera superne pulchritudinis.*

How delightfully Hildegard plays with the word *cubiculum* in this passage. The word hovers teasingly between the meanings of "bedchamber" (where a woman ought to remain hidden), "woman's body" (into which can be breathed the breath of life or "the fiery danger of horrible lust"), and "womb" ("in which every creature lies hidden").

A somewhat different matter with respect to problems of translation has to do with Hildegard's title as head of a community of nuns. Although popularly referred to in modern work as "Abbess," Hildegard does not enjoy this title in the letters addressed to her, where she is normally designated *praeposita*, *magistra*, or *priorissa*. The first two we have rendered variously as "mistress" or "superior," and the latter, of course, as "prioress." In one letter (13), in fact, her title of *magistra* is pointedly juxtaposed to "abbess" used of a second person. Only once—in a letter from Frederick Barbarossa (not included in this volume)—is she addressed as *abbatissa*.

It must also be noted that, aside from biblical citations, we have generally eschewed the use of quotation marks in this work, avoided, that is, the attempt to set one speaker off from another. That was a deliberate choice. For Hildegard, it seems clear, saw herself as God's mouthpiece in a time of turmoil, and therefore frequently her voice and His blend so completely that they become utterly indistinguishable. The same is true of the many other voices she employs in her writing: Divine Love, Mercy, et cetera. The following from the letter to the "Shepherds of the Church" (Letter 15r)[38] will illustrate the point. The merging here is not so absolute as in many other passages that might have been cited, but it will serve to make the point clear. For the sake of clarification, we have attempted to sort things out by placing the speaker's identity in brackets:

> From Him the wind blows, saying: *[God]* lacking no power, I have set the firmament with all its ornaments, with eyes to see, ears to hear, a nose to smell, a mouth to taste. *[Hildegard]* For the sun is like the light of His eyes, the wind like the hearing of His ears, the air like His fragrance, the dew like His taste, exuding viridity like His mouth. The moon marks the times of the

seasons, and reveals knowledge to men. And the stars, which seem to be rational, are indeed so, because they are circular, just as rationality embraces many things. [*God*] I shored up the four corners of the earth with fire, cloud, and water.

In such mystic writing, it seems a fruitless—not to say, hopeless—task to clarify by modern punctuation marks that which, apparently, was never intended to be clear.

A note about gender is in order. When Hildegard speaks of people in this world, her language tends to be quite generalized, universal. *Homo, homines* ("human being," "people") occur very frequently, while *vir* ("man"), *viri* ("men"), *mulier* ("woman"), *femina* ("female person") appear only rarely. Indeed, sometimes she uses *homines* when *viri* might well have been the more natural form. Moreover, when the voice from the Living Light speaks directly to her, a *paupercula*—a feminine form, which we have usually rendered "poor little woman"—it is not, as might have been expected, with *O mulier, O femina,* or even with the title made so respectable by the Holy Virgin *O ancilla,* but with the awesome *O homo.* In our work we have attempted to retain this generalized sense of mankind that Hildegard is addressing, but it must be acknowledged that such usage is much more natural to Medieval Latin than to Modern English, and we have not hesitated to vary *mankind* with generic *man*[39] and sometimes to render *homines* with *men*. As long as the distinctions are clear and Hildegard's point is not smothered under, this has seemed to us the proper course. We have striven at all times for clear, well-modulated English prose uncluttered by awkward attempts to skirt around modern sensitivities.

All biblical quotations in the text are followed immediately by notation of exact source (book, chapter, verse, as needed) in brackets. Save for a few instances where the rigors of the context required a fresh translation, all such quotations are rendered by the language of the Douay version.

In conclusion, let us cite Hildegard herself, who seems to indicate the way to render her writings when she signifies the difficulty of putting mystic things into human speech:

> But He who is great and without flaw has now touched a humble dwelling, so that it might see a miracle and form unknown letters and utter an unknown tongue. And this was said to that little habitation: You have written these things in a language given to you from above, rather than in ordinary human speech, since it was not revealed to you in that form, but let him who has the pumice stone not fail to polish it and make it intelligible to mankind.

In this our effort, we trust we have used the pumice stone well to present a still-living Hildegard by treating her mysteries with respect, while, as much as possible within the constraints of her visionary, admonitory genre, rendering her thoughts accurately both in her clarity and her obscurity. For *in his epistolis,* to paraphrase Richard de Bury on the virtue of books, *mortuam quasi vivam inveniebamus,* "in these letters we have found the dead woman as if still alive."

Notes

1. See *Vita* II.i.16; *Scivias*, "Protestificatio."
2. See B. Newman, *Sister of Wisdom: St. Hildegard's Theology of the Feminine* (Berkeley: University of California Press, 1987), esp. pp. 34–41.
3. So the text *manu propria scripsit*. This is extraordinary paleographical evidence of an author physically writing rather than simply dictating, as was usually the case, even with learned writers. A thirteenth-century miniature in a copy of *De operatione Dei* provides some corroboration: Hildegard is depicted transcribing the message from heaven onto wax tablets, while Volmar writes the finished copy in a book.
4. See C. Hart and J. Bishop, trans., *Hildegard of Bingen: Scivias*, (New York: Paulist Press, 1990), p. 59.
5. "Problemata Hildegardiana," *Mittellateinisches Jahrbuch* 16 (1981), pp. 107–14.
6. On *pigmentarius* and the following *vivens odor*, see Hart and Bishop, trans., *Scivias*, "Translator's Note," p. 55. The term *pigmentarius* itself is from the Scripture. See Canticles 5.13.
7. See G. Constable, *Letters and Letter-Collections*, fasc. 17 of *Typologie des Sources du Moyen Âge Occidental* (Turnholt: Brepols, 1976), p. 11, "In view of the way in which letters were written and sent, and also of the standards of literacy in the Middle Ages, it is doubtful whether there were any private letters in the modern sense of the term."
8. Medieval friendship tended to be very profuse and lavish in its terms of expression in any case, and we should resist the propensity to view such expressions as insincere.
9. Constable, *Letters*, pp. 48, 53–54.
10. See A. Haverkamp, "Tenxwind von Andernach und Hildegard von Bingen: Zwei 'Weltanschauungen' in der Mitte des 12. Jahrhunderts," *Institutionen, Kultur und Gesellschaft im Mittelalter. Festschrift für Josef Fleckenstein*, eds. L. Fenske, W. Rösener, and T. Zotz, p. 517 and esp. pp. 543–45 for a dual-column comparison. Also L. Van Acker, ed., *Hildegardis Bingensis Epistolarium: Prima Pars*, in *Corpus Christianorum: continuatio medievalis*, vol. 91 (Turnholt: Brepols, 1991), p. lx.
11. The buying and selling of Church offices, so called from Simon Magus of Acts 8.18–24, who sought to buy grace from Peter.
12. In 1167 in a famous battle, Christian de Buch, archbishop of Mainz, led the imperial forces against the Romans during their siege of Tusculum, and literally demolished their army, killing some 9,000 out of 30,000 men, and taking 5,000 prisoners. But perhaps a specific instance of senseless cruelty will make the point even better. In 1183, the Romans—who were notorious for their capricious vacillation between hatred for, and support of, whoever the reigning pontiff happened to be—captured a number of loyal adherents to the pope. First, they put out the eyes of all of the men but one. Then, they set paper mitres on their heads, labeling each with the name of a cardinal, save for the one intended for the pope, on which they inscribed "Lucius, the wicked simoniac." Finally, they mounted them all backward on asses, and sent them off to the pope, with the only unblinded one left to guide the way.
13. See especially Haverkamp, "Tenxwind."
14. The steadily increasing intensity of the Church decrees against heresy from about mid-twelfth century on into the thirteenth is a clear signal of the growing power and influence of the various sects.
15. It is true that hostile witnesses accused them of all sorts of abuses, especially sexual irregularity and debauchery (standard fare, after all, for heretics), but Hildegard herself is a witness to the austerity of their lives.

16. But see P. Dronke, *Women Writers of the Middle Ages* (Cambridge: Cambridge University Press, 1984), pp. 171–83, who sees the influence of Manichaean ideas on Hildegard's work.

17. See Newman, *Sister of Wisdom*, pp. 34–41.

18. See especially Dronke, "Hildegard of Bingen as Poetess and Dramatist," in his *Poetic Individuality in the Middle Ages: New Departures in Poetry 1000–1500* (Oxford: Clarendon Press, 1970), pp. 150–92. Dronke's essay also contains a critical edition of the *Ordo Virtutum*.

19. *Sister of Wisdom*, pp. 80–82.

20. See also *Victoria bellatrix* at *Scivias* III.xiii.429 and *vis animae . . . contra omnem fallaciam diaboli bellatrix* ("the might of the soul—a female warrior against every deception of the devil") at *Liber divinorum operum* I.iv.91.

21. Many of the letters, for example, have been spuriously reassigned to correspondents of higher social status so as to enhance Hildegard's standing in the world, and, moreover, some letters have been conflated with others. See note 29.

22. J. B. Pitra, ed., *Analecta Sanctae Hildegardis*, vol. 8 of *Analecta Sacra* (Monte Cassino, 1882).

23. Dronke, *Women Writers*, pp. 256–64. In addition, F. Haug, "Epistolae sanctae Hildegardis secundum codicem Stuttgartensem," *Revue bénédictine* 43 (1931), 59–71, examined the texts of several letters in the Stuttgart manuscript. For further particulars on the difficulties of the manuscript tradition of Hildegard's letters, the following are of primary importance: B. Schmeidler, "Bemerkungen zum Corpus der Briefe der hl. Hildegard von Bingen," *Corona Quernea: Festgabe Karl Strecker zum 80. Geburtstage dargebracht* (Stuttgart: Hiersemann Verlag, 1952), pp. 335–66; M. Schrader and A. Führkötter, *Die Echtheit des Schrifttums der heiligen Hildegard von Bingen* (Cologne and Graz: Bohlau-Verlag, 1956).

24. Van Acker elected to defer to Professor Klaes and did not include these letters in his edition. We are very grateful to Professor Klaes for her generosity in supplying us the text of the correspondence before the publication of her edition.

25. L. Van Acker, "Der Briefwechsel der heiligen Hildegard von Bingen: Vorbemerkungen zu einer kritischen Edition," *Revue bénédictine* 98 (1988), pp. 141–68, and 99 (1989), pp. 118–54; Van Acker, ed., *Epistolarium*.

26. *Epistolarium*, "Einleitung," pp. lxiii–lxviii, from which the following remarks are taken.

27. *Epistolarium*, "Einleitung," p. lxiv. Other exceptions are Letter 15 to Philip of Heinsberg and Letter 29 to Arnold of St. Andreas in Cologne for they would later become archbishops. Van Acker has included Letter 23 to the prelates of Mainz in Class I on the grounds that they represented Archbishop Christian I while he was in Rome; Odo of Soissons finds himself here since he would later assume the title of Cardinal-Bishop of Tusculum.

28. *Epistolarium*, "Einleitung," p. lxvi; cf. Schrader and Führkötter *Echtheit*, pp. 158f; "Vorbemerkungen" (1989), pp. 130f, 152ff.

29. See *Echtheit*, pp. 121f.

30. *Epistolarium*, "Einleitung," pp. lxvii–lxviii.

31. Hildegard's vehement letter to Richardis's mother falls into a different class and is not translated in the current volume.

32. Van Acker has informed us in personal correspondence that volume II will contain the remainder of the letters that make up Class II (91–250).

33. As Robert Carver has recently noted (F. Bowie and O. Davies, *Hildegard of Bingen: Mystical Writings* (New York: Crossroad, 1990), p. 60): "Hildegard is capable of

writing with a simplicity and grace that are truly moving. Yet the beauty of what she is describing is often marred by the ineptitude of her expression."

34. See Dronke, *Poetic Individuality*, pp. 178f; Newman, *Sister of Wisdom*, pp. 24f.

35. The mountain of myrrh is an image taken from Canticles 4.6, "*vadam ad montem myrrhae,*" and represents God's presence, as opposed to the mountains representing the Church authorities. Cf. Letter 7.

36. See I. Herwegen, "Les collaborateurs de Ste. Hildegarde," *Revue bénédictine* 21 (1904), 192–203, 302–15, 381–403; Schrader and Führkötter, *Echtheit*, pp. 143ff, 180ff; Dronke, *Women Writers*, pp. 148, 307, note 11; Newman, *Sister of Wisdom*, pp. 22ff.

37. *Sister of Wisdom*, p. 23. See the remarks of Gebeno of Eberbach, the thirteenth-century compiler of an abridgement of Hildegard's works entitled *Speculum futurorum temporum* (Pitra, ed., *Analecta*, pp. 483–88), "Most people dislike and shrink from reading St. Hildegard's books, because she speaks obscurely and in an unusual style—not understanding that this is a proof of true prophecy" (translated by Newman, p. 22).

38. On this matter, see Newman, *Sister of Wisdom*, pp. 26f.

39. The real problem lies principally, of course, in the use of pronouns, a difficulty that is proportionate to the length of the passage, for there is no really appropriate pronoun to be used to refer to *mankind*. What does one say, *it* and *its?*

The Letters

1[1]

Hildegard to Bernard, Abbot of Clairvaux

1146–47

Hildegard was forty-nine years old at the time she wrote this letter to the illustrious Bernard of Clairvaux. At once confident about her gift and hesitant about its implications, she writes to Bernard as her most famous contemporary, seeking support for her work. Here, as throughout her life, she is absolutely assured of her own divine inspiration and illumination by the Holy Spirit, a point that receives special stress here, of course, because of the nature of the request. Nevertheless, the tone of the letter is timid and diffident, a far cry indeed from the thundering tones she will later adopt to condemn the ecclesiastical and secular leaders of her time.

O[2] venerable father Bernard, I lay my claim before you, for, highly honored by God, you bring fear to the immoral foolishness of this world and, in your intense zeal and burning love for the Son of God, gather men [cf. Luke 5.10] into Christ's army to fight under the banner of the cross against pagan savagery.[3] I beseech you in the name of the Living God to give heed to my queries.

Father, I am greatly disturbed by a vision which has appeared to me through divine revelation, a vision seen not with my fleshly eyes but only in my spirit. Wretched, and indeed more than wretched in my womanly condition, I have from earliest childhood[4] seen great marvels which my tongue has no power to express but which the Spirit of God has taught me that I may believe.[a] Steadfast and gentle father, in your kindness respond to me, your unworthy servant, who has never, from her earliest childhood, lived one hour free from anxiety. In your piety and wisdom look in your spirit, as you have been taught by the Holy Spirit, and from your heart bring comfort to your handmaiden.

Through this vision which touches my heart and soul like a burning flame, teaching me profundities of meaning, I have an inward understanding of the Psalter, the Gospels, and other volumes. Nevertheless, I do not receive this knowledge in German. Indeed, I have no formal training at all, for I know how to read only on the most elementary level, certainly with no deep analysis.[5] But please give me your opinion in this matter, because I am untaught and untrained in exterior material, but am only taught inwardly, in my spirit. Hence my halting, unsure speech.[b]

When I hear from your pious wisdom, I will be comforted. For with the single exception of a certain monk[6] in whose exemplary life I have the utmost confidence, I have not dared to tell these things to anyone, since there are so many heresies abroad in the land,[7] as I have heard. I have, in fact, revealed all my secrets to this man, and he has given me consolation, for these are great and fearsome matters.

Now, father, for the love of God, I seek consolation from you, that I may be assured. More than two years ago, indeed, I saw you in a vision, like a man looking straight into the sun, bold and unafraid. And I wept, because I myself am so timid and fearful. Good and gentle father, I have been placed in your care so that you might reveal to me through our correspondence whether I should speak these things openly or keep my silence, because I have great anxiety about this vision with respect to how much I should speak about what I have seen and heard.[c] In the meantime, because I have kept silent about this vision, I have been laid low, bedridden in my infirmities, and am unable to raise myself up.

Therefore, I weep with sorrow before you. For in my nature, I am unstable because I am caught in the winepress,[8] that tree rooted in Adam by the devil's deceit which brought about his exile into this wayward world. Yet, now, rising up, I run to you. And I say to you: You are not inconstant, but are always lifting up the tree, a victor in your spirit, lifting up not only yourself but also the whole world unto salvation. You are indeed the eagle gazing directly at the sun.

And so I beseech your aid, through the serenity of the Father and through His wondrous Word and through the sweet moisture of compunction, the Spirit of truth [cf. John 14.17; 16.13], and through that holy sound, which all creation echoes, and through that same Word which gave birth to the world, and through the sublimity of the Father, who sent the Word with sweet fruitfulness[9] into the womb of the Virgin, from which He soaked up flesh, just as honey is surrounded by the honeycomb.[10] And may that Sound, the power of the Father, fall upon your heart and lift up your spirit so that you may respond expeditiously to these words of mine, taking care, of course, to seek all these things from God—with regard to the person or the mystery itself—while you are passing through the gateway of your soul,[d] so that you may come to know all these things in God. Farewell, be strong in your spirit, and be a mighty warrior for God. Amen.

Notes

1. Within this first group (Letters 1–45r) is the correspondence with high Church officials: popes, archbishops, bishops, etc. On the classification of the Letters, see Introduction, pp. 17–18.

2. In some MSS this letter opens with "In the spirit of the mysteries of God, O venerable father Bernard."

3. The year is 1147, the time of the Second Crusade, of which St. Bernard was, of course, a leading proponent.

4. In one of the autobiographical sections of the *Vita* (see the edited version in Dronke, *Women Writers*, p. 231), Hildegard writes of these early visions: "In the third year of my life I saw so bright a light that my very soul trembled, but because I was still an infant, I was unable to say anything. Then in my eighth year I was dedicated to the spiritual life as an offering to God, and until my fifteenth I saw many things, and I spoke of such things in a very simple way, so that those who heard me wondered where all this had come from—and from whom. And I too wondered at myself, because although I saw these things deep in my soul, I still retained outer vision, and I have never heard that said of any other human being. And so I hid that vision I saw within my soul as best I could. Also, I was quite ignorant of many things in the outer world on account of the chronic illness I have suffered from the time of my mother's milk up to the present day; it has weakened my body and worn down my spirits. Worn out by all these things, I once asked my nurse if she saw anything besides external objects. "Nothing," she answered, for she did not see any of those things. Then, seized with great fear, I did not dare to reveal such matters to anyone. Nevertheless, by speaking or writing, I used to make many assertions about future events, and when I was fully in the sway of this vision I would say many things totally unfathomable to those who listened. But when the force of the vision subsided somewhat—in the course of which I had acted far more childishly than suited my years—I blushed profusely and frequently wept, and many times I would have gladly kept quiet, if I could have. Still, because of my fear of other people, I did not dare to tell anyone *how* I saw.

5. Our rendering of this difficult passage is, we are fully aware, a radical departure from previous readings. In the past, the passage has been interpreted, in the most radical form, to mean that Hildegard did not understand German at all, and, more moderately, that she could speak and understand the language orally but could not read it—neither of which could be true from what we know of her from other sources. In our rendering, the German language is, as it were, merely incidental to the passage. Hildegard's main point in this entire section has been that her learning is of the spirit, wholly inward, and that she herself is ignorant and unlearned (whatever degree of credence we wish to give to this humility formula), and this continues to be her stress here. One might note, for example, that *litteras*, not *Teutonica lingua*, is the antecedent of *quas*. It is *litteras* ("letters," "learning") that she does not know, an acknowledgment that leads quite naturally in the next clause to her remark about reading only on the simplest level, not at all *in abscisione textus*. One might note, too, that in his answer to her Bernard refers to her *interior eruditio*. The muddying *Teutonica*, one suspects, gets into the passage at this point—very awkwardly, to be sure—merely because she is frequently asked, as she is later by Guibert of Gembloux, whether she receives her visions in German or in Latin.

6. This was Volmar of St. Disibod, who was Hildegard's early teacher, and who remained her confidant, secretary, amanuensis, and friend for many years until his death in 1173. Speaking in the *Scivias*, the Living Light says, "Through my love she searched

her soul for one who would run the way of salvation. And she found him and loved him, knowing that he was a faithful man, like to herself in those labors that lead to me. She held him fast, and with the highest zeal they worked together on all these things so that my hidden mysteries might be revealed."

7. *schismata sunt in hominibus*. This is not the schism in the Church (which, in any case, did not begin until 1159), as her qualifying *in hominibus, sicut audio dicere homines* makes clear. She probably has reference to the various schismatic sects with which the twelfth century was rife. When Pope Eugenius III came into France in 1147, for example, he was shocked at the large number of heretics there, and, in fact, he commissioned the recipient of this letter, Bernard, to deal with them. See S. Runciman, *The Medieval Manichee: A Study of the Christian Dualist Heresy* (New York: Viking Press, 1961), p. 119.

8. Hildegard's expression here is *in torculari arbore*, an interesting example of her sometimes intricately complex and interwoven imagery. Here the image seems to be a fusion of the tree of the garden of Eden and the winepress (where the grapes of wrath are trod) of Isaiah 63.3, already being used in the twelfth century as a figure of the crucifixion. Cf. the following from the *Scivias* (I.iii.31.623ff): "A bright light appeared for the assurance and salvation of mankind: the Son of God dressed himself in the poverty of a human body, and shining like a burning star in the midst of shadowy clouds, He was placed on the winepress where wine without the sediment of fermentation was to be pressed out. For the cornerstone itself fell on the winepress, and produced such wine that it gave forth the finest fragrance of sweetness."

9. The word here is *viriditate*, a totally untranslatable term, as one might expect. "Greenness" or "greening" (as it is sometimes rendered), for example, certainly cannot render the immensity of the term for Hildegard. *Viriditas* is of the very essence of life, and larger than life in Hildegard's view of the universe. It might perhaps be best rendered as "life-force," for it, assuredly, has that sense in her imposing cosmological scheme of things. For further on *viriditas*, see C. Meier, "Die Bedeutung der Farben im Werk Hildegards von Bingen," *Frühmitteralterliche Studien* 6 (1972), pp. 280–90; B. Newman, ed. *Symphonia: A Critical Edition of the Symphonia Armonie Celestium Revelationum* (Ithaca: Cornell University Press, 1988), pp. 38f; Bowie and Davies, *Mystical Writings*, pp. 31ff.

10. The image of the womb of the Virgin as a honeycomb or beehive derives ultimately from the notion of bees giving birth virginally. The idea is given full expression in the following stanza of a poem from the so-called Cambridge Songs preserved in a MS of the eleventh century:

> Nulla inter aves similis est api,
> que talem tipum gerit castitatis
> nisi que Christum baiulavit alvo
>   inviolata.

1r

Abbot Bernard of Clairvaux to Hildegard

1146–47

St. Bernard's response to Hildegard is short and (it must be confessed) rather perfunctory. A short time later, however, he speaks in Hildegard's favor before Pope Eugenius at the synod of Trier, and helps persuade him to give approval to her work.

Brother Bernard, called Abbot of Clairvaux, offers to Hildegard, beloved daughter in Christ, whatever the prayer of a sinner can accomplish.

It is perhaps to be attributed to your humility that you appear to have a higher regard for our poor abilities than I myself would admit. All the same, I have made some effort to respond to your letter of love, although the press of business forces me to respond more briefly than I would have liked.

We rejoice in the grace of God which is in you. And, further, we most earnestly urge and beseech you to recognize this gift as grace and to respond eagerly to it with all humility and devotion, with the knowledge that "God resisteth the proud, and giveth grace to the humble" [James 4.6; I Pet 5.5].[1] But, on the other hand, when the learning and the anointing (which reveals all things to you) are within, what advice could we possibly give?[2]

And so we ask all the more, and humbly beseech, that you remember us before God, and not only us but also those who are bound to us in spiritual community.[3]

Notes

1. This is a theme (with the same biblical verses being cited) that Hildegard is to hear again and again. The stress on humility is not, of course, unusual, but it seems particularly prominent in exhortations to Hildegard, because of the problem of gender. See Newman, *Sister of Wisdom*, esp. pp. 34–41.

2. At about the time Bernard was responding to Hildegard's letter, Pope Eugenius was already receiving word of Hildegard's visions, and a copy of an early portion of the *Scivias* was sent to him. Eugenius read from this work to the prelates assembled at the synod of Trier (November 1147–February 1148), and at just this point, Bernard interceded on Hildegard's behalf, with the happy result that Eugenius wrote Hildegard encouraging her to continue her work. Some MSS add the following sentence at this point: "It is said that you see celestial secrets, and, with the illumination of the Holy Spirit, learn things beyond the sight of mortals."

3. Some MSS add the following as a conclusion of this letter: "Since your spirit is joined to God, we are confident that you can be of great service to us and come to our aid. For 'the continual prayer of a just man availeth much' [James 5.16]. We, for our

part, pray for you constantly, so that you may be strengthened for good, instructed about the interior, and directed to the permanent. So, in this way, those who have put their hope in God will not limp in despair for you, but will progress to better and better things, well strengthened in the blessing which you, as we all know, have received from God."

2
Hildegard to Pope Eugenius
1148

Hildegard writes to Pope Eugenius asking him to look with favor upon her writing. Eugenius, a Cistercian monk before becoming pope, occupied the papal seat from 1145 to 1153. Events might well have been vastly different for Hildegard if this remarkable man had not been sitting on the papal throne at this particular time. In that same year of 1147, Eugenius had given his approval to Bernard Silvestris's *Cosmographia*, a work, like Hildegard's, deeply, disturbingly original. As Peter Dronke remarks (*Women Writers*, p. 148), "That both the *Cosmographia* and *Scivias* (the second still 'work in progress,' not completed till 1151) were given the blessing of this pope is of special importance in terms of twelfth-century intellectual history. Two writers who showed such daring in their cosmological conceptions and formulations could so easily, had it not been for Pope Eugene, have been persecuted, the works called in question and condemned by council or synod, as happened with Abelard, William of Conches, or Gilbert of Poitiers."

O gentle father, poor little woman[a] though I am, I have written those things to you which God saw fit to teach me in a true vision, by mystic inspiration.

O radiant father, through your representatives[1] you have come to us, just as God foreordained, and you have seen some of the writings of truthful visions, which I received from the Living Light,[b] and you have listened to these visions in the embraces of your heart. A part of this writing has now been completed.[2] But still that same Light has not left me, but it blazes in my soul, just as it has from my childhood. Therefore, I send this letter to you now, as God has instructed me. And my spirit desires that the Light of Light shine in you and purify your eyes and arouse your spirit to your duty concerning my writings, so that your soul may be crowned, which will be pleasing to God. In their instability, many people, those wise in worldly things, disparage these writings of mine, criticizing me, a poor creature formed from a rib, ignorant of philosophical matters.[c]

Therefore, father of pilgrims, hear Him Who Is: A mighty king sat in his palace, surrounded by great columns girt with golden bands and beautifully adorned with many pearls and precious stones. It pleased this king to touch a small feather[3] so that it flew miraculously, and a powerful wind sustained it so that it would not fall.

Now, He who is the Living Light shining in the heavens and in the abyss and Who lies hidden in the hearts of those who hear Him says again to you: Prepare this writing for the hearing of those who receive me and make it fruitful[4] with the juice of sweet savor; make it a root of the branches and a leaf flying in the face of the devil, and you will have eternal life. Do not spurn these mysteries of God, because they have a necessity which lies hidden and has not yet been revealed. May the odor [cf. II Cor 2.15] be sweet in you and may you not grow weary on the strait way.

Notes

1. While at the synod of Trier, the pope learned of Hildegard's visions through Heinrich, archbishop of Mainz, and he sent two papal legates to St. Disibod to obtain a copy of Hildegard's writing. What they returned with was the portion of the *Scivias* that had been completed at that time, from which the pope himself read before the prelates assembled at Trier. This reading made a deep impression on the audience, and from that followed the pope's letter to Hildegard granting apostolic license to continue with her writing.

2. It is hard to know just how much of the *Scivias* the pope saw at this time (that is, during the synod of Trier), certainly not the whole, we know with some assurance. For, a full ten years in the writing, the work was not completed until 1151.

3. This happy image of herself as prophet/writer sustained like a feather *(penna)* by a powerful wind (the Holy Spirit) is used frequently in the letters. Cf. also *Scivias* I.iv.196ff: "O daughter, flee, for the Mighty Giver, against whom no one can prevail, has given you wings *(pennae)* to fly. Fly quickly, therefore, over all these impediments. And, greatly comforted, I accepted those wings and flew swiftly over all things poisonous and deadly."

4. The word here is *viridem*. See Letter 1, note 9 above.

3

Hildegard to Pope Eugenius

1148–53

Note the difference in tone in this second letter to Pope Eugenius. Van Acker dates this letter between 1148 and 1153. From Hildegard's assured—even blunt and severe—attitude, an early date is not, one would think, very likely. Here, Hildegard is in full stride as the harsh, acrimonious prophet who has received the word from on high. It is one thing to adopt such a tone in a visionary, allegorical work like the *Scivias*, which was certainly being written in 1148; it is quite another to do so in a personal letter. The letter was likely written closer to 1153 than to

1148, though 1153, the year of Eugenius's death, is obviously the *terminus ad quem*.

Because of the foolishness of those who are too blind to see and too deaf to hear and too mute to speak, those whose treachery and thievery will lead to their own destruction—because of such, He Who is not silent speaks: And what does He say? The flashing sword strikes, cutting down the wicked.

O you who are, in your calling, the refulgent breastplate and the first root in the new marriage of Christ, O you who are divided into two parts (in the one, because your mind has been renewed in the mystic flower, the companion of virginity; in the other, because you are the main branch of the Church), hear Him who is mighty in name and who flows in the torrent: Do not destroy the sight of the eye, nor cut off light from light, but be absolutely equitable, lest you be held accountable for the state of those souls placed in your bosom. And do not allow them to be sunk in the lake of perdition through the power of high-living prelates. A jewel lies on the road, but a bear comes along and seeing that it is very fine stretches out his paw to pick it up and carry it off. But, suddenly, an eagle swoops down and snatches the jewel, wraps it in the covering of its wings, and carries it into the palace of the king. And this jewel shines so splendidly before the king that he sets great store by it, and because of his love of this jewel, he gives the eagle golden slippers, and praises it highly for its uprightness.[1]

Now, you who sit as Christ's representative on the throne of the Church, choose the better part [cf. Luke 10.42] so that you may be the eagle who overcomes the bear; in this way, you may adorn the halls of the Church with those souls entrusted to you. Thus you may snatch yourself from this world and enter the regions above in your golden slippers.

Notes

1. Viewed in light of the political climate of the day, the real figures are perhaps not difficult to recognize beneath the allegorical masks. Can it be other than that the bear represents the emperor; the eagle, the pope? The jewel lying on the road is, surely, independent ecclesiastic power, and the golden slippers represent divine approval of papal resistence to the erosion of ecclesiastic privilege.

4

Pope Eugenius to Hildegard

1151

The letter that occasioned this response from Eugenius has, unfortunately, not survived. Hildegard had written Eugenius in a final, desperate attempt to keep her beloved Richardis in her community. Eugenius here denies her request in effect, by referring the matter to others on grounds that assure no change. The rather long exhortation in the middle of the letter warning against the sin of presumption may perhaps, as Peter Dronke suggests (*Women Writers*, p. 156), be read as Eugenius's sense that, in this matter, Hildegard has stepped beyond her bounds—unless, of course, it simply repeats the usual, formulaic warnings against feminine pride.

Bishop Eugenius, servant of the servants of God, to Hildegard, beloved daughter in Christ, mistress of Mount St. Rupert, greetings and apostolic blessing.

We rejoice, my daughter, and we exult in the Lord, because your honorable reputation has spread so far and wide that many people regard you as "the odour of life unto life" [II Cor 2.16], and the multitudes of the faithful cry out, "Who is she that goeth up by the desert, as a pillar of smoke of aromatical spices?" [Cant 3.16].[1] Therefore, since it is clear to us that, up to this present time, your soul has been so kindled by the fire of divine love that you have no need of any exhortation to perform good works, we consider it superfluous to exhort you further or with a prop of words attempt to support a spirit which already sufficiently rests on divine virtue.

All the same, because a fire is increased by the bellows and a swift horse is impelled to greater speed by the spurs, we feel it incumbent upon us to remind you that the palm of glory belongs not to the one who begins but to the one who finishes the race, as the Lord says, "To him, that overcometh, I will give to eat of the tree of life, which is" in the middle of paradise [Apoc 2.7]. And so bear in mind, my daughter, that the ancient serpent who cast the first man out of Paradise longs to destroy the great (like Job) and, having consumed Judas, seeks power to sift the apostles [cf. Luke 22.31]. Moreover, as you know, many are called but few chosen [cf. Matt 22.14], so bring yourself into that small number and persist all the way to the end in your holy calling, and instruct the sisters entrusted to your care in the works of salvation so that, with them, you may be able with the help of the Lord to come to that joy "that eye hath not seen, nor ear heard, neither hath it entered into the heart of man" [I Cor 2.9].

Finally, we have delegated that matter you wished to consult us about[2] to our brother Heinrich, archbishop of Mainz. His task will be to make sure that the Rule is strictly observed in that monastery entrusted to that sister (the nun that you delivered up to him)—either that or to send her back to your supervision.[3] The transcript of my letter to him will give you the details.

Notes

1. How swiftly Hildegard's reputation seems to have spread in a few short years.
2. This "matter" is the subject on which Hildegard had appealed to the pope, after having exhausted all other efforts. Hildegard's most beloved nun, Richardis, had been elected abbess of Bassum, a move that Hildegard opposed from the beginning, and which she continued to strive to undo. In the *Vita* (II.ii.23) Hildegard is quoted with respect to Richardis, "For when I was writing the *Scivias*, I greatly loved a certain noble girl,

the daughter of the aforementioned margravine, just as Paul loved Timothy, and she joined herself to me in all things in diligent friendship and grieved with me in all my sufferings until I finished the book." See also Letter 12, Headnote.

3. As Peter Dronke notes (*Women Writers*, p. 156), "As Bassum was at that moment a more renowned Benedictine foundation than the Rupertsberg, this was a wholly hypothetical alternative."

5
Hildegard to Pope Eugenius
1153

Although Hildegard never once names him in the letter and although the letter itself is somewhat less than pellucid, Heinrich, Archbishop of Mainz, is the subject of this letter. Because of political complications with Barbarossa and also, probably, because of his own somewhat less than honorable character, Heinrich was removed from office. From very early on, Heinrich had been ardently supportive of Hildegard. It was he, for example, who brought Hildegard and her early work the *Scivias* to the attention of Pope Eugenius. Both here and in an epistle (Letter 7) to the two papal legates Eugenius sent to investigate the matter, Hildegard demonstrates her appreciation and loyalty to Heinrich.

He who knows and discerns all creatures, Who rouses them and is watchful over them, the Living Eye sees and says[a]: the valleys are complaining against the mountains,[1] and the mountains are falling into the valleys. What does this mean? Subordinates are no longer disciplined by the fear of God, and madness sends them scaling the heights of the mountains to rail at their superiors. And they are too blind to see the error of their evil ways. But they say, I am useful and therefore I should be preferred[2] for my usefulness. Thus they disparage everything that prelates do, because they scorn the notion that they are inferior to their prelates. Such subordinates are black clouds; they have not girded their loins; they scatter the seedlings of the field, saying that they are worthless. And they do this because they are full of the poison of envy. Foolish is the indigent man who envies another's fine clothes but does not wash the filth from his own ragged garments.

The mountains, on the other hand, leap over the key to the way of truth,[b] and they do not prepare the way so that they might fly to the mountain of myrrh [cf. Cant 4.6]. Just so, the stars are overshadowed by a dense cloud. The moon holds firm, and yet the stars cry out that it is falling. But the sun dims them all, because, caught up in the whirlwind, they cannot shine forth.

Wherefore, o great shepherd, vicar of Christ, illuminate the mountains and chastise the valleys. Give precepts to the teachers and discipline to the subordinates; give justice anointed with oil to the mountains and the obligation of obedience mixed with a sweet fragrance to the valleys, and make their paths straight so that they might not appear worthless to the Sun of righteousness [cf. Mal 4.2]. Purify your eyes so that nothing escapes your notice. Let your mind be watered by the pure fountain so that you may shine with the Sun and imitate the Lamb.

This poor little woman trembles because she speaks with the sound of words to so great a magistrate. But, gentle father, the Ancient Man and Magnificent Warrior says these things. Therefore, listen: The High Judge commands you to eradicate oppressive and impious tyrants, to cast them from your presence, so they may not stand in your company to your shame. Furthermore, have compassion on both public and private afflictions, because God does not reject the wounded, nor does he spurn the grief of those who tremble before Him.

Wherefore, o shepherd of the sheep [cf. John 10.2], hear these things concerning the priest who brings weariness to many. The Light says: The mysteries of God know the judgment over every person according to his merits. Yet many people, in their perverse overconfidence, are willing to be subjected to examination, but they have no idea how I make my judgments. In their high estimation of their own worth, they deceive themselves, and are like wolves seizing their prey [cf. Ezech 22.27]. Thus although certain people may deserve to be judged for their sins, it does not please me for them to take judgment into their own hands at their own discretion. By no means! Rather, it is your duty to judge with the maternal charity of the mercy of God [cf. Luke 1.78], Who does not cut off the poor and the needy from Himself, since he wishes mercy rather than sacrifice [cf. Hosea 6.6; Matt 9.13, 12.7]. As it is now, however, the vile seek to wash away their vileness with their own depravity, while they themselves are deaf and polluted lying in the ditch [cf. Matt 15.14, Luke 6.39]. Lift them up; give aid to the weak.

Notes

1. Hildegard frequently uses "mountains" as an image of the higher ecclesiastical offices, and "valleys," of subordinates. Here, atypically, she explains her usage quite openly.

2. The word we translate here as "preferred" is *prelatus*. The other forms of the word which cluster around this one—*prelatos, prelatorum*, etc.—we have translated simply as "prelate." Hildegard seems clearly to intend the pun.

6

Hildegard to Pope Eugenius

1153

Hildegard asks the pope to "thoughtfully weigh" the words of this letter. One wonders if he did, and if he did, what he thought of them, for the message of this enigmatic, allegorical letter is certainly not clear—beyond perhaps a general exhortation to call the straying Christian people back to the fold. Compare the vision here with the visions of the *Scivias*.

O shepherd of the people, hear this, that you may live forever.

The Living Light has said to me: Speak to the audacious people who find only terrors in the vanity of their erroneous ways, and say unto them: A certain lord had a marble city, and hunters came and sought to destroy its upright laws, the principles of that flower which the virginal mind created. And, behold, a towering mountain of beautiful polished stones appeared, facing the east. And upon that mountain there was a large building made of ordinary wood and stones.[1] Then, there came many rivers, as if from the middle of the east, flowing into that building. And therein also was the powerful odor of good wine, mixed with water. Then there rushed into that building a large number of people, all bent over and crooked. But others stood in the valley before the mountain and made their way to those who were walking all bent over in that building. And, behold, on that same mountain there stood another edifice, a building of white marble and unhewn stone, like a great tower, facing the north. And in this building there was hanging a radiantly bright bottle filled with the finest balsam, like a blazing fire; and there was oil flowing everywhere on the floor of that building. But, from time to time, there came a wind from the north troubling that balsam and oil. Then many of the people who were sprinkled with the oil and were sealed with that balsam on their foreheads [cf. Apoc 7.3][2] went into the building. And there came a voice from heaven saying: These are the sealed. And those who were sealed in this way were not able to wash away the sign, but remained sealed, just as those who have been reborn in Christ must preserve their baptism. And those who were sealed did not cross over to those who were not sealed, nor did they associate with them, for if they had done so they would have been called foolish and worthless. Those who were not sealed, however, crossed over to those who were and associated with them. In this way, they chose the best part [cf. Luke 10.42], just as a star increases its brightness in a cloud, and a woman is crowned in her virginity. There was also a huge man girt with a golden sash [cf. Apoc 1.13] standing over those buildings, with his right arm on the marble one and his left on the other.

Understood properly, this man stands for the two instruments of ecclesiastical authority. For the omnipotent Father has established a noble part, independent and distinct from secular cases, burning brightly in its secrets before God. Yet there are certain treacherous people who despise it and seek to destroy its justice—which was made manifest in the Son of God. Yet this mountain of justice, burnished with many merciful judgments, ascends from the place of truth, from which arises a useful institution, tending toward God (and therefore assisting mankind), providing a light for man's benefit. Therefore, many teachings and the fragrance of orthodox writing flow from the vigor of truth to it, but some people frequently reject them without justification. It is for this reason that there are many walking about all bent over with corruption, so much so that other people who gape after earthly things imitate their depravity. Yet that part of the mountain mentioned before rises up in its integrity to resist the devil, burning in its secrets before God, having its best part in God, presenting a model of compassion. Still, the many temptations sent by the devil often sully the best part and that compassion. Many people, nevertheless, cross over and pursue true compassion, choosing the best part for themselves. Whence they are said to be sealed before God. And those who receive the seal of this part remain in it tenaciously, just as in their own baptism. Thus it is that they do not descend to associate with those who do not have that seal, so that they will not become useless or foolish. Yet those who do not have the seal ascend to associate with that order and, therefore, are greatly multiplied in blessings. This is what the man girt with the golden sash stands for: he shows that he is both God and man, Who rules both the sealed and the unsealed with his mighty arm. He protects the one group so that they may burn vigorously in him, casting aside the things of this world; and he covers the others with his mild arm so that, through divine protection, they may do good service by offering the light of truth to their neighbors.

Now, you who are the father of the people thoughtfully weigh these words which have been sent to you from the most high Judge for the sake of those who have gone astray. For pride always seeks to oppress humility. This is no more proper than if the moon sought to fight with the sun, seeking to make her brightness like his.

Notes

1. This rhetorical device of describing a building, or various rooms within a building, in moral terms seems almost habitual with Hildegard. It is, P. Dronke remarks (*Women Writers*, p. 161), "something Hildegard had learnt from the second-century prophetic treatise *Pastor Hermas*."

2. It is unclear who the "sealed" represent, but see Letter 15r where she speaks of the clergy as *signati* "sealed." Also see *Scivias* III.xii.4: "*And some of them were sealed in the faith, but some, not. And so the conscience of those who have faith shine with the radiance of wisdom, but the conscience of the others is black from their neglect.* Thus they are clearly distinguished. For the former have fulfilled their faith with works, but the latter have extinguished it in themselves. Certain ones do not have the sign of faith, however, because they chose to know the true, living God neither in the old Law nor in the new Grace."

7

Hildegard to Bernard and Gregory, Cardinals

1153

This letter is addressed to Bernard of St. Clement and Gregory of St. Angeli, the two cardinal legates Pope Eugenius sent to Germany to negotiate with Frederick

Barbarossa over his tensions with Rome, especially his removal from office of "unsuitable" bishops, including Heinrich of Mainz, who is the real subject of this letter. See Letter 5, Headnote.

The Fountain of Waters cries out to you, his followers: In my powerful and eternal name, chastise and correct those wicked traitors and furtive opportunists who have been turned into lead through their twisted sins, those who are scattered from the north[1] through the iniquities of the devil, and who maliciously strike out at their superiors through their great wickedness. Therefore, cast them out of their pastoral seat, which bears the penalty of dogs.[2] For even though certain prelates walk in darkness because of the instability of their ways, it is still not proper for them to be cast down by subordinates.[3]

Therefore, look into these matters with a pure eye lest your own honor be tainted, for, in consequence, this reflects on Him, Who was, and is, upright and just in all His ways in all His servants and Who foresaw all these things before the foundation of time. May He who spurns neither the orphan nor the pauper make your eyes pure [cf. Ps 10.14], because you are the mountain of myrrh and incense [cf. Cant 4.6], towering over the valleys of the filthy pit. Therefore, listen to Him Who is always watchful with living eyes and Who is not wearied by storms, the storms that are the portion of those who are like idols [cf. Ps 10.7], as if they were gods in their prosperity. Yet since you wish to be honored like a great mountain in the King's palace, spread abroad the justice of the Most High for His glory. This is your proper task, because of your illustrious name.

Now, therefore, look to the Fiery Giver who endows mankind with discernment. What person can pit his voice against that which thundered above the heavens and overcame the abyss, ornamenting it with the covering of maternal fruitfulness? And what wings of the winds in their swiftness can outrun that voice? Mankind's voice, after all, cannot make a small feather fly so that no sword can move against it.[4]

Now you, O emulators of the Most High, the Living Fountain cries out these things to you, because it is not fitting for you to have the eyes of the blind nor even a trace of the morals of vipers and the thievery of brigands, stripping bare the altar of God. Why, therefore, are you doing this? But because you are doing so, you are not able to loosen the Lord's shoestring [cf. John 1.27]. Therefore, discipline yourselves.

Notes

1. Associated with Satan and the fallen angels through the prophecies of Jeremiah and Ezechiel, north is always an evil direction in Hildegard's work, as in medieval thought generally.

2. Hildegard's phrase *(penam de canibus)* has an odd ring, but see Widukind, *Res Gestae Saxonicae* II.6, where the Saxon king imposes a penalty on certain military leaders: *dedecore canum, quos portabant usque ad urbem regiam quam vocitamus Magathaburg*, i.e., "the disgrace of dogs, which creatures they were required to carry all the way to the

royal city which we call Magdeburg." We are indebted to Timothy Reuter for calling Widukind to our attention through E-mail from Munich.[1]

3. Since we know that this letter concerns Heinrich, archbishop of Mainz, the sense of this enigmatic language seems to be that those churchmen clamoring for Heinrich's ouster—since they, of course, would be Heinrich's subordinates—should themselves be chastised and brought into line.

4. There is a problem of ambiguity here: Hildegard's inattentive shifting from the one voice (God's) to the other (mankind's) renders the last sentence of the paragraph, at least on a first reading, meaningless. At least two scribes were troubled by the sense and sought to correct it, for two of the MSS add *potest* ("can it") at the end. Hildegard apparently intended the "voice" in this last sentence to be mankind's, not God's as it would appear to be from the context. We have handled the problem by simply making explicit the seeming intention.

8
Hildegard to Pope Anastasius
1153–54

Anastasius was already in his eighties when he was chosen pope in 1153, elected on the very day of the death of his predecessor Eugenius. He himself died the very next year, in 1154, his period of office lasting from 12 July 1153 to 3 December 1154. The reason for Hildegard's harshness toward this pope—at least, so one gathers from the scanty evidence available—is his reputation (probably undeserved) for coming to terms too easily with the emperor, and compromising away ecclesiastical privilege.

O you who are the estimable defense and the bulwark of a beautifully adorned city, which has been established as the bride of Christ, hear Him who is eternal and does not grow weary.

You, O man, who are too tired, in the eye of your knowledge, to rein in the pomposity of arrogance among those placed in your bosom, why do you not call back the shipwrecked who cannot rise from the depths without help? And why do you not cut off the root of evil which is choking out the good and beneficial plants of sweet taste and delightful aroma?[1] You are neglecting the King's daughter who was entrusted to you, that is, heavenly Justice herself. You are allowing this King's daughter to be thrown to the ground: her beautiful crown and tunic torn asunder by the crudeness of those hostile people who bark like dogs and who, like chickens trying to sing at night, raise up their ineffectual voices. They are charlatans, crying out, ostensibly, for peace, but, all the while, biting each other in their hearts, like a dog that wags its tail among those known to him, but bites the honorable knight indispensable to the king's household. Why do you put up with depraved people who are blinded by foolishness and who delight in harmful things, like a hen which cackles in the night and terrifies herself? Such people are completely useless.

Listen, therefore, O man, to the One who loves the power of discernment, so that He himself has established the great instrument of uprightness to fight against evil. But you are not exercising this faculty when you do not root out the evil which seeks to choke the good. Rather, you are allowing evil to raise itself up arrogantly; and you do this because of your fear of those wicked people who lie in wait in the night, and who love the money of death more than the King's beautiful daughter, Justice.

And yet all the works of God are resplendently bright. Hear, O man. For the heavenly Father, before the beginning of the world, intoned in his secret: O my son. And the sphere of the world arose, taking up this word intoned by the Father, while the various species of creatures still lay hidden in the darkness. In that same word that was written, "And God said: Let there be" [Gen 1. 6], the various kinds of creatures came forth. Thus through the word of the Father and because of the word of the Father all creatures were made by the will of the Father.

And God sees all things and foreknows all things. But evil, neither by rising nor falling, is able of itself to make anything or create anything or do anything, because it is nothing but a false choice, an opinion contrary to God's will, and it is through this wrong choice that one does evil.

But God sent his Son into the world, so that He might overcome the devil (who knew evil by embracing it, and made it desirable to mankind) and so that those who had perished through evil might be redeemed. Wherefore God rejects perverse works, like fornication, murder, theft, rebellion, tyranny, and the deceitfulness of sinful people, since He has crushed these things through the Son who has completely scattered the spoils of hell's tyrant.

Wherefore, O man, you who sit on the papal throne, you despise God when you embrace evil. For in failing to speak out against the evil of those in your company, you are certainly not rejecting evil. Rather, you are kissing it. And so the whole world is being led astray through unstable error, simply because people love that which God has cast down.

And you, O Rome, when you are lying at the point of death, you will be so shaken that the strength of your feet, upon which you have stood so far, will no longer sustain you. For you do not love the King's daughter, that is, Justice, with a blazing passion, but with a dull sloth, so that, in fact, you banish her from your presence. Indeed, she is ready to flee from you, if you do not call her back. Yet the high mountains[2] will offer help to you still, raising you up and supporting you with the branches of lofty trees, so that your nobility (that is, the majesty of your betrothal to Christ) will not be completely destroyed. Thus you will retain some vestiges of your beauty, until the snow of the morals of hostile derision comes, which ends in insanity. Beware, therefore, of becoming entangled in pagan rites, lest you fall.[a] Now, hear Him who lives and will never die. The world is now lascivious, and will later become sad. Then will come such great terror that people will not care whether they are killed or not. In the midst of all this: times of wantonness, times of contrition, times of the thunder and lightning of iniquity. For the eye rages, the nose robs,³ the mouth kills. Yet healing will come forth from the heart when the dawn appears like the splendor of the first sunrise. Those things which will follow in the new desire and the new fervor, however, must not be spoken now.⁴

But He who is great and without flaw has now touched a humble dwelling, so that it might see a miracle and form unknown letters and utter an unknown tongue. And this was said to that little habitation: You have written these things in a language given to you from above, rather than in ordinary human speech, since it was not revealed to you in that form, but let him who has the pumice stone not fail to polish it and make it intelligible to mankind.⁵ᵇ

But, you, O man, since you are clearly the shepherd appointed by God, rise up and run quickly to Justice, so that you will not be accused before the great physician of failing to cleanse his sheepfold and of neglecting to anoint his flock with oil. Still, when a man's will has not consented to wrongdoing and when he himself has not been overwhelmed by desire, he will not be condemned absolutely. The flaw of ignorance can be cleansed by the lash.

Therefore, you, O man, stand on the strait path, and God will save you and bring you back into the abode of blessing and election, and you will live forever.

Notes

1. The image of the garden with fragrant plants is one of Hildegard's favorite tropes in the letters. Cf. *Scivias* I.ii.741ff.

2. Here, once again, *mountains = prelates*.

3. Van Acker's text actually reads "The nose tastes or has understanding" *(sapit)*, a reading that ill-fits the context of violence here. We have translated "The nose robs" *(rapit)*, which is the reading of two MSS—although, it must be admitted, the sense is scarcely improved.

4. Following Christ's own admonition (Acts 1.7), Hildegard regards some events in the salvation history to come, as well as some present mysteries, as forbidden to be revealed, at least completely, and warns against rash inquiry into things not to be searched out. See, for example, *Scivias* III.vii.474–80: "Anyone who searches out what God was before He created the world or what God will be after the last day will be cut off from his portion of the sacred communion, for such things are not to be known by a finite mortal weighed down with sins." See also *Scivias* III.x.171ff and III.xi.826ff.

5. This letter is cited in the *Vita* (II.i.14), but the writer apparently found this passage all too enigmatic and attempted to bring some clarity to it by adding *"in Latina lingua."*

9

Hildegard to Pope Hadrian

1154–59

This is Hadrian IV, Nicholas Breakspear, the first and only English pope. He was consecrated in office on 5 December 1154 and served until his death on 1 September 1159—hence Van Acker's dating. If this letter is an exhortation to Hadrian to take stern measures with the unruly, ever-fickle Romans, it was perhaps unneeded. Hadrian took the unusual and bold step of putting the city under interdict soon after coming into power. This letter with its allegorical creatures and its vague allusiveness is one of the most difficult to grasp the sense of—or to translate. For Hildegard's use of allegorical animals, see *Scivias*, especially Book III.

He who gives life to the living says: O man, because you allow the fierce rage of she-lions and the mighty strength of leopards, you will fall victim to them yourself, and you will come to realize that there is shipwreck in the capture of booty, because you have been given to all those who run to you in weariness. But you have an intelligence keen enough to confront the fierce character of men, and by raging against them, you will rein in those careening horses which never leave off running down the paths of plunder. But, for all that, you are at times in conflict with your own better self in your partiality toward the putative probity of certain people when you conceal the coffers of those who died fighting on the plains. For this reason you will experience a battle of great ferocity, but you will destroy the chattel of those remaining, who fall into the pit because of their hardness of heart. Yet you have the power of the mighty key [cf. Matt 16.19], which does not go gladly to the Passover in the form of a sard.[1a]

Lest you fall into the whirlwind, therefore, in your heart seek the salvation of waters so that you may find rest in gentleness to the distress and hurt of those who have been wounded by the wounds of disorder. In this you will imitate the Savior, who redeemed you. And God will never desert you, but you will see by His light.

Note

1. This is quite obscure. For the Latin text, see the Endnote. On the sard, cf. Ex 28.17 and Apoc 21.

10

Hildegard to Pope Alexander III[1]

1173

> This letter is one of the frequent complaints Hildegard is forced to voice against her former community of St. Disibod. In 1173 Hildegard's friend and secretary, who had served her faithfully for over thirty years, the monk Volmar, died. Volmar had also served as provost of the convent, and on his death, the troublesome Helengerus, abbot of St. Disibod, refused to replace him. Hence Hildegard's letter here. The pope's intervention brought about the election of Gottfried, who served as provost only a short time, until his death in 1176. Gottfried took advantage of his position, however, to begin a *Vita* of Hildegard. By the time of Gottfried's death, Hildegard was already in touch with Guibert of Gembloux, who became her secretary in 1177 and served in that capacity until her death.

O lofty and glorious one, first appointed through the Word of God through whom every creature, rational and non-rational, was made according to its kind, to you has that same Word, by robing Himself in humanity,[2] specially yielded the keys of the kingdom of heaven, that is, the power of binding and loosing [cf. Matt 16.19]. You are also, O most excellent father, the source of all spiritual offices. Some of these sound the trumpet of God's justice in the Church, which shines because it has been clothed with various ornaments [cf. Ps 44.8–10], while others set good examples for other people by imitating the lives of the saints, and if they bring forth good works, they attribute them to God and not to themselves. Rejoicing in those who seek to emulate them, they follow the saints who conquered their flesh and, fighting against the sins of the devil, fortified themselves with the clear victory of heaven's army, and with good will looked upon God, just as the angels do.

And so, O mild father, imitate that kindly father who joyfully received his penitent son at his return and killed the fatted calf for his sake [cf. Luke 15.20ff]; and emulate also that man who washed with wine the wounds of the one beaten by robbers[a] [cf. Luke 10.30ff]. By these examples understand the harshness of reproof and the godliness of compassion.[3] And be the Morning Star which precedes the sun, a guide to the Church, which, for far too long, has been lacking in the light of God's justice because of the dense cloud of schism.[4] And with God's zeal seize the penitents and anoint them with the oil of mercy, because God desires mercy more than sacrifice [Hosea 6.6; Matt 9.13, 12.7].

Now O gentlest father, my sisters and I bend our knees before your paternal piety, praying that you deign to regard the poverty of this poor little woman. We are in great distress because the abbot of Mount St. Disibod and his brothers have taken away our privileges and the right of election which we have always had, rights which we have been ever careful to retain. For if they will not grant us reverential and religious men, such as we seek, spiritual religion will be totally destroyed among us. Therefore, my lord, for God's sake, help us, so that we may retain the man we have elected to that office. Or, if not, let us seek out and receive others, where we can, who will look after us in accordance with the will of God and our own needs.

Now again we ask you, most pious father, not to despise our petition or our messengers, who on the advice of our faithful friend took up our cause. May you grant that which they seek to obtain from you, so that after the end of this life, which is already hastening toward evening, you may come to that inextinguishable light and hear the sweet voice of the Lord saying, "Well done, good and faithful servant, because thou hast been faithful over a few things, I will place thee over many things: enter thou into the joy of thy lord" [Matt 25.21, 23]. Incline the ears of your piety to our supplications, therefore, and be the bright day to us and to them, so that from the kindness of your generosity we may give thanks to the Lord together, and you may rejoice forever in eternal happiness.

Notes

1. Alexander spent most of his long reign (1159–81) resisting the power of the empire, from the very beginning when his election was disputed by the anti-pope Victor IV, through two succeeding anti-popes, until reconciliation with Frederick I in 1177.

2. *per indumentum humanitatis sue.* This image of Christ's putting on the robe of mankind's flesh at the incarnation is a particular favorite of Hildegard's. She returns to it again and again.

3. At times, Hildegard can sound extremely harsh in her condemnations, but usually (and it is a common theme in her writing), as here, she stresses justice tempered by mercy.

4. The schism began in 1159 with the disputed election of Alexander III and Victor IV. After Victor's death Barbarossa chose another anti-pope, and, after him, another. The schism lasted until 1177 with the reconciliation between Barbarossa and Alexander III.

10r
Pope Alexander III to Wezelinus

1173

In answer to Hildegard's request, the pope appoints Wezelinus, Hildegard's nephew, to look into the matter. Wezelinus acquitted himself well in this disagreeable task, for through his efforts, Abbot Helengerus of Mount St. Disibod assigned the monk Gottfried to Hildegard to serve as provost and secretary.

Alexander, servant of the servants of God, to our beloved son, abbot of St. Andrew in Cologne, greetings and apostolic blessings.

On behalf of our beloved daughter in Christ, Hildegard, prioress of Mount St. Rupert in Bingen[a] and of the sisters of that place, you should know that it has come to our attention that when, according to their custom, they had elected for themselves a master and provost from the monastery of St. Disibod, the abbot of that place was unwilling to acknowledge the election of the person from his monastery, and even up to the present time still refuses to assign that person to them. Wherefore since it is proper that there be provision for the aforementioned sisters in those things which pertain to the salvation of their souls, we mandate to your discretion through apostolic writings that you call together both sides to your presence once you have made inquiry into this and have more clearly understood this matter of the election of the provost. Then decide the case with proper justice. And if these sisters cannot have a provost from that monastery, see to it, at least, that they have a competent one from another.

11

Hildegard to Hartwig, Archbishop of Bremen

After 1148

This letter has little more to say than greetings and compliment. Is this one of those instances where the "meat" of the letter was delivered by the messenger himself? Hartwig belonged to the noble and highly connected von Stade family. His mother Richardis was an early and strong supporter of Hildegard, and his sister, also Richardis, was Hildegard's most beloved nun.

May the One Who saw you on the first day look upon you and direct you to His will, He Who gave you eyes to see and wings to fly, and Who made mankind a mirror of the fulness of all his miracles, so that the knowledge of God shines in him, as it is written, "You are gods and all of you are sons of the most High" [Ps 81.6].

When a person's reason imitates God, he touches God, Who has neither beginning nor end, for the knowledge of good and evil reveals God. Such is the wheel of eternity.

May God see to it that you flee that evil which arose on the first day and which, lacking good will, stands always opposed to God. May He also make windows in you which shine in the heavenly Jerusalem [cf. Heb 12.22], windows beautifully glazed with the virtues.[a] And may He cause you to fly in the embraces of God's love, just as the one anointed by God's spirit said: "Who are these, that fly as clouds, and as doves to their windows?" [Is 60.8].

For I, a poor little form of a woman, have seen the light of salvation in you. Now, fulfill the precepts of God which his grace gives, and the Holy Spirit teaches you.

12

Hildegard to Hartwig, Archbishop of Bremen

1151–52

This letter is one in a series of efforts by Hildegard to retrieve the nun Richardis, Hartwig's sister. Soon after moving to Mount St. Rupert, Hildegard suffered her greatest loss: Richardis, her beloved disciple, who had assisted her with the *Scivias*. Richardis, apparently out of her own wishes, was elected abbess of Bassum, but Hildegard, at first, refused to grant permission for her move. This letter to Hartwig, asking him to intervene in the matter is actually a late entry in the controversy. Hildegard had already written in complaint to Richardis's mother, as well as a missile of a letter to the archbishop of Mainz (Letter 18r), who had written to Hildegard demanding that she release Richardis to her new post. In a final effort, Hildegard wrote an appeal to Pope Eugenius, the text of which has not come down to us, though the pope's response has (Letter 4).

You are a man worthy of great praise, as one must be who holds the episcopal office in direct succession from almighty God Himself.[a] Therefore, may your eye see God, your intellect grasp His justice, and your heart burn brightly in the love of God, so that your spirit may not grow weak. Be zealous to build the tower of celestial Jerusalem [cf. Heb 12.22], and may God give you that sweetest mother Mercy as your assistant. Be a bright star shining in the darkness of the night of wicked men, and be a swift hart running to the fountain of living water [cf. John 4.10]. Be alert, for many shepherds are blind and halt nowadays, and they are seizing the lucre of death, choking out God's justice.

O dear man, your soul is dearer to me than your family.[1] Now hear me, cast down as I am, miserably weeping at your feet. My spirit is exceedingly sad, because a certain horrible man has trampled underfoot my desire and will (and not mine alone, but also my sisters' and friends'), and has rashly dragged our beloved daughter Richardis out of our cloister.[2] Since God knows all things, He knows where pastoral care is useful, and so let no person of faith canvass for such an office.[b] Thus if anyone, in his madness, willfully seeks to gain ecclesiastic office, he is a rapacious wolf seeking the delights of power more than the will of God. The soul of such a person, therefore, never seeks spiritual office with proper faith.[3] Therein lies simony.

It was, therefore, inappropriate for our abbot, in his blindness and ignorance, to involve this holy soul in this affair and, in the blindness of his spirit, to encourage such great temerity. If our daughter had remained content, God would have fulfilled his glorious purpose for her.

I do not oppose any selection God has made, nor would I ever do so. Therefore, in the name of Him who gave His life for you and in the name of his holy Mother, I beseech you, you who hold the episcopal office in the order of Melchisedech [cf. Ps 109.4; Heb 5.6, 6.20], to send my dearest daughter back to me.[4] If you do so, God will give you the blessing which Isaac gave to his son Jacob [cf. Gen 27.27–29] and which He gave through his angel to Abraham for his obedience [cf. Gen 22.15–18].

Hear me now, and do not cast off my words, as your mother, your sister, and Count Hermann have all done. I am doing you no harm not consonant with the will of God and the salvation of your sister's soul, but I seek to be consoled through her and her through me. What God has ordained, I do not oppose.[c]

May God grant you the blessing of the dew of heaven [cf. Gen 27.28], and may all the choirs of angels bless you if you listen to me, God's servant, and if you fulfill God's will in this matter.

Notes

1. *amabilis anima tua pre genere tuo.* The remark is not, it seems clear, an invidious one, that is, that he is dearer to her than his family since they have already turned down her request. It is rather an attempt to put the case on the proper footing: that spiritual matters take precedence over familial influence and power, which is her whole argument here. Our thanks to Barbara Newman for her assistance in helping us understand the point being made.

2. Hildegard is speaking of Abbot Kuno of St. Disibod, for whom she has little affection in any case, since, among other things, he had attempted to prevent her move to Mount St. Rupert.

3. Here, as elsewhere, Hildegard, in her grief, comes perilously close to accusing Richardis of simony, though much of the blame is shunted off onto Kuno. Interestingly, Richardis was still with Hildegard when she wrote similar warnings about seeking office against God's will. See *Scivias* III.vi.474ff and III.ix.561ff.

4. Bassum lay in Hartwig's diocese, and thus he would indeed have had the authority to return Richardis.

13
Hartwig, Archbishop of Bremen, to Hildegard

1152

This touching letter informing Hildegard of the sudden, unexpected death of Richardis represents the last, sad duty of the brother, in this case, the brother who had stood firm against all of Hildegard's attempts to retrieve Richardis. It is almost as if Hildegard had been right all along (a thought which must surely have been in the minds of all those who had held firm against her), that Richardis should never have left her side. To her everlasting praise, Hildegard's answer to this letter is magnanimous and forgiving.

Hartwig, archbishop of Bremen, brother of the abbess Richardis, sends that which is in the place of a sister and more than a sister, obedience, to Hildegard, mistress of the sisters of St. Rupert.[1]

I write to inform you that our sister—my sister in body, but yours in spirit—has gone the way of all flesh, little esteeming that honor I bestowed upon her. And (while I was on my way to see the earthly king) she was obedient to her lord, the heavenly King. I am happy to report that she made her last confession in a saintly and pious way and that after her confession she was anointed with consecrated oil. Moreover, filled with her usual Christian spirit, she tearfully expressed her longing for your cloister with her whole heart. She then committed herself to the Lord through His mother and St. John. And sealed three times with the sign of the cross, she confessed the Trinity and Unity of God, and died on October 29 in perfect faith, hope, and charity [cf. I Cor 13.13], as we know for certain. Thus I ask as earnestly as I can, if I have any right to ask, that you love her as much as she loved you, and if she appeared to have any fault—which indeed was mine, not hers—at least have regard for the tears that she shed for your cloister, which many witnessed. And if death had not prevented, she would have come to you as soon as she was able to get permission. But since death did intervene, be assured that, God willing, I will come in her place. May God, who repays all good deeds, recompense you fully in this world and in the future for all the good things you did for her, you alone, more even than relatives or friends; may He repay that benevolence of yours which she rejoiced in before God and me. Please convey my thanks to your sisters for all their kindness.

Note

1. It would be difficult to cite a more poignant and at the same time more obdurate insistence on recognition of the proper hierarchy. Even in this grieving report of Richardis's death, Hartwig stresses the difference in social station: his sister's office was the higher, *"Richardis abbatisse," "Hildegardi magistre sororum."*

13r

Hildegard to Hartwig, Archbishop of Bremen

1152

> This is Hildegard's magnanimous, sad response to Hartwig's letter informing her of Richardis's death. All acrimony gone, all hints of simony laid aside, Hildegard's letter is a eulogy on the beauty and holiness of her beloved nun.

O how great a miracle there is in the salvation of those souls so looked upon by God that His glory has no hint of shadow in them. But He works in them like a mighty warrior who takes care not to be defeated by anyone, so that his victory may be sure.

Just so, dear man, was it with my daughter Richardis, whom I call both daughter and mother, because I cherished her with divine love, as indeed the Living Light had instructed me to do in a very vivid vision.

God favored her so greatly that worldly desire had no power to embrace her. For she always fought against it, even though she was like a flower in her beauty and loveliness in the symphony of this world.[a] While she was still living in the body, in fact, I heard the following words concerning her in a true vision: "O virginity, you are standing in the royal bridal chamber."[1] Now, in the tender shoot of virginity, she has been made a part of that most holy order, and the daughters of Zion rejoice [Zeph 3.14, Zach 2.10, 9.9]. But the ancient serpent had attempted to deprive her of that blessed honor by assaulting her through her human nobility.[2] Yet the mighty Judge drew this my daughter to Himself, cutting her off from all human glory. Therefore, although the world loved her physical beauty and her worldly wisdom while she was still alive, my soul has the greatest confidence in her salvation. For God loved her more. Therefore, He was unwilling to give His beloved to a heartless lover, that is, to the world.[3]

Now you, dear Hartwig, you who sit as Christ's representative, fulfill the desire of your sister's soul, as obedience demands. And just as she always had your interests at heart, so you now take thought for her soul, and do good works as she wished. Now, as for me, I cast out of my heart that grief you caused me in the matter of this my daughter. May God grant you, through the prayers of the saints, the dew of His grace and reward in the world to come.

Notes

1. Hildegard is quoting herself. See *Ordo Virtutum*, v. 104.
2. This, apparently, is an oblique reference to Hildegard's muted simony charge, Richardis's gaining the office through the influence of her family.

3. *Sed Deus illam plus dilexit. Idcirco noluit Deus amicam suam dare inimico amatori, id est mundo.* The blending of secular and divine love in this paragraph, or, perhaps better, the expression of divine love in earthly terms is simply exquisite: the beautiful, highborn lady, beloved for both her beauty and her wit and wooed by two very different lovers, is carried off by the worthiest of the two.

14
Arnold, Archbishop of Cologne, to Hildegard

1150–56(?)

The archbishop of Cologne writes to ask Hildegard to send him a copy of the *Scivias*. Van Acker indicates some little latitude (1150–56) for the date of this letter, and even then with an additional question mark. If the requested book "which you wrote under the inspiration of the Holy Spirit" is indeed—and there seems no reason to doubt that it is—the *Scivias* ("whether it is complete or not"), one would think that an earlier date (say, 1150–52) might be more appropriate, since the *Scivias* was finished in 1151.

Arnold, archbishop of Cologne by the grace of God, to Hildegard, a blazing lantern in the house of the Lord at Mount St. Rupert. May you forever remain in the protection of the God of Heaven.

If you are well, with all things around you being directed by the Lord, we rejoice. Thanks to your merits with the Lord, we also are well. We are, however, unable to visit you as we had planned some time ago. Nevertheless, we entrust ourselves to you as far as we can at the present time, putting our hands into yours, joining our faith to yours, completely commending ourselves to you.

In the meantime, please do not hesitate to send, through the good offices of the present messenger, that book which you wrote under the inspiration of the Holy Spirit. For whether it is complete or not, we are neither willing nor able to do without it—not because we wish to tempt God, but because we long to see His miracles.

14r
Hildegard to Arnold, Archbishop of Cologne

1150–56(?)

> Hildegard's response notifies the archbishop that she has sent her "book of truthful visions" out to him. Once again she affirms that nothing in the book is from her own will, but all from the Living Light. Then, oddly, she claims the same thing for the present letter, a curious remark indeed for a letter which merely indicates that she is fulfilling the interlocutor's request. There is, clearly, something amiss with the text as we have received it. The version in the *Patrologia* is much longer and does indeed report a vision in detail. But see Van Acker, *Der Briefwechsel* (1989), p. 140, for details.

Now then, O shepherd of your people, I—poor little woman that I am—sent my book of truthful visions to you, just as you requested. I remind you that it contains nothing originating from human wisdom nor from my own will, but rather it contains those truths which the unfailing Light wished to reveal through his own words. Indeed, this very letter which I am now writing to you came in a similar manner, not from my intellect nor through any human mediation, but through divine revelation.

15
Dean Philip[1] and the Clerics of Cologne to Hildegard

1163(?)

> Philip writes Hildegard to request a copy of the sermon she recently preached at Cologne.

Philip, unworthy dean, and the entire chapter of the cathedral of Cologne send greetings to that venerable partaker of the portion which Mary chose [cf. Luke 10.42], Hildegard of St. Rupert in Bingen, who, in the purity of her heart, gazes upon God in the present life, and, in the life to come, face to face [cf. I Cor 13.12].

Because we esteem your maternal piety, we want to inform you that after your recent visit to us at God's command when, through divine inspiration, you revealed the words of life to us,² we were greatly astonished that God works through such a fragile vessel, such a fragile sex, to display the great marvels of His secrets.

But "the spirit breatheth where he will" [John 3.8].³ For since it is abundantly clear that the Spirit has chosen a dwelling pleasing to Himself in your heart, understandably we come to you in admiration as if to the living temple of God to offer up prayers, and we seek responses of truth from your heart, as if from the very oracle of God.ᵃ We sincerely beseech you, blessed lady, to commend our desires earnestly to God, since they pertain to the welfare of souls. And if your soul, clinging to God as usual, sees anything concerning us in a true vision, please inform us in a letter. We further request that you commit to writing and send us those things that you said to us earlier in person, since, given over as we are to carnal lusts, we all too readily ignore spiritual matters, neither seeing nor hearing them.

Farewell, beloved lady. May God whom you love with your whole heart be with you.

Notes

1. Philip of Heinsberg will later (1167) become archbishop of Cologne, and exchange letters with Hildegard in that capacity. An able and powerful administrator, he favored Barbarossa during the schism, and served as imperial chancellor. It was apparently Philip who later as archbishop of Cologne commissioned Guibert of Gembloux to produce his life of Hildegard.

2. On her third preaching tour which took place some time between 1161 and 1163, Hildegard preached at Cologne. Later in this letter, Philip asks for a written copy of the sermon delivered at that time, and Hildegard's response, Letter 15r, apparently fulfills that request.

3. It is interesting to note how frequently this verse is used to justify God's use of a woman. See also Letter 20.

15r

Hildegard to the Shepherds of the Church

1163(?)

With this letter, Hildegard fulfills Philip's request for a copy of the sermon preached at Cologne, a scathing public sermon charging the clerics of Cologne with negligence in their cure of souls. As a result of their neglect and of their sinful ways, she charges, people are being seduced away from the True Way by the Cathars (who were known for their chastity and virtue) and it is toward the sect of the Cathars, especially active in Cologne, that she directs her most piercing, mordant criticism. Indeed, the stress throughout on the sanctity of the created world seems directed at the Cathar doctrine of the inherent evil in all created things. The appendices furnishing material from the Riesenkodex may not be entirely spurious, that is, non-Hildegardian, but as Barbara Newman suggests (*Sister*, p. 234, note 89), may be material inserted from sermons on a like theme that Hildegard preached on other occasions.

"The one who was, and is, and is about to come" [Apoc 1.4] speaks to the shepherds of the Church: He Who Was was about to make all creation, so that it had the testimony of testimonies in itself by doing all His works just as He wished. He Who Is made all creation and showed the testimony of testimonies in all His works, so that each created thing appeared. He Who Is About To Come will purge all things, and He will re-create them in a different way, and He will wash away all the blemishes of the times and the seasons, and He will make all things ever new, and after the purgation He will reveal unknown things. From Him the wind blows, saying: lacking no power, I have set the firmament with all its ornaments, with eyes to see, ears to hear, a nose to smell, a mouth to taste. For the sun is like the light of His eyes, the wind like the hearing of His ears, the air like His fragrance, the dew like His taste, exuding viridity like His mouth. The moon marks the times of the seasons, and reveals knowledge to men. And the stars, which seem to be rational, are indeed so, because they are circular, just as rationality embraces many things. I shored up the four corners of the earth with fire, cloud, and water, and in this way I joined together all the boundaries of the world like veins. I formed rocks from fire and water like bones, and I established earth from moisture and viridity like marrow. I stretched out the abyss like feet which hold up the body, around which the exuding waters serve as its foundation. Everything was made in this way so as not to fail. If the clouds did not have fire and water, there would be no firm bond, and if earth did not have moisture and viridity, it would crumble like ashes. And if the other luminaries did not have the light of the sun's fire, they would not shine through the waters, but would be invisible.[a]

These are the materials for the instruction of mankind, which he comprehends by touching, kissing, and embracing, since they serve him: by touching, because a man remains in them; by kissing, because he gains knowledge through them; by embracing, because he exercises his noble power through them. Thus mankind would have no freedom of possibility if they did not exist with him. So, they with mankind, and mankind with them.[1]

O my children, you who feed my flocks as the Lord commanded, why do you not blush, since none of the creatures desert the precepts they received from the Master but, rather, bring them to perfection?[2] I set you like the sun and the other luminaries so that you might bring light to people through the fire of doctrine, shining in good reputation and setting hearts ablaze with zeal.

I did this in the first age of the world. For I chose Abel, I loved Noah,[3] I instilled in Moses the precepts of the law, I established as prophets those who most loved me. Thus Abel prefigured the priesthood; Noah, the papal office; Moses, the regal messenger; and the prophets, the many other offices.[4] Moreover, Abel poured forth his brightness like the moon, because he revealed the time of obedience in his burnt offering; and Noah, like the sun, because he brought the edifice of obedience to perfection;[5] and Moses, like strong planets, because he received the law through obedience. And the prophets, like the four corners which hold up the boundaries of the world, persevered mightily when they rebuked the whole world for its terrible iniquity, and thus made God known.

But your tongues are silent, failing to join in with the mighty voice of the resounding trumpet of the Lord, for you do not love holy reason, which, like the stars, holds the circuit of its orbit. The trumpet of the Lord is the justice of God, which you should meditate upon zealously in holiness, and through the law and obedience of your office make it known to the people at the proper time with holy discretion, rather than pounding them mercilessly with it.

But you are not doing this on account of the waywardness of your own will. Thus the luminaries are missing from the firmament of God's justice in your utterances, as when the stars do not shine, for you are the night exhaling darkness, and you are like people who do not work, nor even walk in the light because of your indolence. But just as a snake hides in a cave after it has shed its skin, you walk in filth like disgusting beasts.

Oh woe, just as it is written: you ought to be "Mount Sion in which thou hast dwelt" [Ps 73.2]. For, blessed and sealed in the celestial persons, you ought to be the little habitation redolent of myrrh and incense, in which God also dwells. But you are not so. Rather, you are quick in your pursuit of adolescent lust, incapable, like children, of even speaking of your own salvation. You do whatever your flesh demands. Wherefore it is said about you: "Lift up thy hands against their pride unto the end; see what things the enemy hath done wickedly in the sanctuary!" [Ps 73.3]. For the power of God will crush and destroy your necks which have become stiff with iniquity, for they have been puffed up as with the breath of the wind, since you neither know God nor fear men. Indeed, rather than despising iniquity, you have no desire to cast it out of yourselves. You do not see God nor even wish to do so, but you look at your own works and judge them according to your own standards, that is to say, by doing or abandoning at your own pleasure.

Oh, what great evil and enmity this is! that a person is unwilling to live an upright life, either for God's sake or mankind's, but, rather, seeks honor without work and eternal rewards without abstinence. Such a one, in his supposed sanctity, vainly longs to cry out, as the devil does, I am good and holy. But this is not true.

What do you say now? You do not have eyes,[6] since your works do not shine before men with the fire of the Holy Spirit, and you do not meditate on good examples for them. Therefore, the firmament of God's justice in you is lacking in the light of the sun, and the air has lost the edifice of virtues, sweetened by a pleasing fragrance. Whence it is said: "They have eyes and will not see. They have noses and will not smell" [Ps 113.5, 6]. For just as the winds blow and penetrate the whole world, so should you be mighty winds teaching all people, just as it is said: "Their sound has gone forth into all the earth" [Ps

18.5]. You are worn out by seeking after your own transitory reputation in the world, so that, at one moment, you are knights, the next slaves, the next mere jesting minstrels, so that in the perfunctory performance of your duties you sometimes manage to brush off the flies in the summer.[b]

Through the teaching of the Scriptures, which were composed through the fire of the Holy Spirit, you ought to be the corners of the Church's strength, holding her up like the corners that sustain the boundaries of the earth. But you are laid low and do not hold up the Church, retreating instead to the cave of your own desire. And because of the tedium brought on by your riches, avarice, and other vain pursuits, you do not properly teach your subordinates, nor indeed do you even allow them to seek instruction from you. For you say, We can't do everything. But you ought to steep them in the precepts of the law, and thereby restrain them, lest any of them, in his frailty (his marrow, as it were), do whatever he wishes, just as the earth is steeped and restrained by humidity and viridity, lest it turn to ashes. On account of you, however, they are scattered like ashes and always do whatever they wish.[c]

You ought to be a pillar of fire going before them [cf. Ex 13.21] and crying out to them, performing good works before them, saying: "Embrace discipline, lest at any time the Lord be angry, and you perish from the just way" [Ps 2.12]. For the Lord's law consists of discipline through love and fear. Thus both natures—the spiritual and the carnal—must be exercised righteously, lest the Creator threaten those He has created, because they are not walking in His ways.

But you are deceiving yourselves when you say, We have no control over any of them, because if you were to chastise your subordinates properly through the reason which God gave you, they would not dare to resist the truth, but, as far as they could, they would say that your words are true. But because you are not doing this, it is said of you: "They were troubled, and reeled like a drunken man; and all their wisdom was swallowed up" [Ps 106.27]. For you are troubled, since you have no regard for the good in yourselves, and thus do not walk properly. You reel and stumble, since your works do not give you the right answer, and, like a drunk man, you do not know what you are doing. This is because you wilfully do whatever you want. Whence all the wisdom which you sought so hard to find in Scripture and in instruction has been swallowed up in the pit of your own will, since you did those things you learned by touching and tasting merely to fulfill your own desires in the fatness of your flesh, just like a child who does not know what he is doing because he is a child.

Therefore it is again said to you: Unlike the feet that hold up the body, you are not presenting a wholesome and stable example of morality before the people, so that you can surround them by the Scriptures, just as the abyss is completely surrounded by oozing waters. But you say, We don't have time now for talking, and there is not even time for us to be heard as there used to be. And I reply, Abel did not fail to perform his sacrifice, despite his brother's hatred, but he presented it to his Lord, even though he was killed for it. And Noah sweated profusely, greatly dismayed at the terrible judgment that all creation was to be drowned, for he greatly feared death when he stood above the cloud.[7d] When others saw him, they cried out, What is that fool doing? The winds will surely destroy him. Nevertheless, he fulfilled God's command.[8] Similarly, Moses the lawgiver suffered cruelly at the hands of his brothers and neighbors, but, for all that, he did not abandon the law. Rather, he fulfilled God's commands. Also, in their obedience to God, the prophets were killed by infidels, as if by rabid wolves.

But you are unwilling, in this short and comfortable life, to endure injuries at the hands of the people, and thereby you are laying up infinite torments for yourselves. You ought to be the day, but you are the night. For you will be either the day or the night. Choose, therefore, where you wish to take your stand. You are not the sun and moon and stars in the firmament of God's law and justice. Rather, you are the darkness, in which you lie as if you are already dead.

Whence the devil says to himself about you: Just as I had intended, they busy themselves with feasting and riotous living. But my eyes and ears and belly, and my very veins, are full of their froth, and my breasts, with their vices. For they refuse to labor for their God, and they consider Him nothing. Therefore, I will begin to wage war on them, and, by playing my games with them, I will lead them astray, since I do not find them laboring in the field of their Lord, as He commands them. O you, my disciples and followers, you have been punished publicly far more than they. And because this is so, rise up against them, strip away all their riches and honor, despoil and destroy them. Thus says the devil to himself, and in this way he will fulfill the judgment of God against many people. But I Who Am say to those who hear me: When this time comes, ruin will fall upon you at the hands of certain people, you wicked sinners, and they will pursue you relentlessly, and they will not cover up your works, but will lay them bare, and they will say about you: These are scorpions in their morals and snakes in their works. Moreover, in their zeal toward the Lord, they will curse you, saying "the way of the wicked shall perish" [Ps 1.6]. For they will mock your wicked ways and sneer at you.

But the people who will do this, themselves seduced by the devil and serving as his emissaries, will come with wan faces and, clothing themselves in sanctity, will ally themselves with great secular princes.[9] And they will say to them about you: Why do you keep them with you and how can you stand to have them near you, when they are polluting the whole earth with their iniquity?[10]

The people who say these things about you will walk about in black robes, with proper tonsure, and will appear to men serene and peaceful in all their ways. Moreover, they do not love avarice, and do not have money, and, in their secret selves, they hold abstinence as so great a virtue that they can scarcely be reproached. The devil, however, is within these men, revealing himself to them in the obscuring lightning, just as he was at the beginning of the world before his fall. And he makes himself, as it were, like the prophets, saying: People foolishly imagine that I appear like rabid and unclean animals or come in the guise of flies, but, in reality, I fly on wings in the flashing thunder and deceive them so fully that they fulfill my will perfectly. In this way, I will make myself like the almighty God in the wonders I perform.

For the devil works through the spirits of the air,[11] who, because of men's wicked deeds, buzz around in the air in countless hordes like the flies and gnats which plague people in the sweltering heat with their sheer numbers. For the devil deceives them in this way because he does not dissuade them from chastity, but indeed permits their desire to be chaste.[12] Therefore, they do not love women, but flee from them. And thus they appear in public as if they were filled with sanctity, and say with mocking words: Before now, all other people who wanted to remain chaste burned themselves up like roast fish. But no pollution of the flesh or lust dares to touch us, because we are saintly and filled with the Holy Spirit.

Wake up![e] The misguided people of today have no idea what they are doing, no more than those who went before us in times past. For, at that time, others who err in the Catholic faith will fear them and will serve them slavishly, imitating them as much as possible.[13] And when the full gamut of this error has been run, these people will everywhere persecute and exile the teachers and wise men who remain true to the Catholic faith—but not all of them, because some of them are mighty knights for God's justice. Moreover, they will not be able to affect certain congregations of saints, whose way of life is upright. For this reason, they advise princes and wealthy men to coerce teachers, wise men, and clerics with club and staff so that they may be made "just." And in some cases this will be accomplished, causing others to tremble with fear.[14]

In the beginning of this their seduction into error, they will say to women: it is not permitted for you to be with us, but because you do not have good and upright teachers, obey us and do whatever we say, whatever we command, and then you will be saved. And in this way they draw women to themselves and lead them into their own error. Therefore, they will say in the pride of their puffed-up spirit: We are completely victorious.[15]

But I Who Am say: Thus the iniquity which will purge iniquity will fall upon your heads, just as it is written: "He made darkness his covert, his pavilion round about him: dark waters in the clouds of the air" [Ps 17.12]. And, because of your wicked deeds, which are devoid of light, God will wreak His vengeance upon you, and He will be so hidden in that vengeance that you will have no hope of deliverance. For no one will call out for mercy for you, but everybody will say that you are wicked. The law and doctrine are from heaven, and, if you were an ornament of virtue and a fragrant garden of delights, God should have been living in you through these.

But you are a bad example to others, since no rivulet of good reputation flows from you, so that, with respect to the soul, you have neither food to eat nor clothes to wear, but only unjust deeds without the good of knowledge. Therefore, your honor will perish and the crown will fall from your head. Thus injustice calls forth justice, and it seeks out and searches for every scandal, just as it is written: "For it must needs be that scandals come: but nevertheless woe to that man by whom the scandal cometh" [Matt 18.7]. Thus the wicked deeds of mankind must be purged through tribulation and contrition,[16] and many woes are laid up for those also who, through their irreligious acts, bring misery upon others. These are people of no faith, seduced by the devil, and they will be the scourge to discipline you rigorously, because you do not worship God with pure hearts. And they will not cease to torment you until all your injustice and your iniquities are purged.

These, however, are not those deceivers who will come before the last great day when the devil has flown on high, just as he began to fight against God in the beginning, but these are their precursors. Nevertheless, after their perverse worship of Baal and their other depraved works are made known, princes and other great men will rush upon them, and will kill them like rabid wolves, wherever they can be found. Then the dawn of justice will arise, and your last days will be better than those before, and, on account of your past trials, you will be devout, and you will shine like pure gold, and thus you will remain through long ages.[17]

At that time many people will be amazed that such mighty storms heralded this time of mercy. But those who lived before these times fought mightily against their desires to the great peril of their bodies, but they were unable to extricate themselves. In your times, however, you will be engaged in restless wars on account of your desires and your unsettled morals, and, through them, you will be reduced to nothing.

Whoever wishes to escape these dangers, therefore, let him beware lest with darkened eyes he run into the nets of these woes. But let each, to the best of his ability, escape them through good works and the safe harbor of uncorrupted will, and God will provide him with His aid.

Poor little timorous figure of a woman that I am, I have worn myself out for two whole years so that I might bring this message in person to the magistrates, teachers, and other wise men who hold the higher positions in the Church. But because the Church was divided,[18] I have kept quiet.

Appendix I[19]

And so again I say: God sets the works which He Himself made as an example for those who fall away from Him, since they are not bearing good fruits, just as a father sets good examples before his sons when they turn away from him and act dishonorably. In His benevolence, God gave His teaching to Adam, but Adam failed through the devil's counsel. Thus he lost his heritage in paradise and the brightness which he wore like a shining garment, and he put on a woeful garment in its place, and went out into a land of darkness. Then the devil rejoiced because he had made a fool of man, and he continued to do so until the time of Abel, who loved God with a perfect will, and he showed that will in his good work. But then the devil laid hold of Cain and caused him to kill his brother. God saw these things in his mind as if they were written in a book. But the devil was ignorant of these mysteries, because they were intelligible only to holy divinity. For virginity was adorned in Abel through the performance of his priestly duties and in the blood of his martyrdom, all of which was brought to full consummation in the Son of God.[20] Then, in Noah, God prefigured the foundation of the celestial kingdom through the building of the ark when He brought forth a new world.[21] For at that time the earth produced a new juice, that is, wine, in which there is life and death, and through it the devil persuaded Noah's son to dishonor his father's nakedness [cf. Gen 9.20–25]. As a result, that son, stripped of the blessing of liberty, became a slave. Afterward, through circumcision and true revelation, God disclosed the walls of that foundation in Abraham and his barren wife [cf. Gen 17]. For circumcision was the downfall of the devil and the wound of death. The first woman was also barren of life, but the Church through faith was teeming with life. Through murder and other wicked works, the devil maliciously made some of the generation of Abraham into objects of scorn so that they fell from God's blessing. But the finger of God wrote the law for Moses [cf. Ex 31.18; Deut 9.10], and thereby raised the lofty towers of the aforementioned foundation. As a result, the devil sank to new depths of evil (long premeditated, and now openly revealed) when, in the guise of Baal, he claimed to be God. Thus God punished the children of Israel with many plagues. Then the unicorn came and slept in the lap of the Virgin[22] when the Word of God became flesh [cf. John 1.14] and completed the foundation of the kingdom. For through virginal nature, He completely fulfilled the sacrifice of Abel by the blood of martyrdom. The ancient serpent tried to entrap Him, however, because he didn't know who He was since he did not know the mysteries in the mind of God, and thus he urged the Jewish people not to be persuaded by His miracles but to seize Him when He was sold by His disciple.[23] Wherefore they were sold into various countries and lost their own country. But through his disciples, the Son of God taught the faith to leaders, princes, and kings, and set His Church, like Noah's ark, upon other lofty mountains, and filled it with publicans and sinners, as well as the just. He also began obedience in Abraham, and He Himself, as the incarnate Word, was obedient to His father even unto death [cf. Phil 2.8], and for circumcision He gave baptism in the name of the holy Trinity, commanding His disciples to baptize all believers. And through baptism the serpent was confounded and strangled, and death was wounded and defeated. Then the Church gave birth in a way different from Eve's, since she was sterile of life. Mary's grace was greater than the harm Eve had done.[f] But the ancient serpent persuaded the Jews and infidels to persecute His saints and kill them. The Son of God, however, achieved the banner of victory in all His works, and just as He gave the law to Moses, He commanded His disciples to teach all people, establish teachers, and adorn the Church in all its orders. And this they did through the inspiration of the Holy Spirit who wrote true doctrine in their hearts. Because the Word of God was made flesh, it pleased God that all the orders of angels, which were known by name, be spiritually represented among spiritual people, such as priests, bishops, and the other spiritual orders of this kind.[24] Then the Church appeared like dawn among spiritual people, and was so refulgent in virtue that it had a defense like a shield and protection like a breastplate for their defense. And so spiritual people were greatly honored by God and men up to the time of a certain tyrant, who began to be a worshipper of Baal, serving idols.²⁵ When the spiritual people saw this, they at first sighed and trembled. But then later they departed from their original unity, each one following his own desires, and turned away from the covenant which God had promised through the Holy Spirit. Abandoning one divine precept after another, just as the Jews had done, each order wilfully established laws in accordance with its own desires, and turned aside from upright life and sound doctrine.²⁶ Then, like Adam, they were stripped of the garment of obedience, and began to live according to the flesh. And they did this like a dark land, just as, after his disobedience, Adam was called "the dark one" by God. For just as they had, previously, shone brightly in the Church, they no longer gave off light, but became like the darkness of the whirlwind. In this they were like Adam, who was obscured by a dark cloud through disobedience, and, walking in darkness, no longer gave off light, neither for himself nor for others.²⁷

Again, I heard a voice from the Living Light saying: O daughter of Zion, the crown of honor will fall from the heads of your children, and their riches will diminish, because they did not take advantage of the time that I gave them for overseeing and teaching their subordinates. For I gave them breasts to nourish my little ones, and because they failed to perform this task fittingly and at the proper time many of these little ones, like children far from their homes, have died from hunger, because they were not refreshed with correct doctrine. Moreover, these people have a voice, but they do not cry out, and they were given work but they do not labor. Without merit, they wish to have glory; and merit, without work. Whoever wishes to have glory with God must cut off his own will, and whoever desires to have merit with God must work for it. But because you are not doing this, you will be accounted the slaves of slaves, and slaves will be your judges. Your freedom will fall from you, just as my blessing departed from Canaan. These scourges will be the precursors of other, worse ones to come.

*Appendix II*²⁸

For the devil brought about a flaw in the work which God began in the first man, when he spewed out the poison of his vices upon the spiritual people. But God will preserve in righteousness those people He has chosen, just as He also preserves some people from this latest error,²⁹ so that they may do away with it. Thus the devil will be confounded in the tail of this error and will hide himself away like a snake in a cave, just as, in this latest error, he will also be brought to confusion. For God foresaw all His works in Adam (whose bones and flesh He made from the mud) when He breathed the breath of life into him. When the spirit goes out of a man, however, his flesh and bones become ashes, but on the last day they will be renewed. God's creation of man from mud prefigured the old law, but the resurrection of man's flesh and bones from the mud shows the spiritual law, which the Son of God brought forth through Himself. Moreover, he who is raised up from his ashes will be eternal, and, rewarded with sanctity and the true law, he will see the face of his Creator, because, then, he will be truly renewed, just as it is written, "Send forth thy spirit, and they shall be created: and thou shalt renew the face of the earth" [Ps 103.30]. This means: O, God, Creator of all things, you will send forth your Spirit at the last trumpet, and men will rise, immortal, so that from then on they will neither grow, nor wither, nor decay. And so you will renew the face of man, that is to say, his body and spirit will be one in knowledge and perfection. God, Who has neither beginning nor end, will do this. For God has need of nothing, because He is perfect in Himself. When God created man, He placed in him all His miraculous works, and entrusted to him every edifice of the virtues, through which man makes his way to that One Who loves him very much, because He is Love [cf. I John 4.8, 16]. For God is like a head of a household who entrusts his goods to a close friend, so that, in return for his good work, he may receive his reward. Now, O children of God, hear and understand what the Spirit of God says to you so that you will not lose the better part. And the Spirit of God says to you: Look to your city and your district, and cast out those wicked men from your midst, for they are like the Sadducees and worse than Jews. For as long as they are with you, you cannot be safe and free from anxiety. The Church weeps and mourns over their iniquity, which is defiling her children. And so drive them out, lest your city and congregation perish, for long ago the banquet of the royal wedding was prepared in Cologne, and to this day its streets still resound.

Notes

1. *Sed et homo nullam licentiam possibilitatis haberet, si ista cum eo non essent. Sic ista cum homine, et homo cum illis.* This letter is perhaps Hildegard's fullest, most detailed expression of man the microcosm. In the remainder of the letter, note the intricate ways she uses to re-express the idea of the larger world of the universe reflected in the little world of man.

2. This idea is, of course, not new with Hildegard. It was perhaps given the most notable—certainly, the most influential—expression in twelfth-century thought by Alanus de Insulis in *De Planctu Naturae*. Alanus's vision of a monumental personified Nature, on whose robe was figured all the creatures of the world, with a rip in the garment only in that place where man was represented, is the most famous literary, allegorical representation of this idea.

3. At this point some MSS add "I showed myself to Abraham." And below after Noah's prefiguration, they have "Abraham, the renewal of the offspring."

4. *Vnde etiam Abel sacerdotium prefigurabat, Noe principale magisterium, Moyses regale nuntium et prophete plurima magisteria.* The only one of these four that is absolutely clear is Abel, who prefigures the priesthood. Since they all have to do with religious functions, however, Noah, with the "principal office," would seem to prefigure the papacy. In Letter 8, for example, Hildegard refers to the pope as sitting *in principali cathedra*. The function of Moses, as the regal messenger, is less clear, and the prophets, with their many offices, are clearly intended to be generalized.

5. Here, some MSS add "and Abraham, like strong planets, when he established circumcision," and then after Moses replace "strong planets" with "the other stars."

6. Note how nicely she carries out her microcosm/macrocosm thought pattern ("For the sun is like the light of His eyes" just above) and how well she ties it into the biblical passage cited just below.

7. Van Acker suggests that Hildegard may have confused Noah with Moses in Ex 24.15–16: "And when Moses was gone up, a cloud covered the mount. And the glory of the Lord dwelt upon Sinai, covering it with a cloud six days: and the seventh day he called him out of the midst of the cloud."

8. Some MSS add at this point: "And Abraham, too, despite the pain of his heart and the love for his son, did not refuse to bind up his son as a burnt offering."

9. I.e., the Cathars.

10. Some MSS add here "These are the drunken and the lecherous, and unless you cast them out of your midst, the whole Church will be destroyed."

11. Hildegard speaks frequently of the spirits of the air, or airy spirits, as she does in a passage from the *Vita* (II.ii.27) where she describes how certain *aerei spiritus* came and talked with one another about their plans for her.

12. Some MSS add here: "And again he [the devil] says to himself, 'God loves chastity and continence, and so I will make a show of these among them.' In this way does the ancient enemy, through his airy spirits, 'inspire' *[inflat]* men to abstain from sexual sins."

13. Some MSS add: "Then the people will rejoice at their way of life, because they will appear to be just."

14. Some MSS add: "Yet, as Elijah said, many of the just who are not taken in by these errors nor uprooted from their fundamental beliefs will be preserved."

15. Some MSS add at this point "Yet, later, they will engage in secret lechery with these women, and thus the iniquity of their sect will be laid bare."

16. Cf. *Scivias* III.v.187ff: "When a person understands that he has acted contrary to God's will, he must be purged either by a bodily punishment or by the penalty of penitence or by tortures in the next life."

17. Some MSS add the following at this point: "For the first dawn of justice will then arise in spiritual people, just as, at first, it began with a small number, and they will not want to have great power and wealth which destroy souls, but they will say: ' "Woe to us, because we have sinned" ' [Lam 5.16]. For from their past fear and grief they will be strengthened for justice, just as the angels were strengthened by the love of God when the devil fell. And thus, afterwards, they will live in humility and will not desire to rebel against God by performing wicked deeds, but, cleansed of their many errors, they will remain in the mighty strength of uprightness."

18. The schism began in 1159 when the cardinals elected two popes, Alexander III and Victor IV. The latter was given Barbarossa's approval, and he retained his schismatic position until his death in 1164. At this point Barbarossa, in blatant defiance of the Church, elected his own pope, Paschal III, and, after him, another, Calixtus III. The schism lasted until 1177, when Barbarossa and Alexander III were reconciled.

19. This portion of Letter 15r, attested by only two MSS, Van Acker prints only as an appendix. To be read in the context of the letter as a whole, it should be inserted, as in the MSS, at line 14, p. 58, immediately after the sentence, "Rather, you are the darkness, in which you lie as if you are already dead."

20. For Abel is the Old Testament antetype of Christ.

21. The *Glossa ordinaria* interprets the ark as a figure of the Church, as in the following interpretation of God's sealing the door of the ark: *"Nemo enim intrat in Ecclesiam, nisi per sacramentum remissionis peccatorum, quod de latere aperto emanavit."* Note how carefully Hildegard works out her argument by her recurrent use, as here, of the word *foundation*.

22. The unicorn of *Physiologus* and *Bestiary* has become fully Christianized. This is one of the earliest (oblique though it is) references to the Holy Hunt, where the

simple maiden used to capture the mighty unicorn has been transformed into the Holy Virgin. In the *Physica* (viii.5), Hildegard writes at length of the unicorn in purely naturalisic, non-allegorical, terms.

23. This is the Abuse of Power conception of the Redemption, whereby Satan, completely unaware (and kept unaware) of the divinity of the Christ, oversteps his bounds and has an absolutely sinless man killed. He thereby forfeits his original prey and opens the way to the harrowing of hell and the fulfillment of the plan of redemption.

24. The orders of the angels are, in ascending order, angels, archangels, virtues, powers, principalities, dominations, thrones, cherubim, and seraphim. As Barbara Newman notes ("Intro," Hart and Bishop, *Scivias*, p. 30), Hildegard took the idea of the celestial hierarchy mirroring the ecclesiastical hierarchy from Pseudo-Dionysius.

25. Probably Henry IV, with whom Hildegard felt a new, evil, "womanish" age began.

26. Note Hildegard's essential conservatism. This is a condemnation of new religious orders.

27. At this point a third MS picks up the text of this questionable passage.

28. This is Van Acker's second appendix to this letter, again attested by only two MSS. In the MSS, the text appears after line 25, p. 60, following the sentence, "But let each, to the best of his ability, escape them through good works and the safe harbor of uncorrupted will, and God will provide him with His aid."

29. That is, from the error of the Cathars?

16
Philip, Archbishop of Cologne, to Hildegard

1167–73

The archbishop of Cologne inquires about Hildegard's health and requests that she impart to him any admonitions about Cologne that she receives from God.

Philip, archbishop of Cologne by the grace of God, sends greetings to his beloved sister, Hildegard. Wondrously infused with the Holy Spirit as you are, I pray that, in celestial glory, you may see Him, in whose embraces you long to be.

Although we are so widely separated from each other that we cannot enjoy mutual company and conversation, still the love of Christ will keep together those who are joined in spirit. Whence it is, beloved mother, that when the long-desired opportunity to travel on the road to see you at last presented itself this year, your sickness and weakness of body disturbed and dismayed not only my heart but also the hearts of the many who in our land embrace you in Christ, for we are always hopeful for your bodily health and your eternal salvation.

Therefore, we decided and thought it proper to make inquiry and to be made certain about your condition. Moreover, we wanted to inform you that every day we are so perturbed by the whirlwinds and storms of secular matters that, at times, we can scarcely lift the eyes of our mind to heaven. But because many people know that you are endowed with divine gifts—for which the faithful congregation of the Church rejoices—we, too, give thanks, according to the measure of our judgment, knowing that man spends his life in a covering of flesh, but, as the Apostle says, is transformed in heaven [cf. Phil 3.20f]. Therefore, endowed with such a dowry, like a woman who has come upon a fine pearl [cf. Matt 13.45f], we request that you inquire of God's mystery and pass on to us whatever words of admonition God grants to you. For as the one who speaks the truth says, there is no benefit in wisdom and treasure that has been hidden away [cf. Ecclus 20.32]. Farewell.

16r
Hildegard to Philip, Archbishop of Cologne

1167–73

In response to Philip, Hildegard admonishes him to fulfill his episcopal function by bringing his wayward subordinates in line, to be a shining example to them pointing the way to the True Light. Note the emphasis on justice leavened by mercy, Hildegard's usual message.

In the inspiration of a true vision, I saw and heard these words: Fiery Love, which is God, says to you, What does one call a star that shines under the sun? It is, of course, called "luminous," because, aided by the sun, it gives off more light than other stars. But what if that same star were to hide its light so that it was dimmer than the lesser stars? If it did that, it would lose its glorious name and be called blind, for its light would not be seen, although it is called "luminous." So too a knight who goes into battle without armor will most assuredly be trampled down by the enemy if he does not protect himself with a breastplate, a helmet, or a shield. Consequently, he will be captured in great distress.

But you who are called a bright star because of your episcopal office, giving off light through the name of the high priest, you should not be hiding your light (that is, the words of justice) from your subordinates. Still, you freqently say to yourself: If I attempted to discipline my subordinates[1] with fearsome words, they would consider me merely a pest, because I am not strong enough to control them. O how I wish I could have their friendship without having to say anything! But it does you no good to talk and act this way. What should you do then? First of all, what you should *not* do is terrorize them with awesome words stemming from your office as bishop and the aristocracy of your birth, snatching at them like a hawk, nor should you use dangerous words like a club to browbeat them. Rather, temper words of justice with compassion and anoint them with the fear of God, making clear to them how dangerous injustice is to their souls and their felicity. Most certainly, most certainly, most certainly. Then, will they listen to you.

Do not adapt yourself to their filthy and unstable ways, and don't worry about whether you please them or displease them in your actions, for if you do, you will appear to lower yourself in the eyes of God and men. Such an attitude, in any case, is not appropriate to your office. Take note, for example, that hog slop fattens pigs, but if it is mixed in with the fodder given to clean animals that chew the cud, those animals waste away. So it is with you: if you were to join the company of sinners and take on their filthy habits, you would be polluted. Wicked men would then rejoice and upright men would be distressed, saying, Ach! Woe! What kind of bishop do we have? He is not shining light on the strait paths for us.

Rescue your people and turn them away from injurious infidelity. Do these things lest you be stripped of the breastplate of faith, and show them the way of justice as revealed in the Holy Scripture. Put the helmet of hope on your head and cover yourself with the shield of true defense [cf. Ephes 6.14ff], so that in all woes and dangers you will, to the best of your ability, be the defender of the Church. Also, hold the light of truth, so that you may be an upright knight in my army—for I am true love—and so that, in the shipwreck of this world and in the heavy battles against iniquity, you may be an active and powerful knight, in order that you may shine like a bright star in eternal felicity.

Now, O father, you who hold the episcopal office, do not have contempt for the poverty of the person writing these things to you, for I did not write and send them forth through my own will nor that of any other person, but I merely wrote those things I saw and heard in a true vision, while I myself was fully alert in mind and body. I am also fulfilling your command that I should send some advice to you.

Note

1. This important theme of the discipline of subordinates is one that occurs again and again in the letters. Cf. *Scivias* II.v.1503ff.

17

Hildegard to Philip, Archbishop of Cologne

1170–73

A caustic admonition to Archbishop Philip ("change your name from wolf to lamb") cautioning him to amend his own life and become a respectable example for his subordinates.

O you who hold that office which is from God and not from men, since God, the director of all things, has established that certain men may serve as His vicars, be ever aware of the way that you represent Christ.

In a vision I saw, as it were, the sun shining with excessive heat upon mud filled with worms, and these creatures stretched themselves out in the joy of the heat, but, eventually not being able to bear the excessive heat, they hid themselves away, and the mud sent forth a noisome stench. I saw also that the sun shone in a garden, in which roses and lilies and all kinds of herbs grew, and the flowers grew abundantly by the heat of the sun, and the herbs sent forth innumerable roots and gave forth an exceedingly delightful odor, so that many people, suffused with this lovely fragrance, rejoiced in this garden as if it were paradise. And I heard a voice from above saying to you: Make your decision, O man, whether you wish to remain in this garden of delights or to lie with the worms in that stinking excrement. You must determine whether you will be a lofty temple beautifully adorned with towers, in whose windows one can see the eyes of doves [cf. Cant 1.14; 4.1] or whether you will be a wretched hovel thatched with straw, scarcely large enough to hold a peasant and his family.

The worm-filled mud is the first root of original sin, which sprang forth through the wiles of the ancient serpent, and which virginity choked off when the Son of God was born from the Virgin Mary. For the garden of all virtues arose in Him, Whom even bishops ought to imitate. It is fitting for them to ascend to the heavenly temple through the lofty teaching of the episcopal office, just as a dove looks on high with its eyes, but not with the eyes of a hawk. That is to say, bishops ought not to act in accordance with the morals of this world, making wounds which they have not anointed with oil.

Free yourself from the lowly ways of avarice, so that you do not pile up more than you have, for avarice is always poor and needy, but does not give the joy felt by the indigent who desire no more than what they already have. Scatter avarice like straw and trample it underfoot, for it destroys all honorable standards, as a moth destroys clothing. Avarice is always a beggar and is like a peasant's wretched hovel, which has no room to preserve honorable ways. But you are lying next to this hovel, like a mound of dirt which the worms dig up and overturn. That is to say, most bishops, who should be lifting people's minds through correct doctrine, are hoarding their thoughts in their own treasure houses, and are neglecting the words that they ought to be speaking to others, and with which they themselves should be refreshed.

O father, I say to you in truth that I saw and heard all these words in a true vision, and I have written them to you in reponse to your command and petition. Therefore, do not be amazed at these things, but reflect on all your life from your childhood up to the present time. Also, change your name, that is, from wolf to lamb, because wolves gladly seize the sheep. And take part in the banquet prepared for the prodigal son, who ran to his father to confess his sins, saying: "Father, I have sinned against heaven, and before thee" [Luke 15.18, 21]. Then, all the choirs of the angels rejoiced over him, and were amazed that, despite the gravity of his sins, God conferred so much grace upon him. And join with the flowers and the herbs, so that the people may rejoice in your sweet fragrance because they have an honorable and helpful shepherd. Thus you will deserve to hear the voice of the Lord: "Well done, good and faithful servant, enter thou into the joy of thy Lord" [Matt 25.21, 23].

18
Heinrich, Archbishop of Mainz, to Hildegard

1151

Hildegard had refused to release the nun Richardis to her duties as the newly elected abbess of Bassum. This letter from Heinrich, in whose diocese Bingen lay, is a command that she do so.

Heinrich, archbishop of the see of Mainz by the grace of God, sends his grace with fatherly affection to Hildegard, beloved mistress of the community at Mount St. Rupert the Confessor.

Although we have heard of your many wonderful miracles, we have been slothful, we know, by not visiting you as often as we could. But burdened as we are by so much business, we are sometimes scarcely able to lift our heart to those things which are eternal, and we do it slowly at that. But to come to the point, we hereby inform you that some messengers, monks of a certain noble church have come in petition to us with respect to a sister who is a nun in your monastery.[1] They earnestly request that this sister be given up to them, since she has been duly elected abbess. Thus by the authority of our position as prelate and father, we give you this command and, in commanding, enjoin you to release this sister immediately to those who seek and desire her. If you accede to these requests, you will know our gratitude from now on in even greater measure than you have known it so far; but if not, we will issue the same command to you again in even stronger terms, and we will not leave off until you fulfill our commands in this matter.[a]

Note

1. The nun Richardis. See Letter 4, Headnote, and, especially, Letter 12, Headnote.

18r

Hildegard to Heinrich, Archbishop of Mainz

1151

In response to Heinrich, Hildegard rejects his authority to command her on this issue. Citing the divine inspiration of the Living Light, she stoutly defends her decision to refuse permission for Richardis to leave, harshly charging those who oppose her with simony and willful disregard of God's will.

The Bright Fountain, truthful and just, says, These legal pretexts brought forward to establish authority over this girl have no weight in God's eyes, for I—high, deep, all-encompassing, a descending light—neither initiated nor wanted them. Rather, they have been manufactured in the conniving audacity of ignorant hearts.[a] Let all the faithful hear these things with the open ears of their hearts, and not with the outward ears, like a beast which hears the sound, but not the meaning of a single word. The Spirit of God says earnestly: O shepherds, wail and mourn over the present time, because you do not know what you are doing when you sweep aside the duties established by God in favor of opportunities for money[1] and the foolishness of wicked men who do not fear God.

And so your malicious curses and threatening words are not to be obeyed. You have raised up your rods of punishment arrogantly, not to serve God, but to gratify your own perverted will.

Note

1. Note the suggestion of simony once again with respect to Richardis's election.

19

Hildegard to Heinrich, Archbishop of Mainz

1153

This short little missive is vitriolic in its condemnation of Heinrich.

He Who Is says: You have been found wanting, and I say to you: The heaven of the Lord's vengeance has been opened, and now the ropes have been lowered against His enemies [cf. Ps 139.6]. Rise up, however, because your days are short,[1] and remember that Nebuchadnezzar fell and that his crown perished [cf. Dan 4.21ff]. And there have been many others who have fallen when they rashly exalted themselves to heaven. Ach! you piece of dust, why are you not ashamed at exalting yourself to the heights when you ought to be in the muck? Now, therefore, let madmen blush. But as for you, rise up, and abandon your curse by fleeing from it.

Note

1. Indeed, at this point, Heinrich has only a few months to live.

20

Arnold, Archbishop of Mainz,[1] to Hildegard

1158–60

Arnold, Heinrich's successor as archbishop of Mainz, asks for Hildegard's prayers and support.

Arnold, archbishop of Mainz by the grace of God, sends his grace with fatherly esteem to Hildegard, virgin dedicated to God and mistress of Mount St. Rupert the Confessor.

We know that "the spirit breatheth where he will" [John 3.8], distributing his gifts to each as he wishes [cf. I Cor 12.11]. We say this having no anxiety about you. For if once He made tillers of the field and dressers of sycamore trees into prophets [cf. Amos 7.14], and caused an ass to speak [cf. Num

22.28ff], how can we be surprised if He teaches you with his inspiration? We must not deny the gifts of God, nor can we. Therefore, dear lady, we ask you to support us in your prayers to the Lord, so that we may at least spend our days in the fear and love of our Creator, and thus, having done well, may merit to have a long life of continuing happiness.

Note

1. Through the patronage of Frederick Barbarossa, Arnold became archbishop after the deposition of Heinrich in 1153. Arnold thus owed his position to the emperor, and Frederick did not hesitate to exact the tribute. He insisted—despite Arnold's repeated excuses—that the archbishop accompany him on his Italian campaign. To complicate matters, when Arnold sought to exact the war-tribute from the citizens of Mainz, they obstinately refused to comply, and he excommunicated the entire city. The violent conflicts and unceasing confrontations resulted in Arnold's murder on 24 June 1160, at the portal of the church cloister of St. James before the walls of Mainz. It is perhaps Hildegard's understanding of the dangerous political situation that lends urgency to her response to Arnold's letter.

20r
Hildegard to Arnold, Archbishop of Mainz

1158-60

Hildegard's answer to Arnold is quite general in its moral advice, but nevertheless leaves the impression that Hildegard feels that he is not fulfilling the duty of his episcopal office.

O father, the Living Light has given these words to me for you: Why do you hide your face from me? You do this as if you are perturbed and angry at the mystical words which I bring forth not from myself, but as I see them in the Living Light. Indeed, things are shown to me there which my mind does not desire and which my will does not seek, but often I see them under compulsion.[a] Therefore, I pray to God that you not consider His help as something foreign[1] to you and that your mind may be devoted to pure knowledge, so that you may gaze into the mirror of salvation. Thus you will live forever.

May the bright light of God's grace never be cut off from you, but may the mercy of God protect you, so that the ancient traitor may not deceive you. Now, however, may your eye live in God, and may the viridity of your soul never dry up.[b] The Living Light says to you: Why do you not stand firm in your awe of me? And why do you overcome and cast aside anything that stands in your way, like an overzealous thresher of wheat?ᶜ Such action goes against my will. Therefore, rise up to God, for your time will come quickly.

Note

1. If the prose sounds a little awkward here, it is because we are attempting to preserve Hildegard's pun on *auxilium/exsilium*. The entire passage in Latin reads: *Posco tamen a Deo quod auxilium suum tibi non sit quasi exsilium.*

21
Hildegard to Conrad, Archbishop of Mainz

1162(?)

Hildegard congratulates Conrad on becoming the new archbishop of Mainz and exhorts him to rule justly. Conrad was archbishop of Mainz from 1162 to 1165. Steadfastly refusing to recognize the anti-pope Paschal III, he held with Pope Alexander III in opposition to Barbarossa. As a result of his loyalty to the pope, he lost his see, and never regained it, even after the reconciliation between pope and emperor.

I saw and heard these words in the True Light: The day calls forth the day and puts an end to pestilence, just as it is said: "Day to day uttereth speech, and night to night sheweth knowledge" [Ps 18.3]. For God is reason, and all justice is in God. Thus all good and just things have proceeded from Him to mankind and all creatures. And His creative act is pure in Him, as it is written: "All things were made by Him" [John 1.3]. Day would not be bright if it did not have knowledge, that is, knowledge of darkness which reveals praise of the day. Just so, the malevolence and the faithlessness of the devil reveal God, because neither faithlessness nor grievous wars can prevail against Him. God did not make evil, but He overcame it, making it into his footstool [cf. Ps 109.1; Heb 1.13, 10.13], because "without Him was made nothing" [John 1.3].

You are now, O son of God, at the very invocation of the day. Therefore, take up the shield of faith [cf. Eph 6.16], and diligently hold the beautiful justice of God in the embraces of your heart, as you would clasp your dearly beloved to your bosom, and, in all your works, flee from the darkness of injustice, because God is truthful. In doing so, you will become one of the elect, the legitimate son, rather than the son of the concubine injustice [cf. Gen 16, 21.1–21; Gal 4.22ff].

But gird yourself with justice and the love of eternal felicity. Moreover, in the dawning of this new day, do not give heed to those who spurn God and reject His works, as it is written: "Deliver, O God, my soul from the sword: my only one from the hand of the dog" [Ps 21.21]. In this way, you will escape from the sword which falls on evil men, and avoid the infidelity of the words of men who, like dogs, reject God. Now, however, may God teach you to be a faithful servant so that you may live forever.

22

Conrad, Archbishop of Mainz, to Hildegard

1163–65(?)

Conrad responds to Hildegard seeking her prayers for the onerous administrative burden that he has taken on.

Conrad, by the grace of God archbishop of the see of Mainz, sends the devotion of his grace—both paternal and filial—to Hildegard, beloved mistress of the sisters at St. Rupert in Bingen.

Although we are overburdened with onerous duties, we are writing you a brief letter because we long for your affection with all our heart and mind. And because we know that you have been inspired by the Holy Spirit, we long to hear your words of exhortation. For while we strive to serve this earthly kingdom with our body, we often neglect to serve the heavenly King with our spirit.[1] Therefore, we entrust ourselves to your prayers and the prayers of your sisters so that, aided by them, we may with God's merciful help be rescued from the whirlwinds and storms of this age, by which we are greatly fatigued.

We want you to be assured that we are ready and able to help you in all your needs as far as God has granted us the ability.

Note

1. An echo of the medieval commonplace of the dangers to one's immortal soul of accepting a high ecclesiastical office. The theme is most strikingly expressed in those widespread stories of a monk, elected bishop, who, after an early death, returned to reveal that because he had accepted the office, he was damned—or, if he had refused the office, that he was in paradise.

22r

Hildegard to Conrad, Archbishop of Mainz

1163–65(?)

Another general letter of admonition from Hildegard to the archbishop exhorting him to rule justly, for his authority comes directly from God.

The mystic vision says to you: O man in authority, Christ has appointed you as his representative, for all power is from God [cf. Rom 13.1]. No one has ever been found to compare with God, who is the Father of all, because all things proceed from Him. Therefore, he is king of all and the priest who became man and offered up an unblemished sacrifice to set mankind free. According to his own solemn oath, He is priest, as it is written: "The Lord hath sworn, and he will not repent: Thou art a priest for ever according to the order of Melchisedech" [Ps 109.4]. Indeed, in order to conquer evil, God foreordained that he would become man, with no sin, with no need of penitence, with none of the divisions and contradictions of sinful mankind. This was foreshadowed by Melchisedech.

Therefore, you, O man, you who are now in the broad daylight, hasten before night comes when no man can work [cf. John 9.4], and strive with true power to teach God's precepts to your people, and rule them in true justice, as God rules them. And govern them with mercy, zealously, since God himself has freed them. For all such power and authority to govern is from God. But also, in your compassion, "make unto you friends of the mammon of iniquity; that when you shall fail, they may receive you into everlasting dwellings" [Luke 16.9].

Now, O father and, after Christ, master, hear this poor little creature writing to you the things I have seen in the True Light, so that you may stretch out your hand to all of us who in our need run to you for refuge. And in return for the joy you offer them, you will be received into the eternal joy of the tabernacles, and will live in the eternal blessedness for which God created you. Amen.

23

Hildegard to the prelates at Mainz[1]

1178–79

This is perhaps the most famous—certainly the most intriguing—of all Hildegard's letters, because of her elaboration of the idea of music as a means of recapturing the original joy and beauty of paradise. Placed under interdict for her failure to obey the prelates of Mainz, Hildegard and her community felt the loss of music—specifically singled out by the interdict—most intensely, as one can see from what follows. In this letter, as Peter Dronke points out (*Women Writers*, p. 197), Hildegard "works out her own philosophy of music: music becomes not only the *musica mundana*, the cosmic harmony familiar from Boethius's *De Musica*, but a way of understanding history—Adam and Lucifer, the Old Testament prophets and the New Testament Church—and a way in which human beings can still incarnate heavenly beauty in an earthly mode. The symbolism then turns into micro-cosmic allegory—music is the human body and soul, and the principles with which they are informed—an allegory that is dynamic and in no way forced, arising effortlessly out of Hildegard's pattern of thoughts and images." Despite the compelling argument that Hildegard makes, the prelates of Mainz paid absolutely no heed to this letter, and persisted inflexibly with the interdict.

By a vision, which was implanted in my soul by God the Great Artisan before I was born, I have been compelled to write these things because of the interdict by which our superiors have bound us, on account of a certain dead man buried at our monastery, a man buried without any objection, with his own priest officiating. Yet only a few days after his burial, these men ordered us to remove him from our cemetery. Seized by no small terror, as a result, I looked as usual to the True Light, and, with wakeful eyes, I saw in my spirit that if this man were disinterred in accordance with their commands, a terrible and lamentable danger would come upon us like a dark cloud before a threatening thunderstorm.[a]

Therefore, we have not presumed to remove the body of the deceased inasmuch as he had confessed his sins, had received extreme unction and communion, and had been buried without objection. Furthermore, we have not yielded to those who advised or even commanded this course of action. Not, certainly, that we take the counsel of upright men or the orders of our superiors lightly, but we would not have it appear that, out of feminine harshness[2] we did injustice to the sacraments of Christ, with which this man had been fortified while he was still alive. But so that we may not be totally disobedient we have, in accordance with their injunction, ceased from singing the divine praises and from participation in Mass, as had been our regular monthly custom.[b]

As a result, my sisters and I have been greatly distressed and saddened. Weighed down by this burden, therefore, I heard these words in a vision: It is improper for you to obey human words ordering you to abandon the sacraments of the Garment of the Word of God,[c] Who, born virginally of the Virgin Mary, is your salvation. Still, it is incumbent upon you to seek permission to participate in the sacraments from those prelates who laid the obligation of obedience upon you. For ever since Adam was driven from the bright region of paradise into the exile of this world on account of his disobedience, the conception of all people is justly tainted by that first transgression. Therefore, in accordance with God's inscrutable plan, it was necessary for a man free from all pollution to be born in human flesh, through whom[d] all who are predestined to life might be cleansed from corruption and might be sanctified by the communion of his body so that he might remain in them and they in him for their fortification. That person, however, who is disobedient to the commands of God, as Adam was, and is completely forgetful of Him must be completely cut off from participation in the sacrament of His body, just as he himself has turned away from Him in disobedience. And he must remain so until, purged through penitence, he is permitted by the authorities to receive the communion of the Lord's body again. In contrast, however, a person who is aware that he has incurred such a restriction not as a result of anything that he has done, either consciously or deliberately, may be present at the service of the life-giving sacrament, to be cleansed by the Lamb without sin, Who, in obedience to the Father, allowed Himself to be sacrificed on the altar of the cross that he might restore salvation to all.[e]

In that same vision I also heard that I had erred in not going humbly and devoutly to my superiors for permission to participate in the communion, especially since we were not at fault in receiving that dead man into our cemetery. For, after all, he had been fortified by his own priest with proper Christian procedure, and, without objection from anyone, was buried in our cemetery, with all Bingen joining in the funeral procession. And so God has commanded me to report these things to you, our lords and prelates. Further, I saw in my vision also that by obeying you we have been celebrating the divine office incorrectly, for from the time of your restriction up to the present, we have ceased to sing the divine office, merely reading it instead. And I heard a voice coming from the Living Light concerning the various kinds of praises, about which David speaks in the psalm: "Praise Him with sound of trumpet: praise Him with psaltery and harp," and so forth up to this point: "Let every spirit praise the Lord" [Ps 150.3, 6]. These words use outward, visible things to teach us about inward things. Thus the material composition and the quality of these instruments instruct us how we ought to give form to the praise of the Creator and turn all the convictions of our inner being to the same. When we consider these things carefully, we recall that man needed the voice of the living Spirit, but Adam lost this divine voice through disobedience. For while he was still innocent, before his transgression, his voice blended fully with the voices of the angels in their praise of God.[f] Angels are called spirits from that Spirit which is God, and thus they have such voices by virtue of their spiritual nature.

But Adam lost that angelic voice which he had in paradise, for he fell asleep to that knowledge which he possessed before his sin, just as a person on waking up only dimly remembers what he had seen in his dreams.[g] And so when he was deceived by the trick of the devil and rejected the will of his Creator, he became wrapped up in the darkness of inward ignorance as the just result of his iniquity.

God, however, restores the souls of the elect to that pristine blessedness by infusing them with the light of truth. And in accordance with His eternal plan, He so devised it that whenever He renews the hearts of many with the pouring out of the prophetic spirit, they might, by means of His interior illumination, regain some of the knowledge which Adam had before he was punished for his sin.[h]

And so the holy prophets, inspired by the Spirit which they had received, were called for this purpose: not only to compose psalms and canticles (by which the hearts of listeners would be inflamed) but also to construct various kinds of musical instruments to enhance these songs of praise with melodic strains. Thereby, both through the form and quality of the instruments, as well as through the meaning of the words which accompany them, those who hear might be taught, as we said above, about inward things, since they have been admonished and aroused by outward things. In such a way, these holy prophets get beyond the music of this exile and recall to mind that divine melody of praise which Adam, in company with the angels, enjoyed in God before his fall.

Men of zeal and wisdom have imitated the holy prophets and have themselves, with human skill, invented several kinds of musical instruments, so that they might be able to sing for the delight of their souls, and they accompanied their singing with instruments played with the flexing of the fingers, recalling, in this way, Adam, who was formed by God's finger, which is the Holy Spirit. For, before he sinned, his voice had the sweetness of all musical harmony. Indeed, if he had remained in his original state, the weakness of mortal man would not have been able to endure the power and the resonance of his voice.[i]

But when the devil, man's great deceiver, learned that man had begun to sing through God's inspiration and, therefore, was being transformed to bring back the sweetness of the songs of heaven, mankind's homeland, he was so terrified at seeing his clever machinations go to ruin that he was greatly tormented. Therefore, he devotes himself continually to thinking up and working out all kinds of wicked contrivances. Thus he never ceases from confounding confession and the sweet beauty of both divine praise and spiritual hymns, eradicating them through wicked suggestions, impure thoughts, or various distractions from the heart of man and even from the mouth of the Church itself, wherever he can, through dissension, scandal, or unjust oppression.

Therefore, you and all prelates must exercise the greatest vigilance to clear the air by full and thorough discussion of the justification for such actions before your verdict closes the mouth of any church singing praises to God or suspends it from handling or receiving the divine sacraments. And you must be especially certain that you are drawn to this action out of zeal for God's justice, rather than out of indignation, unjust emotions, or a desire for revenge, and you must always be on your guard not to be circumvented in your decisions by Satan, who drove man from celestial harmony and the delights of paradise.

Consider, too, that just as the body of Jesus Christ was born of the purity of the Virgin Mary through the operation of the Holy Spirit so, too, the canticle of praise, reflecting celestial harmony, is rooted in the Church through the Holy Spirit. The body is the vestment of the spirit, which has a living voice, and so it is proper for the body, in harmony with the soul, to use its voice to sing praises to God. Whence, in metaphor, the prophetic spirit commands us to praise God with clashing cymbals and cymbals of jubilation [cf. Ps 150.5], as well as other musical instruments which men of wisdom and zeal have invented, because all arts pertaining to things useful and necessary for mankind have been created by the breath that God sent into man's body. For this reason it is proper that God be praised in all things.

And because sometimes a person sighs and groans at the sound of singing, remembering, as it were, the nature of celestial harmony, the prophet, aware that the soul is symphonic and thoughtfully reflecting on the profound nature of the spirit, urges us in the psalm [cf. Ps 32.2, 91.4] to confess to the Lord with the harp and to sing a psalm to Him with the ten-stringed psaltery. His meaning is that the harp, which is plucked from below, relates to the discipline of the body; the psaltery, which is plucked from above, pertains to the exertion of the spirit; the ten chords, to the fulfillment of the law.[j]

Therefore, those who, without just cause, impose silence on a church and prohibit the singing of God's praises and those who have on earth unjustly despoiled God of His honor and glory will lose their place among the chorus of angels, unless they have amended their lives through true penitence and humble restitution. Moreover, let those who hold the keys of heaven beware not to open those things which are to be kept closed nor to close those things which are to be kept open, for harsh judgment will fall upon those who rule, unless, as the apostle says [cf. Rom 12.8], they rule with good judgment.

And I heard a voice saying thus: Who created heaven? God. Who opens heaven to the faithful? God. Who is like Him? No one. And so, O men of faith, let none of you resist Him or oppose Him, lest He fall on you in His might and you have no helper to protect you from His judgment. This time is a womanish time,[3] because the dispensation of God's justice is weak. But the strength of God's justice is exerting itself, a female warrior battling against injustice, so that it might fall defeated.[k]

Notes

1. In 1178 Hildegard had permitted the burial of a certain nobleman—whose name has not come down to us—in consecrated ground at Mount St. Rupert. This seemingly innocuous decision was to lead to the bitterest confrontation that Hildegard, now eighty years old, had ever faced in her long career. For the dead nobleman had once been excommunicated, and there remained some question of whether he had been absolved from that interdict. At least so alleged the prelates of Mainz, who ordered Hildegard, under pain of excommunication herself, to have the corpse exhumed and cast out of holy ground. The motives of the prelates, however, are suspect, especially on account of the haste with which they acted, while their archbishop was away in Rome serving as

mediator between Frederick Barbarossa and Pope Alexander III—not to mention the apparent ease with which Hildegard could locate eyewitnesses to affirm the truth of the absolution. In any case, Hildegard was obdurate, resolutely refusing to give up the body. (The "protocol" of her canonization reports that she made the sign of the cross over the grave with her *baculus,* causing the tomb to vanish without a trace.) Hildegard remained splendidly defiant, suffering, at this late stage in her life, all the consequences of excommunication, seeking all the while to have the decision overturned.

2. How cannily Hildegard plays her masculine audience!

3. This is a frequent theme in the letters and the other works: the loss of the "virility" of the earlier Church. Hence a woman, paradoxically, has been called by God to help restore this lost virility. In one of the numerous autobiographical sections in the *Vita,* Hildegard writes, "Eleven hundred years after the Incarnation of Christ the doctrine of the apostles and the burning justice which had been firmly established in the Christians and spiritual people began to falter and turned into hesitation." And then she makes the specific application to herself, *"I was born in those times."* See Newman, *Sister of Wisdom,* pp. 238-49.

24

Hildegard to Christian, Archbishop of Mainz[1]

1179

The prelates of Mainz of the previous letter had acted in the name of their archbishop, Christian, who was away in Italy serving as mediator between Pope Alexander III and Frederick Barbarossa. Here, Hildegard informs Christian of the causes of the conflict and the steps she had taken to resolve it, and prays for his assistance.

O most gentle father and lord, appointed to be Christ's representative as shepherd of the flock of the Church, we humbly give thanks to almighty God and to your paternal piety that you have received our letter compassionately, poor though we are, and that in your mercy you have deigned to send a letter to our superiors in Mainz on our behalf when we were sorely tried and perplexed.[2] We give thanks also for the kind words expressed with your usual clemency, which (brought by Hermann, dean of the church of the Holy Apostles in Cologne) so consoled and cheered us in our trials and tribulations that we have run to you in all confidence, like daughters to their cherished father. Therefore, gracious lord, we your servants, who sit in the grief of our trials and tribulations and have humbly cast ourselves at your feet, now tearfully lay bare to you the full truth concerning the cause of our intolerable grief. We are confident that the fire of Love, which is God, will so inspire you that your paternal piety will deign to hear the cry of lament, which, in our tribulation, we raise to you.

O mild father, as I informed you earlier in a letter, a certain young man who was buried in our cemetery had been absolved from excommunication for some time before his death and had been fortified with all the sacraments of the Christian faith. When our superiors at Mainz ordered us to cast him out of our cemetery or else refrain from singing the divine offices, I looked, as usual, to the True Light, through which God instructed me that I was never to accede to this: one whom He had received from the bosom of the Church into the glory of salvation was by no means to be disinterred. For to do so against the will of His truth would bring great and terrible danger down upon us. Yet I would have humbly obeyed them, and would have willingly yielded up that dead man, excommunicated or not, to anyone whom they had sent in your name to enforce the inviolable law of the Church—if my fear of almighty God had not stood in my way.[a]

Thus although we did cease singing the divine offices for some time (though not without great sorrow), the Mighty Judge, whose commands I have not dared to disobey, sent the true vision into my soul. And forced by this, despite a grievous illness, I went to our superiors in Mainz, where I presented in writing the words I had seen in the True Light, just as God Himself instructed me. Thus might they know the will of God in this matter. There, in their presence, I tearfully sought pardon, and with weeping and humility asked for their compassion. Yet their eyes were so clouded that they could not look at me with any trace of compassion, and so, full of tears, I departed from them.

But a great number of people did have pity for us, although, despite their good will, they could offer us no real assistance. Yet my[3] faithful friend, the archbishop of Cologne, came to Mainz bringing with him a certain knight, a free man. And this man was willing to offer sufficient testimony that he and the aforementioned dead man had been partners in that transgression and that the two of them had likewise received absolution from excommunication, in the same place, and at the same hour, by the same priest. And that very priest was there present and verified the truth of this matter, and, acting in your name, obtained permission for us to celebrate the divine offices in security and peace until your return.[b] Now, however, although we still have the utmost confidence in your compassion, most gracious lord, we have just received your letter from the synod forbidding us, once again, to celebrate those offices, a letter delivered to us by our superiors upon their return from Rome. Yet, having confidence in your paternal piety, I am assured that you never would have sent that letter if you had known the truth of the matter. And so, most gentle father, by the order which you yourself gave, we find ourselves again under that previous restriction and are suffering even greater grief and sadness.

Now, in a vision—and you have never, I remind you, given me trouble about my visions before[c]—I have been ordered to say with heart and mouth: It is better for me to fall into the hands of men, than to abandon the command of my God [cf. Dan 13.23]. Therefore, most gentle father, for the love of the Holy Spirit and the piety owed to the eternal Father, who sent his Word into the womb of the Virgin to blossom there[4] for the salvation of mankind, I beseech you not to look down upon the tears of your grieving and wailing daughters who out of fear of God are enduring the trials and perplexities of this unjust injunction. May the Holy Spirit be so poured out on you that you may be moved to compassion for us and so that at the end of your life you may in return receive compassion.

Notes

1. At the Diet of Würzburg in 1165, Frederick attempted to force recognition of his anti-pope, Paschal. Conrad, archbishop of Mainz, fled the diet and joined forces with Pope Alexander. Whereupon Frederick replaced him as archbishop with this man, Christian de Buch, who served in this capacity until his death in 1183. Serving also as chancellor to the emperor, Christian, who was a superb general, led Barbarossa's forces in his campaign against Alexander III. Later, however, he played an important role in bringing about the reconciliation of the emperor and the pope at the Peace of Venice in 1177.

2. Compassionate letter or not, the archbishop did not immediately lift the interdict, although some relief—however short-lived—was forthcoming to Hildegard and her nuns, as will be seen later in this letter.

3. Van Acker's text reads here *fidelis amicus tuus*, but he notes that the *fidelis amicus meus* of the *Patrologia* may be the correct reading. In any case, the friend is Philip of Heinsberg, who was archbishop of Cologne in 1189.

4. Our "to blossom there" is a free rendering of Hildegard's ever-recurring *viriditas*. The Latin text reads *qui pro salute hominis in suaui viriditate misit Verbum suum in Virginis uterum*, a literal rendering of which would give "who sent His Word into the womb of the Virgin in sweet viridity."

24r
Christian, Archbishop of Mainz, to Hildegard

1179

At last, in March of 1179, only some six months before Hildegard's death, the archbishop writes from Rome making it possible for the interdict to be lifted.

Christian, archbishop of Mainz by the grace of God, to Hildegard, revered lady and beloved in Christ, and to all the brides of Christ who serve God with her, with a prayer that they might ascend from virtue unto virtue and see the God of gods in Zion [cf. Ps 83.8].

Although in the wondrous and praiseworthy power of God and the mercy of our Savior, we are woefully inadequate, nay rather completely unworthy, yet, dearest lady in Christ, having the utmost confidence in your faithful prayers that we may be made worthy, we honor with our thanks Him from whom descends "every best gift, and every perfect gift . . . coming down from the Father of lights" [James 1.17]. For He has been pleased, and rightly so, with your soul and has illuminated it with His true and unfathomable light, and His continuing grace has been granted to your saintly devotion, to sit with Mary at the feet of the Lord [cf. Luke 10.39] and receive visions of the heavenly Jerusalem.

Dearest lady in Christ, these obvious signs of your holy life and such amazing testimonies to the truth oblige us to obey your commands and to pay especial heed to your entreaties. Thus we are rightly obliged to cast the gaze of our heart to whatever we know has been granted to your saintly prayers. And having the greatest confidence in your sanctity (next only to that we owe God), we hope, through the sacred odor of your prayers, to attain God's eternal grace. We also hope that this sinful soul of ours, made the more acceptable through your saintly intercession, will obtain the mercy of its Creator.

Hence, with regard to the tribulation and affliction which you and yours are enduring because of the suspension of the divine offices, the clearer your innocence in this matter becomes to us, the more firmly we sympathize with you. Nevertheless, the Church held that the man buried in your churchyard had incurred the sentence of excommunication while he was alive, and although some doubt remained concerning his absolution, the fact that you disregarded the outcry of the clergy and acted as if this would cause no scandal in the Church was a very dangerous act, since the statutes of the holy fathers are inviolable. You should have waited for definitive proof based on the suitable testimony of good men in the presence of the Church.[a]

Yet we wholeheartedly sympathize with your affliction, as is only right, and therefore we have written back to the church at Mainz to this effect: we grant you the privilege of celebrating the divine offices again, on the condition that proof of the dead man's absolution has been established by the testimony of reliable men. In the meantime, saintly lady, if we have caused you annoyance in this matter, either out of guilt or ignorance, we earnestly beseech you not to withhold your compassion from one who seeks pardon. May you deign to pray the Father of mercies to present us unblemished to your sight and to the church at Mainz, for the glory of God and the honor of your church and for the salvation of our soul. May the Lord preserve your wholeness and holiness.[1]

Note

1. Our "wholeness and holiness" seeks to preserve Christian's pun *sanitatem et sanctitatem*.

25

Eberhard, Archbishop of Salzburg,[1] to Hildegard

1163–64

As a staunch ally of Pope Alexander III, Eberhard feels the heat of the tense political situation and seeks Hildegard's prayers. Note his feeling for the need of secrecy in his closing request that she send her answer under seal.

Eberhard, by the grace of God, archbishop and servant of the church of Salzburg, although unworthy, to Hildegard, sister and mistress of St. Rupert in Bingen, I pray—whatever effect the prayer of a sinner may have—that after the victory over this flesh you may enter with the wise virgins into the embraces of the heavenly bridegroom [cf. Matt 25.10].

A sinner set in this vale of tears, I am worn down by the many whirlwinds and storms of this age, having endured terrors within, combats without [cf. II Cor 7.5]. Therefore, beloved lady, I earnestly beseech that you deign to pour forth your prayers for me so that divine compassion may open the heart of unfailing love to me and mercifully rescue me from all my distress. For on account of the schism now in the Church, the emperor is attempting to use force against us.[2]

O virgin worthy in God's sight, in your love please remember that when I was at Mainz when the emperor held court there, I very earnestly commended myself to your saintly prayers, so that through your intercession the condition of my life might improve in the Lord and have a blessed ending. At that time, you promised me, your humble servant, that (after you had received my letter) you would hasten to write back to me reporting whatever God deigned to reveal to you. Humble still, I am now asking, O saintly woman, the payment of this promise. Farewell, O virgin of God, and keep me in your remembrance. Please send whatever response you have under seal.[a]

Notes

1. Eberhard served as archbishop of Salzburg from 1149 until his death in 1164. A powerful and thoroughly independent personality, he was a commanding and authoritative figure in the complex political situation of the twelfth century. Although staunchly, fearlessly supportive of Alexander III, he was frequently in the company of the emperor, and, thus, served as a pacifying influence in the relations between the two.

2. In opposition to Frederick Barbarossa's "anti-pope" Victor IV, Eberhard was one of the staunchest allies among the high-ranking German prelates of Alexander III. In this early era of the schism, Hildegard had taken no stance. For however irregular the election, Victor IV had, after all, been elected by the cardinals. But when the emperor chose his own pope after Victor's death (1164), Hildegard took a very firm

stand, sending off a scorching letter to Frederick—and this despite the fact that Frederick must, in a very large sense, be considered her patron. In 1163, for example, he had granted a charter of imperial protection in perpetuity to Mount St. Rupert.

25r
Hildegard to Eberhard, Archbishop of Salzburg

1163–64

Hildegard responds to Eberhard with praise for his unflagging service to the Church, and (in typical Hildegardian fashion) points out to him that such service is not different from efforts toward his own personal salvation, that the two are one and the same. For the image of the two walls joined by a cornerstone with which the letter begins, compare *Scivias* III.ii.

O you who are the representative of the Son of the living God, your present condition, as now revealed to me, is like two walls joined by a cornerstone. One of these is like a bright cloud; the other, partially obscured by shadows. And the two are kept rigidly apart, never mixing with one another. These two walls are your labors, joined together by your spirit. The bright side stands for your exertions and your sighs for the narrow road that leads to God. The shadowy side, on the other hand, represents your labors for the people under your authority. This is your true difficulty: you esteem your private efforts for your own salvation, the bright side of the wall, as something personal, while you look upon temporal duties as something foreign to you. This is why you are so frequently exhausted in your spirit. For you do not understand that your striving for God and your labor for His people are the same thing.[1] For your eager panting after heavenly things and your care of the people in God's name can be perfectly integrated. Even Christ Himself clung to heavenly things, while, at the same time, He devoted Himself to the people, as is written, "You are gods and all of you the sons of the most High" [Ps 81.6; cf. John 10.34]. Here is the sense of that verse: "gods" in heavenly matters and "sons of the most High" in the care of the people.

Therefore, father, steep your labors in the fount of wisdom, from which Divine Love and Obedience drank, those two daughters clad in regal garments. For Wisdom along with Divine Love, set all things in order bringing forth many streams, just as she says, "I alone have compassed the circuit of heaven" [Ecclus 24.8]. For through his own obedience, God has given mankind a precept: Divine Love is the vestment which, in the order of angels, looks upon the face of God, but the vestment of obedience is the garb of the Lord's humanity. These two maids are knocking at your door, and Divine Love is saying to you, I long to remain with you, and I want you to put me on your bed and love me diligently. For when you search wounds and wash them in your compassion, then I lie in your bed, and when you treat simple, good-living people with kindness in God's name, then I am your beloved. But Obedience also says to you, I remain with you through the law and the precepts of God. Therefore, hold me earnestly in your strength, not as your overseer but as your dearest friend. For you took me up at your baptism, and, in the discipline of submission, you held me as you advanced, and in your high office you embraced me when you were obedient to the commands of God. Divine Love is my source, for I was born from her.

O father, Wisdom speaks to you again, Be like the head of a household who patiently hears the foolishness of his sons, and yet does not cast aside his prudence. In the same way, I join together the heavenly and the earthly for the benefit of the people. Therefore, search and cleanse wounds, and embrace simple, good-living people. In this way, God assisting, you will have joy in both facets of your life.

Now, father, I, poor little woman that I am, see that your will chooses the door of virtue which will come to you, so that in those virtues with the grinding down of your body, you will complete the cycle of earthly life.[a] May the One Who Is, He Who searches out all things, keep your soul and body in His salvation.

Note

1. This seems to be a firmly held conviction of Hildegard's. For her, service to the Church *is* service to one's own personal salvation. It is for this reason that she almost never gives an affirmative to the large number of people who consult her about abdicating an administrative position in order to seek out a solitary monkish life.

26
Hillinus, Archbishop of Trier,[1] to Hildegard

1152(?)

The archbishop of Trier asks for a few words of consolation from Hildegard, upon whom God has poured His grace so abundantly.

Hillinus, archbishop and humble servant at Trier, unworthy though I am, to Hildegard, most beloved sister, with prayers that she follow the Lamb and the Bridegroom "whithersoever he goeth" [Apoc 14.4].

It has pleased the wisdom of God, which chooses "the weak things of the world that he may confound the strong" [I Cor 1.27], to choose a pleasant habitation for itself in your virginity. And so He has abundantly poured forth the grace of His light in the spirit of wisdom and fuller knowledge. By the pouring out of this light, He intended, I believe, to stimulate the minds of others to efforts more conscientiously directed toward salvation [cf. Heb 6.9], and, with you as mediator, O venerable mother, O woman to be embraced in genuine love, to illumine their thoughts.

O beloved virgin in Christ, the true vine, in whose shade you rest and whose fruit is sweet to your throat [cf. John 15.1; Cant 2.3], it now remains for you to further extend the shoots of this vine over this stormy sea, and, for the benefit of souls everywhere, to draw off the nectar of the cup of heaven which you have imbibed, freely giving what you have freely received [cf. Matt 10.8]. In this way, you will not be accused of hiding under a bushel the lamp that was lit for the benefit of your neighbors [cf. Matt 5.15; Mark 4.21; Luke 8.16; 11.33].

Therefore, holy mother, I join all those who fly to the harbor of your consolation, and, with firm hope of obtaining my desire, I beseech your maternal compassion in the name of holy love, and ask that you deign to distill some drops in written form to me, a poor sinner—drops which you have drawn from the King's own wine cellar—and send them along to me by the bearer of this letter.[a] I ask this favor, for I know that, even in this life, you miraculously drink the abundance of His will to the full. I make this request not only for His sake who has shown that these things are possible, but also so that truth may quell those rumors that cause certain people to doubt your divine inspiration.[2]

May God, Who began a good work in you [cf. Phil 1.6], bring it to perfection in the life of the living.

Notes

1. Hillinus served as archbishop of Trier from 1152 until his death in 1169. Earlier, as a minor prelate in Trier, he was present at the Synod of Trier (1147–48), where Hildegard's work was read in full audience.

2. An interesting offhand comment on rumors skeptical of Hildegard's divine inspiration. In the *Vita* (II.ii.22), Hildegard is quoted about the criticism directed at her: "Why is it that so many mysteries are revealed to this foolish, untaught woman and not to strong and wise men? . . . Many wondered whether this revelation were from God or whether from dry spirits of the air, which lead many astray."

26r

Hildegard to Hillinus, Archbishop of Trier

1152(?)

Hildegard exhorts Hillinus to hold the tower of his office staunchly, even if the ramparts (the priests) are breached and the streets (the people) are ransacked.

Wisdom cries out, saying: The present time is a squalid, womanish time.[a] O alas, Adam, the root of the whole human race, was a new testament of all justice. Afterwards, in his race the manly spirit rose up and went out in three throngs, like a tree spread out into three branches. The first throng was of such a nature that the sons of Adam chose according to their own capacity. The second was such that men rashly became murderers. The third, that they committed whatever idolatry or similar evils they wished. Now this tree has dried up, and the world has been turned upside down through many dangers.[b] This time looks back to the time when the first woman gave the nod of deception to the first man. But man has more physical strength than woman. Yet woman is a fountain of wisdom and full joy, which man brings to perfection.[c] But, alas, this present time is neither cold nor hot [cf. Apoc 3.15]; it is squalid. After this, a time will come which will bring forth manly strength in the midst of great dangers, fear, injustice, and ferocity. At that time, the error of errors will blow like the four winds which inundate the world with slander amidst great dangers.

Now, therefore, O shepherd, hear what the justice of God has in store for you, because the grace of God has not put you in office in vain. The fact is, however, that when you do perform good works, you become tired all too quickly, and when you are called to the symphony, so that you pause to pray, you immediately dry up.

Oh, you who are Christ's representative, listen again: a certain king held a city in great honor, and he entrusted it to three of his men so that they might carefully guard it. To the first, he entrusted the tower; to the second, the streets; to the third, the walls and its ramparts. You have been stationed in the tower, your people on the streets, and your clergy on the ramparts. But if the wall of the city is breached and its streets ransacked, continue to guard the tower all the same, and be stalwart so that the whole city will not be destroyed and reduced to rubble.

The likeness of the dove teaches you, and the Word of God is knowledge in you. Now, therefore, stay vigilant: discipline those entrusted to you with an iron rod [cf. Ps 2.9], teach them, anoint their wounds; and you will live forever.

27
Arnold, Archbishop of Trier,[1] to Hildegard

1169

Arnold, Hildegard's nephew, writes to inform her of his recent election to the archbishopric of Trier, which office he held from 1169 to 1183. An intriguing personal note enters in with Arnold's criticism of his brother Wezelinus, whom he considers a mere flatterer of Hildegard: are the two contentiously vying for the affection of the famous seer?

Arnold, by the grace of God humble archbishop-elect of Trier, sends greetings and love to his beloved kinswoman in Christ, Hildegard of St. Rupert, from Him who is salvation and love.

Friendship among relatives is a heavenly thing, because old age neither thwarts nor weakens it, and when it is true, it does not stagnate, but, rather, grows and improves daily. And so since we have embraced in the arms of true love from our earliest years, I am surprised that you have more regard for a flatterer than for a true friend, since the prophet says, "But let not the oil of the sinner fatten my head" [Ps 140.5]. We consider our brother, the prior of St. Andrew's, as your flatterer, but we wish to be considered your true friend.

But because we know our success is a source of joy for you, we thought that you, beloved, should be notified that through God's grace our situation has improved. Still, because that which one regards as a punishment is no blessing, we declare before God and you that the position to which we have been called (against our will, God knows) was never, as is usual in such cases, a source of temptation or comfort to us, because our ignorance, our fragility, laments our insufficiency and deplores our infirmity. And because we do not know who has called us to such an office, we are afflicted by great anxiety. If we knew it to be God, we would have faith that He who had begun a good work in us would also bring it to perfection [cf. Phil 1.6], since our promotion to this office resulted from necessity rather than any virtue of our own.

And we know that "God in his holy place" [Ps 67.6] has worked salvation among you by visiting his people [cf. Luke 7.16] to mercifully liberate a woman possessed by the devil.[2] Thus we earnestly beseech you to give an account of the method by which that liberation was achieved. Moreover, whenever you look to the True Light, please impart to us some saving grace through your letters, and, after the example of Moses, intercede for us by lifting up your hands to the rock of refuge, while we fight against Amalech in the valley of worldly miseries [cf. Ex 17].

We are writing back to you in the presence of the abbot of St. Eucharius, our faithful and beloved friend, and he has helped us by seasoning our words with his sweetness. Therefore, we also ask that you send your response back through him.

Notes

1. Arnold was archbishop of Trier from 1169 to 1183. He was Hildegard's nephew, the brother of Wezelinus.
2. Hildegard was called upon to help this woman—a noblewoman named Sigewize—because, it was reported, the demon himself crying out through the woman's voice declared that only a certain "old woman" on the upper Rhine could be of any assistance. Hildegard somewhat reluctantly took on the task, first by writing and sending to them a kind of mimetic scenario to be acted out, and later by working with her at Mount St. Rupert itself. See Letters 68–69. Also see Dronke, "Problemata Hildegardiana," pp. 117ff.

27r
Hildegard to Arnold, Archbishop of Trier

1169

In accordance with her usual theme, Hildegard exhorts Arnold to preserve justice in his new administrative position, and she, perhaps, warns him against jealousy of his brother, though, in truth, the admonition is so general that it is difficult to tell.

O, you are a tree planted by God, just as Paul says: All power is from God [cf. Rom 13.1], because, according to the highest authority, every power has been named in the invocation of His name, and through that invocation a tree derives its viridity from the honor of His name.[a] May you preserve yourself from that which is not of God and which is done with the left hand, lest you fall in the falling sickness of pride, like the first angel, Satan, who set himself in opposition to God to steal furtively that honor which many people today wilfully snatch for themselves, totally disregarding the means to that end. Such an attitude is nothing in God's eyes, because "without him was made nothing" [John 1.3], and thus God destroys whatever stands apart from Him.

Therefore, as far as you are able though God's grace be solicitous to give testimony to the people through God's commandments, which are as luxuriant as the leaves of a tree. For the burden of your office has many tribulations, such as poverty, which binds you in, because riches and money do not love heavenly things. In this way, God reins in man's desires so that he will sigh for heaven, his homeland. Thus it is fitting that a poor man love a poor man and a rich man acknowledge a rich man, because wisdom gives a ring to the poor man, but denies an earring to the rich.[b]

Wherefore, with regard to your office, keep this in mind: "I have not hid thy justice within my heart: I have declared thy truth and thy salvation" [Ps 39.11]. Here is the interpretation of this passage: God's Justice does not conceal herself, but makes her paths wide and is not ashamed to run on them. Justice also does not hide her wounds by preferring evil to good, but Injustice says that life is hell, and that one must run in both directions at once. Justice, on the other hand, does not steep herself in this fallacy, nor does she kiss Injustice with a multiplicity of words; rather she tramples it underfoot. Likewise, Truth does not praise those works which are done apart from God, but, like a brave knight, prepares herself to oppose them in battle.

Now let Justice be your shield, and dress yourself in her truth, as with a breastplate, so that you may appear well armed before God and not a fugitive in the company of vanity, and learn to suck the breasts of Justice. Also, learn to heal the wounds of penitent sinners with mercy, just as the great Physician has bequeathed to you a salutary example for restoring the people to health.

For through the instruction of His name, you have been placed in the viridity of that blessed man who did not listen to the wicked devil, wicked indeed because he did not love good. Beware of boasting in your treasure, for in the end money is deceitful, because it fails one as easily after one year as after thirty. But rejoice on Mount Zion, where the help of the Most High is eternal in eternity, and where every spirit praises the Lord [cf. Ps 150.6].

Be, also, an ivory mountain, from the windows of which spears fly in the upright judgment of justice against your adversaries. Run also to the heights of the law and justice of God, like a mountain goat, lest you fall unarmed through instability, and may your sons rise up from the side of the Church and cry out to you for the food of justice. And so learn good doctrine so that you may satisfy them.

As you asked, I have looked to the True Light, and I could scarcely see the beginning of good works. And so, now, be more zealous in doing good works so that, afterward, I may write more things to you by the grace of God. And be a faithful friend to your soul, so that you may live forever.

Finally, concerning the possessed woman you inquired about, we have seen many miracles which are impossible to put into writing now. But we know that the breath of the devil grew weaker and weaker day after day until he came forth at last and the woman was freed from the weakness caused by the devil. And during the time she was possessed, she suffered from an infirmity that, at that time, she was unaware of. But now she has recovered fully in both body and soul.

28

Hildegard to Arnold, Archbishop of Trier

1169–70

Hildegard exhorts Arnold to preserve humility in his high office.

O servant and close friend of God, consider the example of a day which begins clear and beautiful and remains so until the evening, never clouded over by storms, as opposed to a day which dawns brightly but soon becomes a dangerous, stormy time, so that the foul ending destroys the promise of the beautiful beginning. Thus beware lest you attribute to yourself alone those good qualities which are yours in both your spirit and your works. Rather, attribute them to God, from whom all virtues proceed like sparks from a fire. Remember, too, that you are ashes and that you will return to ashes, and, therefore, give God the honor which you owe Him for the gifts which you acknowledge in yourself. For whoever is aware that he has good qualities, but ascribes them to himself alone, that person is like an infidel who worships only the works of his own hands.

Therefore, dear son of God, gird yourself with true humility and cast off vainglory, and you will be like the bright day which is never clouded over by storms, with your good beginning being brought to perfection by a good end. Thus you will not be like that day which has a bright beginning but a stormy ending. May the fire of the Holy Spirit never be extinguished in you, so that, persevering joyfully in His mystery, you may reach the height of blessedness.

Finally, O servant of God, with all the devotion of my heart I commend to your prayers my beloved son, the abbot of St. Eucharius, who calls me Mother, unworthy though I am. On his behalf, please pray to almighty God to bring the good intentions of his heart to fruition, and to make him such a man in this present life that he may deserve to attain the joys of eternal life. I also will gladly pray for him, to the best of my ability with my God's help. And I beseech you through God's love to kindly remember me before the Lord.

29

Arnold, Superior of St. Andrew in Cologne, to Hildegard

Before 1169

The self-reviling in this letter goes far beyond the usual humility formula. Arnold seeks help from Hildegard for his poor, wretched self, from her divine revelations if possible, if not from her ordinary wisdom.

Arnold, Superior of St. Andrew in Cologne (although unworthy), to Hildegard, lady and dearest mother, with a prayer that she may always flourish in the Lord.

Dearest lady, you know, not only from our conversations but also through divine revelation, how sorely my soul is tried by the tribulations of temptation, both inwardly and outwardly. Now, therefore, because I am weak and because I see in myself no progress at all toward God, I have written to you, my lady, fully prepared to follow your commands implicitly, whether founded in divine revelation or simply in the wisdom of your counsel. Do not spare me, I beseech you. Do not hide my iniquity from me. I fear for the tattered remains of my impoverished spirit, and I am terrified that I am being sucked down into the abyss. Therefore, O dearest mother, strong in Christ, please intercede for me, and pray for my wretched soul.

May the Lord be with you and yours.

30

Hildegard to Eberhard, Bishop of Bamberg

1157

In this short letter, Hildegard seeks help from Eberhard (bishop of Bamberg from 1146 to 1170) for Gertrude, widow of Count Hermann von Stahleck. As sister of King Conrad III and of Duke Frederick II of Schwabia, and aunt to Barbarossa, she was of the highest nobility. Gertrude and her husband liberally supported Mount St. Rupert, and after her husband's death, Gertrude dedicated her life to God, and entered the Cistercian monastery of Wechterswinkel. The request made by Hildegard here for a more suitable convent for Gertrude and her nuns was received well by Eberhard, who turned over the hospital belonging to the seminary attached to Bamberg cathedral to this group of dedicated nuns. Thus this generous act of intercession by Hildegard had a happy result, for this new convent became a thriving community.

A certain man rose up in the morning and planted a vineyard. Later, because of much dissension, he turned his eyes to foreign places, and his desire was fulfilled.

Now, O father, look to your daughter Gertrude, who was called forth, a pilgrim, from her own country, just like Abraham, who also left his land. She has given up everything and bought the pearl of great price [cf. Matt 13.46]. Now, however, her mind is being squeezed dry by great anxiety, like a grape in the winepress. Therefore, for the love of Him who was before the beginning and has filled all things with compassion, help her as much as you can, so that the vineyard in this daughter may not be destroyed.

31

Eberhard, Bishop of Bamberg, to Hildegard

1163–64

Eberhard seeks information from Hildegard on a fine theological point. He is currently engaged in a Christological quarrel with Gerhoch of Reichersberg, and he seeks ammunition for his argument from Hildegard, which he receives at length, for Hildegard takes the question very seriously.

Eberhard, bishop of Bamberg by the grace of God, although unworthy, your devoted servant with prayers for eternal blessedness, to Hildegard, venerable sister and superior of St. Rupert.

By favor of heavenly grace, the report of your sanctity resounds in the ears of people everywhere so that we can say in all truth that "we are the good odour of Christ unto God" [II Cor 2.15]. But also "the Lord hath looked down from heaven upon the children of men, to see" if there be any that understand [Ps 13.2] or any who seek God in you. And so, perfumed by the fragrance[a] of your good reputation, we run enthusiastically to the Lord whom you venerate and reverently consult. You surely will not deny to me alone what you have offered to so many. Now, since we are passing through on our way from the imperial court, we wish to submit the following matter to be expounded through your spiritual love, since you are imbued by the Holy Spirit: eternity is an attribute of the Father, equality an attribute of the Son, with the Holy Spirit being the connection between the two.[b] We earnestly desire to have this matter explained through God's revelation to you.

May the Lord be with you, so that we also may be helped by your prayers.

31r
Hildegard to Eberhard, Bishop of Bamberg

1163–64

This letter is really a theological treatise dealing with the various attributes of the persons of the Trinity.

He Who Is, and from Whom nothing is hidden, says, O shepherd, do not allow the sweet flow of the odor of balsam dry up in you, that vitality which must be given to the foolish who do not have the breasts of maternal compassion to suck, and who, therefore, lack sustenance. Therefore, offer the lamp of the King to your people, so that they might not be scattered in bitterness, and you yourself rise up, living, in its light.

Father, I, a poor little woman, am able to expound upon the question you asked me, because I have looked to the True Light,[1] and I am sending along to you the answer I saw and heard in a true vision—not my words, I remind you, but those of the True Light, which has no imperfection.

Eternity is the essential quality of the Father.[a] That is to say, nothing can be added or subtracted from it, for eternity is like a wheel, which has neither beginning nor end. Thus, in the Father, before the beginning of the world, eternity is. Eternity always is and always has been. What is eternity? It is God. For eternity is not eternity except in Perfect Life. Therefore, God lives in eternity. Life proceeds not from mortality, but life is in life. Thus a tree grows only from its life-giving sap, and not even a stone is without its moisture, and every living thing has its own life force. For eternity is itself alive, and is not without the ability to produce life.[b]

How is this so? It was the function of the Word of the Father to bring forth every created thing. And so the Father is not idle in his great might. Hence, God is called the Father, because all things are born from Him. And so, once again, eternity is an essential quality of the Father, because He was Father before the beginning, and was eternal before the inception of His magnificent works, all of which He foresaw eternally. But the state of the Father is not the state of man, which is sometimes uncertain, sometimes past, sometimes future, sometimes new, sometimes old, but that which is in the Father is always stable.

The Father is brightness, and that brightness has radiance, and that radiance has fire: and they are all one. Whoever does not believe this does not see

God, because he is seeking to make a division in an indivisible God. Indeed, the works which God established no longer have their undivided essence, since man has brought about divisions.

Brightness is Paternity, from which all things have their being and by which they are all embraced, for they derive from its power. That same power made man, and breathed the breath of life into him. But also in that same power man has his own potency. How? Flesh produces flesh, and good propagates that which is good: the good is spread abroad by spiritual conversation and is increased by good example in another person.[c] These powers are in man both carnally and spiritually, because one thing proceeds from another. Man highly prizes his useful works, because he conceives them in his mind and brings them into effect by his actions. So, too, it is God's will that His power be manifested in all his creatures, because they are His work.

Radiance gives eyes, and that Radiance which is the Son gave eyes when he said, "Let there be." At that moment all things appeared physically in the Living Eye. And fire, which is God, permeates these two terms, because it is impossible to have brightness without radiance. And if they did not have fire, there would be neither brightness nor radiance. Flame and light lie hidden in fire; otherwise it would not be fire.

Equality is the essential characteristic of the Son.[d] How? All creatures were in the Father before the beginning of time, all in the order He Himself had ordained. Afterward, the Son gave them their physical form. How? It is like a person who conceives an idea of a great work, and then makes it explicit by his word so that it comes forth in praiseworthy form.

The Father ordains, the Son puts into effect.[e] For the Father has ordained all things in Himself, and the Son has brought them to completion. And the light which was in the beginning is from that eternal light before the beginning of the world, and this light, whose radiance is from the Father, is the Son, through Whom all things were made. And the Son clothed Himself in the garment of mankind, whom he had formed from the mud, the garment which, before, had no bodily form.[f] Thus God saw all his works before Him as light, and when He said "Let there be," He gave each kind its own proper garment.

Afterward, God humbled Himself to his own work, and in this way equality to mankind is an essential quality of the Son of God, for He himself put on the garment of humanity, just as the works of God clothed themselves in their physical forms. For God had foreknowledge of all the works which he generated, and, therefore, He stooped into the lowliness of humanity to become a man, because divinity is so perfect that, if He had not clothed Himself in humanity, He could have tolerated nothing in man which opposes the good, since "all things were made by him: and without him was made nothing" [John 1.3]. All things perceived by sight, touch, and taste were made by Him, and He foresaw that all these things were necessary for mankind, some for the embracing of divine love, some for reverence, some for knowledge, some for discipline, and some for discretion.

"And without him was made nothing." This "nothing" is insolent pride. It is an attitude of mind which has regard only for itself, and has faith in nothing. For its wishes are the opposite of God's, and it thinks only of its own fabrications. It is full of darkness, because it despised the light of truth, and because it set in motion that which it could not bring to completion. Thus pride is nothing, because it was neither made nor created by God.[g] It had its beginning in the first angel, when he looked at his own refulgence and became arrogant, because he did not see the Source of his brightness. But he said to himself: I want to be the Lord, and I will acknowledge no one else as Lord. And, immediately, his glory vanished, and he became the prince of Hell.

Then God gave that first angel's glory to His other son, man, and made him so powerful that all created things are subject to him. Thus man was endowed with such great power that, through it all, he never lost his pristine glory. But like the blasphemy by which the devil rejected God, man in his foolishness wanted to be like God in honor, that is, to be as God is. Nevertheless, man did not cast aside that love which he knew God to be. Thus the essence of the devil is absolute darkness, because he did not wish the brightness of God to exist. Adam, on the other hand, did wish the brightness of God to exist, and indeed longed to be in His presence. Hence, man's essence is perfect, because something of that original light remains in him—although he is filled with misery and woe.[h]

The connection between eternity and equality is the Holy Spirit.[i] The Holy Spirit is a fire, but it is not an extinguishable fire that sometimes blazes up and sometimes is put out. It permeates eternity and equality, and binds the two into one, just as a person binds together a bundle of sticks (which, if not bound, flies all asunder). And it is like a blacksmith who unites the two materials of bronze and makes them one through fire. It is a sword brandished in every direction. The Holy Spirit reveals eternity and enkindles equality, joining them into one. The Holy Spirit is fire and life in eternity and equality, because God is living. The sun is radiant with a blazing light, and the fire burns in it. It illuminates the whole world, and it appears as a single entity. But any thing devoid of life-force is dead, just as a limb cut off from a tree becomes withered, because it no longer has the stuff of life in it.[j]

The Holy Spirit is the uniting factor and the life-giving force, for without the Holy Spirit eternity would not be eternity, nor would equality be equality.[k] The Holy Spirit is in both, and the three are one in divinity, that is, God is one.

Rational expression, also, has three forces: sound, word, and breath.[l] The Son is in the Father the same way that a word is in a sound, and the Holy Spirit is in each, just as breath is found both in sound and in word. And these three persons are one God, as I said earlier. The essential quality of the Father is eternity, for there was no one before Him, since eternity (unlike the works of God) had no beginning. The essential quality of the Son is equality, because the Son has never been separated from the Father, nor the Father from the Son. But the essential quality of the Holy Spirit is the connection between the two, for the Son has always remained in the Father, and the Father with the Son, since the Holy Spirit is the fiery life in them, and they are one.

And it is written: "the spirit of the Lord hath filled the whole world" [Wis 1.7]. The meaning of this Scripture is that all created things, visible and invisible, have life imbued with the spirit, and those created things that man does not know, his intellect searches out until he does. For from the sap, flowers; from flowers, fruit. The clouds have their course, and the moon and stars burn with fire. The tree brings forth flowers through invigorating sap, and water, in its rarer essence, has the ability both to make the wind moist and to bring forth rivulets. Even the earth exhales moisture.^m

For all created things have visible and invisible qualities, and that which is seen is weak, but that which is not seen is strong and vital. Since man cannot see these invisible qualities with his eyes, he seeks to grasp them with his intellect. These are the forces of the works of the Holy Spirit.

"And that, which containeth all things" [Wis 1.7]. What is the subject of this quotation? Man. In what way does he contain all things? By ruling, by using, by commanding. God gave him this capacity in accordance with His will.

"Hath knowledge of the voice" [Wis 1.7]. This capacity is rationality which utters sound with a voice. The voice is body; rationality, soul; the warmth of the air, fire; and they are all one.ⁿ Thus when rationality is heard by speaking, by creating with the voice, all its works are brought to perfection, and therefore it has the power to create, because as it commands, so will it be. Consequently, none of the works of God are in vain.²

If someone had a jar full of money, he would be very glad. But if the jar were empty, he would consider it worthless. There is emptiness in all the works of wicked men, and they flee from the fire of the Holy Spirit. At first, through the devil's instigation, they delight in sinning. But when a person realizes that his wicked deeds are worthless and rejects them, he is like the prodigal son, who, after his hunger, remembered his father's bread, and said, "Father, I have sinned against heaven, and before thee" [Luke 15.18, 21]: "Against heaven," because I am heavenly in my rationality; "and before thee," because I know that you are God. Then he repudiates the devil, and at last chooses God as his Lord. Thereupon, all the celestial harmonies stand in awe at the confounding of the devil's wickedness, for that which they had earlier considered useless mud, they now regard as a pillar of cloud supreme in its usefulness, and that which they had at first seen as worthless, they now regard as very beautiful, because they deem worthless all the wickedness of the devil.^o For there is no usefulness in such wicked deeds, but usefulness is achieved through good works. These are the works of the Holy Spirit.

Now, O father and shepherd of the people, may God grant that you reach the light where you will receive the knowledge of true blessedness.

Notes

1. Clearly, this is what Eberhard expected from Hildegard, an answer concerning metaphysical matters directly through inspiration of the Holy Spirit, a means, in his mind apparently, superior to those provided by the abstract logic of the budding scholastic method.

2. What Barbara Newman (*Sister of Wisdom*, p. 20) writes of Hildegard's *Liber divinorum operum* applies equally well to the seer's cosmological vision expressed in this

letter: "First, Hildegard, in typical twelfth-century fashion, saw the world as a divine milieu in which every being is both a sign of the Creator's plenitude and a potential instrument for his action. Her outlook was profoundly theocentric. Second, within this divine milieu, the human being holds the place of honor as the image of God. And in the third place, because the most important activity in life is the salvation of the soul, the cosmos is to be read as one vast and complicated moral lesson."

32
Henry, Bishop of Beauvais, to Hildegard

1148–62

The bishop of Beauvais writes to solicit Hildegard's prayers. Henry, the brother of King Louis VII of France, served as bishop of Beauvais from 1141 to 1162, and, in 1162, became archbishop of Rheims, a position he held until 1175.

Henry, by grace of God, bishop of Beauvais, unworthy though I am, sends greetings to Hildegard, beloved mistress of St. Rupert at Bingen, whatever good the prayers of a sinner, uttered with a contrite and humbled spirit, can accomplish.

Blessed be the Lord who has blessed you with every spiritual blessing [cf. Ephes 1.3]. May religious fervor be spread into the far reaches of the world through your example as one anointed with the fragrance of God's compassion. For God's esteem for you is clear even to me, a sinner, and, far removed from you in body if not in spirit, this is a great consolation to me, overwhelmed as I am by the storms of this age. We have absolutely no doubt whatsoever that by your merits and prayers the compassion of Christ is available to all who faithfully seek the help of your prayers.

Not trusting in our own conscience, we have no confidence of obtaining salvation through our own actions, and so through the love of the Holy Spirit we beseech you (far removed as you are from us) to implore the Lord in your prayers for forgiveness of our sins. Moreover, out of your love for us, please do not be reluctant to write back and send any little comfort or admonition necessary for our salvation. In accordance with His grace, may He who has all power, and from Whom no thought is hidden, deign to answer your prayers for the desire of our heart.

32r

Hildegard to Henry, Bishop of Beauvais

1148–62

Hildegard sends Henry comfort through the voices of personified virtues.

The Living Light showed me the following vision and said, Say to that man: I saw, as it were, the beautiful form of virtue, which was Pure Knowledge. Her face was extremely bright, her eyes like jacinth, and her clothes like a silken cloak. And on her shoulders she had a bishop's pallium like carnelian. She summoned a lovely friend of the king, that is to say, Divine Love, and said, Come with me. And they went along together and knocked at the door of your heart, calling out: We wish to live with you. Therefore, beware: don't close us out, but close out instead vices, secular concerns, and changing winds which rise up like smoke in tornadoes, and like water which flies in storms. For these are the disturbances of the human mind when provoked to anger and similar emotions. Do not, in your weariness, keep silent, but let your voice ring forth like a trumpet in the rites of the Church. Let your eyes be pure in knowledge so that you may not be reluctant to cleanse yourself of the dishonorable dust of the burden you bear. For you are covered with the drops of the night [cf. Cant 5.2]. But the persuasive voice of pride has said to you: Do not cleanse yourself. But this is contrary to our wishes, for we want you to eradicate every vestige of darkness from yourself, and not to be fearful of the many terrors inflicted by your enemies, for they speak neither well nor rightly about you. O knight, keep us with you and give us a dwelling place in your heart, and we will take you with us to the palace of the king.

33

Hildegard to Gero, Bishop of Halberstadt

1160–70

Although Gero's letter to Hildegard has not been preserved, it seems clear from the context of Hildegard's response that he had queried her about the state of some recently deceased person's soul.

In a true vision I saw and heard these words spoken by Wisdom for the people's scrutiny: As a result of God's benevolence, as well as that just man's own merits, he is now numbered among the blessed and the just, that is, the saints.

And Wisdom says again about him: Let the winds be lifted through the four elements, and let them sound this forth with praises among the people: that he has gone before with voice raised in prayer. For when the just have completed their woeful pilgrimage and come at last to blessedness, God's grace should, justly and rightly, be praised in them, for they have been found without trace of wicked deeds committed against God's justice through infidelity or deception. That just man indeed breathed forth sighs which ascended through the mirrored eye of the cherubim to the throne of God.[a]

34
Amalricus, Bishop of Jerusalem, to Hildegard

1157–73(?)

With this request for prayers from the bishop of Jerusalem, it is clear that Hildegard's reputation has spread afar.

Amalricus, by the grace and appointment of God servant and bishop of Jerusalem, though ineffective, sends his very humble prayer and greetings in Christ to Hildegard, beloved daughter and mistress of Mount St. Rupert in Bingen, in the bishopric of Mainz.

From those many people who come from far distant places into our land to bend their knees at the sepulchre of the Lord, we have frequently heard that divine power is at work through you and in you, for which we ourselves offer unceasing thanks as humbly as we can.

We have long desired to correspond with you, beloved daughter, but because an intermediary has been unavailable so far, our desire has been completely frustrated. But now after a long time, an opportunity has arisen, and therefore we thought it appropriate to address you and all your sisters (who, as I hear, are under your supervision in Christ) in the present letter. And so it is that although we are oppressed constantly by overwhelming difficulties—attacked on the one side by the treachery of malignant spirits and on the other by the sword of the pagans—we would, if we had pleasing words at our command, extoll you as the bride of Christ and as a woman always focused on the mysteries of Christ. But it is not necessary to praise with human words one who, by divine grace, has been granted participation in angelic praise. We call those happy who are accounted worthy to converse with you day after day to their hearts' delight. It is not inappropriate at all for us to call those happy who, in the mirror of divine radiance, endeavor daily to learn from the Lord the prize reserved for their merits [cf. I Cor 9.24]. Happy, I say, exceedingly happy, those who have accounted all earthly things vile in contrast to the reward of heavenly things, and who despise, crush under their heel, and denounce all things which seem pleasant, delectable, and enduring to all other mortals in this life. Behold, true daughters of Jerusalem, in whom no blemish has been found [cf. Cant 4.7], in whom the world finds nothing to love, and who also without doubt "follow the Lamb whithersoever he goeth" [Apoc 14.4].

Now, O daughter, with our hearts turned to you, we humbly ask for any consolation revealed to you from heaven. And because we are foundering in the storms of secular anxieties, we also commend ourselves to your prayers and the prayers of all your sisters so that you may piously intercede for us to Him whose chamber you long to enter after you have passed the boundary of this life. And may the Lord bring it about, O beloved, that "thou see the good things of Jerusalem all the days of thy life" [Ps 127.5].

35

Hermann, Bishop of Constance, to Hildegard

1148–66

Hermann, bishop of Constance from 1138 until his death in 1165 or 1166, seeks Hildegard's prayers. Hermann was totally loyal to the emperor and supported his choice of Paschal III as pope.

Hermann, by grace of God bishop of the church of Constance, albeit ineffectual and unworthy, sends greetings to Hildegard, bride of Christ, at the monastery of St. Rupert in Bingen, with wishes that you may increase in divine love and that the outcome of both your corporeal and spiritual life may be most blessed.

The fame of your wisdom has spread far and wide and has been reported to me by a number of truthful people, reports that have made me desire to seek out your solace and support even from these far distant regions and to commend myself to your prayers. For it is very difficult to become the judge of other people's lives when one does not know how to observe moderation in his own.

Therefore, with sincere devotion, beloved lady, I beseech you to come to my aid with your prayers before the Lord, and to fortify me with your response.

For both my own will, as well as secular concerns, almost completely pull me away from my service to God.

35r
Hildegard to Hermann, Bishop of Constance
1148–66

> Hildegard takes Hermann to task for not being just in the performance of his duties.

The most just Light says: Straighten up your mind, O man. For you are disregarding the counsel of the prelates of old, who never, like you, had a mind blown about by the winds of vanity. O, man, what in the world are you thinking! Aren't you ashamed to walk in the darkness of your own appetite? For that Revelation, from whom nothing is hidden, shows through the living eye that the bow of God's zeal is threatening mankind's temerity. Why do you not see where the "mammon of iniquity" [Luke 16.9] lies, through which you justify yourself?[1] Many laborers bring their cases before you, seeking the straight and narrow way. But you flap your lips with empty rhetoric, which is your very essence, and you drive them away, angry and indignant.[a]

And so turn from darkness onto the straight path, and shed some light on the feelings of your heart, lest the Father of all say to you: Why are you stupidly climbing a column that you did not build? For the day grows dark for one who does not labor in the straight path of the journey, and, you especially, beware of this! Rise quickly, therefore, and walk the straight and narrow, before the sun sets on you, and your days wane.

Note

1. The full verse of this scriptural text reads: "And I say to you: Make unto you friends of the mammon of iniquity; that when you shall fail, they may receive you into everlasting dwellings." It was a text frequently used to justify monetary gain, but, as this context makes clear, a text also frequently misused.

36

Hildegard to Hermann, Bishop of Constance

1148–66

In this second letter to Hermann, Hildegard exhorts him, once again, to be faithful to his duties.

The Living Light which reveals miracles says: You who in your calling are a father and shepherd in charge of souls, stretch out your arms, lest your enemy plant tares in your fields [cf. Matt 13.25].

Watch over that garden which the divine gift has planted, and take care that its herbs do not wither. Rather, cut the rottenness out of them, and cast it out, for it chokes off their usefulness. In this way, you will cause them to flourish. For when the sun hides its rays, the earth ceases to rejoice.

And I say: Do not overshadow your garden with the weariness of silence, but in the True Light weed out those things which must be weeded out with discretion. Illuminate your temple with benevolence, and burn incense in your censer, so that its smoke may ascend to the palace of the living God. And you will live forever.

37

Heinrich, Bishop of Liège, to Hildegard

1148–53

There are problems of ascription with respect to this letter, but it seems to have been written by Heinrich of Liège. He is most notable because his name appears in the document of 1163 by which Barbarossa granted imperial protection to Mount St. Rupert. Prominent among the prelates of the Church, he was extraordinarily favored by Barbarossa. Heinrich writes as a grievous sinner requesting Hildegard's prayers.

Heinrich, by the grace of God bishop of Liège, sends greetings to the servant of Christ, Hildegard of St. Rupert in Bingen, with prayers that you serve the King of kings ceaselessly, and that you receive the prize of eternal blessedness [cf. I Cor 9.24].

Plagued by great instability of mind and body, I have determined to write to you, because I greatly need the mercy of God, which, I will not deny, I have offended and provoked by my countless sins. Therefore, beloved sister, because I know for a certainty that God is with you, I urge and beseech you, in the name of His mercy, saintly lady, to stretch out your hand to me as I founder and run to you for refuge. Please let it be your concern to remain vigilant with devoted prayers so that my negligence may be cast from me, and please write back to inform me what the unfailing Living Light reveals that I must do to arouse myself from this somnolence of soul.

May the most merciful God grant that I receive full consolation through your writings, and, through your intercession, that I may, at last, be granted the dwelling place of eternal rest.

37r
Hildegard to Heinrich, Bishop of Liège

1148–53

Hildegard laments the slothfulness and sin that are now in the world, and prays Heinrich to perform his duties well so as to bring back the "lost pearls" to the mountain of God.

The Living Light says: the Scriptures are a path which lead to the lofty mountain where flowers and precious herbs grow, with a fragrant breeze blowing over them, bringing forth their sweet aroma, and where roses and lilies show their bright faces. Yet because of the shadows of dark living air, that mountain was not visible until the Son of the Most High had illuminated the world. For the Sun itself came from the dawn to illumine this mountain, and all the people saw its herbs. The day was very beautiful, and good news came into the world.

But, O shepherds, now is the time for wailing and mourning, because in our day that mountain has been overshadowed by such dark clouds that its sweet fragrance no longer is wafted down to us. But you, O Heinrich, be a shepherd good and noble in your character. And just as the eagle looks to the sun, so you give thought and consider how you can restore the slothful and the prodigal to their homeland and how you can bestow some light on that mountain so that your soul may live. Thus you will hear the beloved voice of the high judge exclaim: "Well done, good and faithful servant" [Matt 25.21, 23], and your soul will radiate light like a knight who is refulgent in battle when his comrades rejoice with him because he has emerged victorious.

And so you, O leader of the people, fight victoriously, correct those who have gone astray, and wash the filth from the beautiful pearls, preparing them for the Most High King. And thus let your mind sigh in its eagerness to bring back those pearls to the mountain, just as the gift of God had originally planted them. Now, may God protect you and free your soul from eternal punishment.

38
Daniel, Bishop of Prague, to Hildegard
1148–67(?)

Daniel, bishop of Prague, seeks Hildegard's prayers, and is prevented only by the great distance and the difficulites of travel from coming to see her in person. Daniel served as bishop of Prague, a suffragan-bishopric of Mainz, from 1148 to 1167. A staunch adherent of the imperial party, he participated in the emperor's Italian campaign, during which he contracted malaria, from which he died in 1167.

Daniel, by the grace of God servant of the people of Prague, and also bishop, although useless and unworthy, sends whatever the small token of prayers uttered with all devotion can accomplish to Hildegard, the bride of Christ and superior of St. Rupert in Bingen.

We glorify God our Lord and magnify His name, because illumined by His spirit you help many in tribulation with comfort and support, and with the assistance of that same spirit, you lead many people to produce the fruit of good works, as we have heard tell about you even in these far-flung places.

And so, saintly lady, you will already have learned that we have a great desire to see you and to enjoy conversation with you in Christ. The great difficulties of travel, however, have kept us from coming to you. But because we have heard that your love has aided many people in their distress, we have been encouraged to seek the assistance of your prayers and advice, beloved lady, for we are shaken by secular tribulations. From the first time we heard your name and the grace bestowed upon you by Christ, we have always remembered you in our hearts. We earnestly pray that that same grace which originates from the true Light may remain with you always.

38r

Hildegard to Daniel, Bishop of Prague

1153–54

Hildegard interprets the fruit of the vineyard that Noah planted after the flood typologically as obedience, and urges Daniel to overcome the instability of his character and be obedient to the true sun.

The voice of life and salvation says: Why will a person chew on a grape and still wish to remain ignorant of the nature of that grape? For this is the grape which came forth from the earth, transformed, after the destruction of the people, after God wiped the earth clean and strained it into a form different from that which the first man had scorned.[1] The reason for his ignorance is because man is frivolous in the instability of his character and in his times of light and darkness. For sometimes a person rises a bit when he is prosperous, but then falls a little when danger comes. In neither case, however, does he give thought to the embraces of the king's daughter, that is, justice and truth.[2] Instead, he knocks her royal crown off, since the shepherd flees and, refusing to fight bravely, does not defend the Church of Christ. Rather, he is like a wanton child, playing, without a care in the world. A person who acts like this wants merely to chew and to gratify his own appetite, just as, by nature, he seeks after food. And so his vision is too dull to see where discernment lies, that discernment which wisdom produced,[3] as may be understood in the figure of the grape. Thus it was that when Adam scorned obedience in the dawn of the world, age after age went to ruin until the great flood, when God cleansed the earth of its terrible iniquity. Then God gave the earth a new vigor when Noah brought forth in his vineyard that noble seed of obedience which Adam, like a wanton boy, rejected in his foolishness. And thus in the time of Noah the earth brought forth the power of the grape, and, after him, consequently, Wisdom arose for our salvation.

Now, O man, you who are wavering and unstable in your character, and do not aggressively seek a remedy for yourself and others, rise up and look at the sun with due moderation. And do not flee from the light or shun it because of the severity of your sins, lest you be ashamed when the mighty King examines your works. Then you will live forever.

Notes

1. *Quid est hoc, quod homo manducat et non uult scire que sit uua, que de terra alio modo sudauit post peremptionem populi, cum Deus terram extersit et cribrauit in alium modum quam primus homo illam derideret?* This is a reference, of course, to the grape (the vineyard)

that Noah planted after the flood (cf. Gen 9.20–21). Hildegard is treating this "momentous grape" typologically. Note, too, that our rather tame rendering "which came forth from the earth" renders *que de terra . . . sudauit*, literally "sweated forth," a concept very important in Hildegard's moisture-filled, fertile world of *viriditas*.

2. Thus it is: one daughter, but two virtues.

3. Again, the word *sudavit*, making the parallel with the grape "sweated forth" by the earth.

39

Odo of Soissons[1] to Hildegard

1148–49(?)

In this humble, even abject, letter, Odo seeks Hildegard's prayers.

Odo of Soissons, a broken reed, the embodiment of evil, food for the devil,[a] sends greetings to Hildegard, saint, friend of God, bride of Christ.

It is written, "having no covering, they embrace the stones" [Job 24.8]. But in our day, alas, all the obstacles to iniquity have been removed: the stones, intended as a barrier to the road of sin; the mountains, ordained to fall upon the heads of sinners; the hills, established to bury those who have fled from Christ. The wicked deeds of men, which have run only half their course, are laid bare before God, and, if no one intervenes, they dash headlong against the stone of transgression and the rock of scandal.

As a direct result of these matters and caught up in them as I am, my lady, cut off from hope I am dashed daily against that rock, and although crushed and broken, I still dare to hope for compassion from God. And so through that same compassion of God, I entreat you not to cast me away, since I depend so fully upon you, and in the name of Him who deigned to be scorned for our sakes, do not scorn me. Please hear my plea, I beseech you, through the precious blood of Jesus Christ, your beloved bridegroom, through that blood flowing from the cross by which He paid your dowry and made you his bride. In earnest prayer and supplication before your bridegroom, seek to learn why, although I have cried out so often to Him from the depths and slime of my sin, He has not deigned to pull me out. Is it His will that I continue to hope for forgiveness and will He grant me a broken spirit and a contrite heart?

Commit to writing the things that you see. Farewell. Repeating my prayer again and again, I beseech you in the name of Christ not to forsake me.

Note

1. Odo was appointed Cardinal-Bishop of Tuscany in 1170.

39r
Hildegard to Odo of Soissons
1148–49(?)

Hildegard counsels Odo to keep his mind concentrated on God and to keep out of matters that do not concern him.

Because I see and hear and know all to the same effect, I write these things according to a true vision of the mysteries of God: O man, you are like a cloud that shifts back and forth and, no matter where it is, has very little light. And indeed it frequently blocks out the sun, so that its light is cut off for a long time. Thus it is written: "For behold they that go far from thee shall perish" [Ps 72.27]. The point of this verse is that those who have the day of good knowledge wither up when they turn away from it to bring forth useless things. They focus instead on the inconstancy of that darkness which, empty and barren, does not seek aid in reason. Such people are lacking in the vitality that comes from God. For Adam shone brightly in the innocence of his sanctity, but he was caught in his sin so that, turning aside from God's commandments, he perished. Then the crown of innocence, the beautiful daughter of the King, was taken from him.

Turn your mind back again to wholesome things, and look into the fountain of dancing water [cf. John 4.14]. Keep out of matters that do not concern you, for every useless thing will wither, since it has not been planted by God. Let your mind be pure in God, keep the hunger for God's justice, stay in the straight path, and God will receive you.

Be content with the labor which you have done for God, and are still doing. But as far as you can, direct your mind and thoughts toward God. As for me, I will constantly pour out my prayers to God for you.

40
Odo of Soissons to Hildegard
1148–49(?)

The master of the University of Paris seeks an answer from Hildegard on a question debated in scholastic philosophy.

Odo of Paris,[1] humble and unworthy master—master by title and position only—sends his prayers and whatever else may be considered worthy of such saintliness and nobility of person to the lady Hildegard, the remarkable virgin of Christ.

Because, lady, you have made yourself the handmaiden of Christ, He has exalted you beyond yourself. Thus it is believed that He has revealed some of the secrets of the virginal bridal chamber to you, even while you are still clothed in the flesh, so that you are believed to be one of those about whom it is sung: the king has brought me into his chamber [cf. Cant 2.4, 3.4].[a] But the prophetic and faithful soul says repeatedly :"My secret to myself, my secret to myself" [Isa 24.16], and King Hezekiah grievously offended God by opening up the storerooms of spices and the treasuries of the temple to the Babylonian messengers [cf. Isa 39.2–8]. Therefore, blessed are those who are so exalted above us sinners that they attain sight of heavenly things, for on their paths they await the spirit of discernment among those who, by God's grace, have acquired treasures for themselves more by overcoming temptation than by receiving revelation, and blessed are those who here below among mankind learn from their visions what they are to reveal and what they are to keep hidden.[2] For since God distributes His gifts to each according to his humility, certain things which might distress the apostolic and ecclesiastical institution are kept under seal and not made known.

Hear these things, O wise woman, for "the woman that feareth the Lord, she shall be praised" [Prov 31.30]. It is reported that, exalted, you see many things in the heavens and record them in your writing, and that you bring forth the melody of a new song,[3] although you have studied nothing of such things. But this does not surprise us at all, because it does not exceed your purity and saintliness, without which no one can attain to such things. But we can know that whatever is revealed to you there about things holy signifies your glory; whatever is hidden here requires a kind of humiliation.[4]

Despite the fact that we live far away, we have the utmost confidence in you, and, therefore, we would like for you to resolve a certain problem for us. Many contend that God is not both paternity and divinity.[b] Would you please explain to us in a letter what you perceive in the heavens about this matter.[5]

Farewell, beloved lady.

Notes

1. Odo took the title of Odo of Paris after he became teacher at the University of Paris.

2. The syntax of the Latin lends some clarity to this messy passage. In the original, the "My secret to myself" passage and the King Hezekiah anecdote are dependent *because* clauses qualifying this long, complicated sentence. The general sense seems to be that not all revelations from heaven should be noised abroad, lest one offend God as Hezekiah did.

3. *atque modos noui carminis edas*. This remark is very significant, for it indicates that Hildegard had acquired some little fame for her musical compositions quite early, even before she finished the *Scivias* in 1151. Elsewhere, in the *Liber vitae meritorum*, Hildegard lists the *Symphonia* as one of the works she had completed between the completion of the *Scivias* and the beginning of this new *Liber* in the year 1158.

4. This passage seems hopelessly corrupt. The *PL* rendering of the MS is *quidquid hic abest agitur*, where *abest agitur* makes no sense. Van Acker has emended to *ab eis agitur*, which scarcely gives better sense, given the entire context of the passage. We have chosen to adopt *PL*'s conjecture *absconditur*, which contrasts nicely with the *revelatur* of the preceding clause, and is also paleographically acceptable.

5. This is one of the semi-heretical theses of Gilbert de la Porrée, bishop of Poitiers, who was soon to be brought up to a hearing at the Council of Rheims. At this Council, held in 1148, Pope Eugenius forbade the reading of his work until "corrected." As Peter Dronke remarks (*Women Writers*, p. 149), "Odo credited Hildegard with a means of judging different from and superior to normal methods of metaphysical enquiry."

40r
Hildegard to Odo of Paris
1148–49

In answer to Odo, Hildegard speaks briefly on the nature of divinity.

I, poor little woman that I am, say this in the smoke of spices on the lofty mountain: the sun sends down its rays and illumines the trivial and unstable affairs of many places. And you also, O master, open up many inroads into the Scripture, and spread your teaching abroad among both the high and the low like streams of water.[a] I, on the other hand, tremble greatly because of my humble condition.

Listen now: a king sat on his throne, surrounded by lofty columns bedecked with fine ornaments and set on bases of ivory. And these columns displayed the king's vestments proudly to all. Then it pleased the king to lift up a small feather from the ground, and command it to fly, as he himself wished. Yet a feather does not fly of its own accord, but the air bears it along. And I, like the feather, am not endowed with great powers or human education, nor do I even have good health, but I rely wholly on God's help.[1]

And I say to you: From a certain very learned man who inquired of me, I heard that the fatherhood of the supreme Father and the divinity of God were not themselves God. And he asked me, a puny little woman, to look very carefully to the the true Light concerning this matter.[2] I looked and I learned, seeing in the true Light—certainly not through my own cogitation—that God is indeed both paternity and divinity, for man does not have the capacity to speak of God in the same way that he would speak of the humanness of a human being or the defining characteristic of a work made by human hands.[b]

The Living Light, therefore, says in the secret word of wisdom: God is complete and whole, and has no beginning in time, and so He cannot be divided by a word as man can, for God is nothing other than entirety, and for this reason nothing can be added to or substracted from Him. For He Who Is is both paternity and divinity, as it is written: "I am who I am" [Ex 3.14].^c And He Who Is is Completeness. How is this true? In the fullness of making, of creating, of perfecting.

Whoever says that God is not paternity and divinity names a point without a circle, and if he wishes to have a point without a circle, he denies Him who is eternal.^d And whoever denies that God is paternity and divinity denies God, because he wants there to be some void in God. And this is not true. But God is plenitude, and that which is in God is God. For God cannot be shaken out nor strained through a sieve by human argument, because there is nothing in God that is not God. And since creation has a beginning, it follows that man's reason discovers God through names, for reason itself, by its very nature, is full of names.^e

Now, again, O man, hear the poor little woman speaking to you in the Spirit: God wants you to make your paths straight and to be subject to Him, so that you may be a living rock in the cornerstone.³ Thus you will not be cut off from the tree of life.

Notes

1. See Letter 2, note 3. Also, Hildegard writes in the autobiographical section of the *Vita* (I.ii.11): "I have a trembling fear, since I have no confidence in my own ability. But I stretch out my hands to God, so that like a feather, which is light and powerless, wafted only by the wind, I may be sustained by Him."

2. For all her humility, Hildegard, it seems clear, is at times not above getting her digs in: this man "flowing in learning" *[doctrina fluente]* had to have recourse to me, a puny woman *[me pusillam]*.

3. I.e., of the New Jerusalem.

41

Gunther, Bishop of Speyer, to Hildegard

1153–54

The bishop of Speyer seeks Hildegard's prayers. Gunther, Count of Henneberg, served as bishop of Speyer from 1146 to 1161. Highly favored by Barbarossa, he served in the emperor's Italian campaign, during which he contracted the plague, from which he died on 16 August 1161.

Gunther, by the grace of God servant and bishop of Speyer, sends greetings to Hildegard, beloved mistress of St. Rupert in Bingen, wishing you eternal salvation in Christ.

We give thanks to God that you are a fragrant aroma to those both near and far and that you offer consolation from the Holy Spirit to all who consult you. Therefore, beloved lady, be assured that it gives us pleasure to see the honor and benefit of your church and that we will gladly use all means at our disposal to work for its advancement.

But now, saintly lady, we earnestly ask that out of your love for us you intercede with God and with your prayers render Him favorable to us. Be assured beyond doubt that if God grants us life, you will not fail to receive honor and remuneration. For it is proper for you to pour out your prayers for us, just as we ourselves are concerned about your own needs. Will you please write back to us?

41r
Hildegard to Gunther, Bishop of Speyer

1153–54

Hildegard writes a stern warning to Gunther that God is watching him through "the windows," and will not ignore his "heinous offense." What the particular offense was is unclear, but as an adherent and staunch supporter of Barbarossa, Gunther is likely, in Hildegard's eyes, guilty of transgressions against the Church. Note, however, her emphasis on forgiveness and mercy.

The Light of divine inspiration says to you, O man: Do not ignore the admonition of the Holy Spirit through negligence in office, because God requires that quality from you that He exhibited when He brought back the lost sheep, when He washed away the sins of mankind, when the mighty warrior overcame the ancient deceiver and utterly confounded him.[a] God is watching you through the windows because he is faithful and merciful. Let no man make mockery of this through his perverted will.

Hear: Do not ignore the reason for God's admonition, lest He strike you with His scourge. In His zeal God will strike down that heinous offense of yours, for even His priests and their companions are holding Him up to mockery. For this reason, He brandishes the bow of his admonition to show that no one can resist Him.

Now, O man, you are enveloped in great darkness. Therefore, rise up quickly after your fall and build a tabernacle in heaven, so that filthy sinners will feel shame at your exaltation when you arise from the darkness where you lie now, scarcely alive because of your works. Your only redeeming quality is, as it were, your intent gaze toward the life to come, which shines in you like the dawn.

Your mind is sifted and shaken by great torments when your gross nature afflicts you with twisted desires. Rid yourself of this terrible attitude. Hear, O man: A certain man had a very fertile plot of land, which he plowed and planted very densely, and it brought forth an abundant harvest. Then the man decided to make that plot into an herb garden, so that aromatic plants would grow there to heal wounds and scars. Thus that land was made better than it was before.

Now, O man, choose which of these two things is more useful to you. For the foundation of the heavenly Jerusalem was first set with stones, stones which were wounded by terrible falls and were defiled by the scars of their vices, but which, afterward, were cleansed of their sins through penitence. The Maker of the world laid that first foundation from unhewn, unpolished stones, and those stones bear up the whole of the city of God. Thus flee the wantonness of the foul shipwreck of this world, and be like the sard and the topaz [cf. Apoc 21.20; Ex 28.17], and be swift as the hart to lap up springs of pure water [cf. Ps 41.2]. Then you will live forever.

42
Hildegard to Godfrey, Bishop of Utrecht

About 1163

Hildegard warns Godfrey (bishop of Utrecht from 1156 to 1177) of the "darkness of schisms" and exhorts him to hold the rod of God's correction firmly in his hand.

The Serene Light says: Light[1] gives life, but darkness brings forth schisms, and nighttime yields sadness. Thus one who wishes to have life must avoid schisms. How does schism arise? It comes about when a person does not sigh to God, nor cling fast to Him, nor say to Him "You are my Creator"—all this, as if God did not exist. But whoever does this is caught up in a circle, seeking always the prosperity of this world. And who can give that to him? Nobody. For in its continuing cycle, prosperity arises sometimes, simply because God created man; and sometimes it fades away, because man's faith in God is weakened. Night is a fitting time for sadness. Thus because of the misdirection of his desire and will, sinful man wraps himself, as it were, in black night,[a] and, frequently, finds himself enveloped in grief, because he cannot hope to find joy in his work.

Therefore, O knight of Christ, subject yourself to God's law as completely as you can, and hold the rod of chastisement in your hand, according to the precepts of God's law, so that you may live forever. Flee the storms of the night, because such is God's will, and look to those living creatures full of eyes [cf. Ezech 1.18, 10.12], so that you may look to God in all that you do. Thus you will be called the dear son of God.

Note

1. Van Acker reads *lex* here, but notes that Pitra "perhaps rightly" emends to *lux*. Hildegard indeed seems clearly to be deliberately contrasting *lux* and *tenebre*.

43

Godfrey, Bishop of Utrecht, to Hildegard

Before 1173

Godfrey, bishop of Utrecht, requests Hildegard's prayers.

Godfrey, by divine grace bishop of Utrecht, to his unique, exceptional, and remarkable sister Hildegard, mistress of the sisters of St. Rupert. Greetings from Him who ordains salvation through Jacob [cf. Ps 43.5].

Dearest sister, ever since I began to love you in Christ never has your memory departed from my mind, for it is sweeter to me than honey and the honeycomb [cf. Ps 18.11]. And indeed, beloved lady, I am compelled to hold you in esteem by the power of God which dwells in you, works through you, and causes you, beyond all others, to be cherished by that Bridegroom who saves all who have set their hope in Him. And since divine love is diffused in your heart, I ask you through that love with which you abound for all people that with all diligence and effort you undertake to pray to God on my behalf, so that I may deserve to be relieved from the burden of my sins in this life.

May the Lord guide you to that place of blessed eternity, eternal blessing, joyful tranquillity, and joy without end. Like one thirsting for the fountain, thus do I desire your reply.

43r

Hildegard to Godfrey, Bishop of Utrecht

Before 1173

Hildegard exhorts Godfrey to rule his people with justice and mercy.

O man, you have been chosen and called by God to work according to His will by imitating Him, since God builds, rules, and anoints all things.

For omnipotent God created the world through His word. And He rules it, sanctifying all things through water, washing away the sins of man. For God created all creatures and He governed them, and He has imbued man, along with all creatures, with His spirit, just as a potter makes all his vessels beautiful with fire. But then the bright day set into dark night when Adam fell through disobedience, and for this reason man has lived in sin and forgetfulness, as if God did not exist. Then because of man's heinous sins, God poured out the flood waters over all the earth. Afterward, the saints, the law, and the prophets arose. Then just as man was not created until every creature announced him, so too the Son of God came last of all, for it was not fitting for Him to appear in an empty time, when no justice could be found.[a] But the Son of God came to redeem the whole world through obedience, the anointing of baptism, and penitence.

Now, O shepherd, beware lest you be in a childish time which does not know God, but see to it that you are in the time of just and holy men, in the time of the revelation of the prophets;[b] and seize justice in all your works, just as God foresaw all things before He made them, and rule your people in accordance with His will.

Moreover, as Christ's representative, give help to the people lest you be like a trumpet that only makes noise but does no work. Be a good aroma of virtue so that you may live forever, and say: "I will extol thee, O God my king: and I will bless thy name for ever; yea, for ever and ever" [Ps 144.1]. For when you understand that you occupy the bishop's seat, praise God in all your ways and exalt Him in your good works, and cogitate on His precepts, repeating them tirelessly to the people. And kiss Him through faith, and embrace Him through your good works. Make your God known by your honorable way of life, and magnify Him as the king just in his judgments so that you may rule your people equitably and anoint them with mercy. See to it, too, that you do not drag pernicious iniquity in your wake, by, that is, accepting bribes for "justice." And invoke His name, standing always in awe of Him, for He is King. And you will do these things all the days of your life, while you live in this world, so that, afterward, you may live for ever and ever.

44
Adelbert, Bishop of Verdun, to Hildegard

1156–63(?)

Adelbert seeks the prayers and aid of Hildegard and her sisters. Nevertheless, "like a blind man pointing the way to the sighted," he does not hesitate to warn her of vainglory.

Adelbert, by grace of God servant and bishop of the church at Verdun, although unworthy, to his dearest mother Hildegard of Mount St. Rupert, with a prayer that she may take joy in her present and everlasting visions from God.

"Blessed be the glory of the Lord from his holy place" [Ezech 3.12], that glory which made you his servant in your tender years. Nevertheless, I, like a blind man seeking to point the way to the sighted, wish to make the following suggestion to you, dearest lady: acknowledge that grace God has shed upon you with humility by giving heed to the prophetic sayings of Balaam of old, for (although he stood against the people of God in his last hour) there is something memorable in his vision when he said: "He that falleth, and so his eyes are opened" [Num 24.4], signifying, truly, humility in his vision. Also, the teacher of the Gentiles said: "Lest the greatness of the revelations should exalt me," et cetera [II Cor 12.7]. Please be aware that I have said these things more out of the fidelity of my affection for you than out of presumption of my learning.

Moreover, you should know that I cannot, right now, come to you, although I am not far from you. Nevertheless, in my adversities I run to you, my steadfast patron, seeking your prayers, and requesting the aid of the sisters, your band of God's handmaidens. For a long time I have not deserved that you write to me, but I pray that, now at least, I may be deemed worthy.

45
Conrad, Bishop of Worms, to Hildegard

Before 1173

Conrad prays for the assistance of that "brightest light" Hildegard. Note at the end of the letter his suggestion that the substance of the letter is to be delivered by the messenger himself.

Conrad, by grace of God bishop of the church at Worms, though unworthy, sends warm devotion with all obedience (although, alas, with but a poor showing of prayer) to Hildegard, beloved sister at Mount St. Rupert.

We give thanks to God, who has placed you as the brightest light on the golden candelabra and has caused the brightness of His light to shine through you far and wide in his house. Wherefore, beloved sister and daughter, we most earnestly beseech you by the rays with which, we fully believe, the sun of justice [cf. Mal 4.2] illumines you: dispel the clouds from our mind, which oppress us with the threatening whirlwind of tribulation and the inundation of inconstant thought.

There are a number of important matters that we would have imparted to you if the sheer volume of words required to explain them to you had not stood in the way. Yet we are speaking to you now through the present messenger as if in person, and we most earnestly call for you to respond and advise us.[a]

45r
Hildegard to Conrad, Bishop of Worms

Before 1173

This letter of general admonition is notable most especially for its metaphor of man as a structure of God's making, in which man's soul flies "within the circumference of his rationality."

You are one who sits on the throne of Christ, holding the iron rod in your hand to rule your sheep. But look to the sun of justice [cf. Mal 4.2] and the hosts of the stars (which are types of virtues[a]), so that you may not lack the food of life, for a good shepherd is one who grows abundantly in good works and who feeds his sheep in the green pastures of righteousness. May He whose word brought forth all creation on the first day and Who will sound the trumpet on the last day to call forth the sons of men grant this to you.

For those who live justly are God's tabernacle, because God dwells in them. Man is a structure of God's making, and God has his mansion in him, because God sent a fiery spirit into man, and this spirit flies within the circumference of his rationality, just as a wall encompasses the breadth of a house.[b] Moreover, one who has not neglected God's law, but has been justified in his works through the precepts of God, that person builds the heavenly Jerusalem. One who acts according to the flesh rather than the spirit, however, will fall from that holy structure. But one who cuts himself off from the desires of his own will adorns that heavenly structure with pearls and precious stones and pure gold [cf. Apoc 21.18ff].

And so make yourself a precious stone, and you will be adorned in the heavenly Jerusalem.

Albon[1]
46
Hildegard to Abbot Wolfard
1153–54

Hildegard writes to allay Wolfard's doubts about the eucharist. Wolfard, like Rudeger later (Letter 89), has, apparently, expressed to Hildegard his concern over his doubts with respect to the doctrine of transubstantiation, the Real Presence in the form of the bread and wine. Although not exactly new in the twelfth century, the doctrine was still novel enough to be the subject of inquiry and to raise haunting doubts, as here. In the preceding century, Berengarius of Tours had argued forcefully for a mere spiritual or symbolic presence in the eucharist. It was in opposition to Berengarius that the Church (through the Roman Council of 1079) first put into official language the doctrine that the bread and wine were "substantially changed" into the body and blood of Jesus Christ. And in 1139 the Second Council of the Lateran pronounced heretical all those who denied the Real Presence in the Eucharist.

The Serene Light which gives words to ruminate upon says: O man, by thinking about the Son of God, you have assurance. Still, however, you hesitate to break the bread which you really wish to eat at the prompting of your mind. Why do you go around in circles, sifting through all manner of things and casting your gaze every which way, attempting to find out where the reality is to be found in the sacrament?[a] Why are you doing this? God builds his tabernacle on whatever is good and just. Rise up to the light, therefore, and you will live forever. For God has established the means through which He receives his burnt offering. Blessed is the person who clings ever to God in everything, for he will never be deceived by the devil. Live, therefore, O man, and be victorious in this shadowy world.

Note

1. At this point, Van Acker begins his second classification of letters: correspondents of minor ecclesiastical rank, for whom we know their specific location. The letters in this section are organized alphabetically by place, and, as much as possible, hierarchically by rank. From this point forward, we will list the place-name, as here, before the letter or series of letters.

47

Hildegard to Prior Frederick

1153–54

A general admonition to Prior Frederick to amend the instability of his ways.

He Who Is says: A king saw a ladder darkened by the changes in time of pestilence. But then the sun shone forth and dispelled the darkness. This delighted the king, and he said: This unstable ladder is tired out, because sometimes it reaches to lofty heights and sometimes is overshadowed by darkness.

And your mind is just like this, O man. For in the bright day of the quest of your soul, you ascend to me in great joy, but in the time of noxious pestilence you cultivate the "falling sickness," as if the matter of salvation were not to be inquired into. Yet ashes by their very nature are ever in motion and unstable. Therefore—in both the brightness of the day and the darkness of the whirlwind—look to me, and always seek out the ointment which heals, and you will live forever. Cherish my perfect law, and flee doubt, and God will save you.

Alpirsbach
48

Godfrey the Monk to Hildegard

1152–53

A letter from one cringing before the majesty of Hildegard, who, he believes, sees all things past, present, and future.

Godfrey, unworthy priest and least among the monks of St. Benedict, sends his pledge of devout obedience with all humility to the most serene and truly blessed Hildegard, endowed with the spirit of divine revelation.

"They that trust in" the Lord, "shall understand the truth: and they that are faithful in love shall rest in him: for grace and peace is to the elect" of God [Wis 3.9]. The truthful reports of many people have taught me and made me sure that these sacred words, uttered by divine wisdom, will be fulfilled in you. And whatever I find verified by Holy Scripture I cling to faithfully, because no word is impossible with God [cf. Luke 1.37]. Therefore, although I have never seen your divine revelations, I have heard of your reputation, which is spreading abroad, and I have never doubted its truth. And so I know in truth that because you have placed your faith in the Lord, you have understanding of His truth, and because, faithful to Him, you have rested in His love, you have received the gift of divine revelation and the spirit of heavenly consolation, and therefore achieved the peace of God's elect.

Now, therefore, because the compassion of almighty God is found more abundantly in you than in any other mortal, I do not, I want you to know, make my request to you in order to tempt you, nor to be arrogant, but to seek God's grace through you humbly. I beseech you to remember the word of the Lord: Do not despise one of my little ones [cf. Matt 18.10]. Please do not, therefore, scorn my letter on account of my insignificance, but for the love of Jesus Christ, mercifully heed my prayers, I pray. And intercede with God for my sins, and with your holy prayers lift up my life, and do not fail to chastise my negligence with a letter of admonition. For I keenly desire the rebuke of your sweetest love. Although I judge myself unworthy of a loving response from you, I desire to receive the reward of my simple trust. For I believe that all the secrets of my heart are laid bare before you by that Spirit through whom you see all things past, present, and future.[a] Never did a day shine more brightly for me than when I came into your presence. And I would walk barefoot just to hear the sound of your voice, which would be altogether pleasant and desirable for me, if only I were worthy to hear your wondrous visions or to receive a letter from you, blessed lady.

May the almighty Father through the power of his Son, our Lord Jesus Christ, and through the accord of the Holy Spirit, deign to grant you length of days so that you may work to amend His holy Church.

48r
Hildegard to the Monk Godfrey
1152–53

Hildegard writes general words of consolation to a distressed monk.

The Living Light says: O man, streams of water flow from me to invigorate your mind.[a] But your mind has been bound up and distressed by unstable morals in the blackness of a scudding wind. And your secret thoughts deceive you sometimes, and sometimes you are led astray by the taste of your own works.[b] But the face of your desire turns toward me in the joyful hope of recovery, which you are not yet able to attain by your work. Very good are those desires which build a tower on the heights of the fragrance of sweet aroma. Therefore, the angels of God rejoice because of the works produced by the creature made by the finger of God, for these works taste God by destroying the food of the unrighteousness of sinners.

Now, O knight, be strong in battle as long as you live in the body, because your enemy does not grow weary, nor does he weaken in battle. Let your works be such that the gentle Father will rejoice over you, and his Word will enlighten your spirit, and the fiery Lover will shed the ointment of salvation and the invigoration of the flower of wisdom upon you.

Altena
49

An Abbess to Hildegard

Before 1173

A very loving, intimate letter from an abbess to Hildegard.

To the lady and mother, Hildegard, beloved and venerable in Christ, intimate companion of His love, from "N,"[1] abbess of Altena, although unworthy, a sinner sitting penitent with Mary at the feet of Jesus, with the hope of seeing her beloved just as He is.

Most beloved of all women, I rejoice in your blessedness, for, as is shown by your very clear delight, you have found the One whom your soul loves as much as mortal can, and even now blissfully spending time with Him in the secret chamber of your heart, you have tasted and seen "that the Lord is sweet" [Ps 33.9].

It seems clear that I must accept with equanimity the fact that you have failed to visit me through your letters for a long time, although I am greatly devoted to you. For I believe that if, just for a second, you could turn the eye of your mind from gazing at your beloved and could set foot outside your peaceful dwelling, you would not fail to console me more frequently through your messenger, who would gladden me by informing me of your well-being, and would bear back news of me to you. For if it is not granted to me to see your beloved face again in this life—and I cannot even mention this without tears—I will always rejoice because of you, since I have determined to love you as my own soul. Therefore, I will see you in the eye of prayer, until we arrive at that place where we will be allowed to look upon each other eternally, and to contemplate our beloved, face to face [cf. I Cor 13.12], in all His glory.

Note

1. The identity of this writer is unknown. Even the initial given, presumably that of the abbess's name, varies in the MSS from *N* to *B* to *H*.

49r
Hildegard to the Abbess
Before 1173

Hildegard's answer to the abbess is austere and brief, merely an explication of a biblical verse, a rather odd answer to such a tender, devoted letter.

O you who are a leader in the brilliant, springing waters of the fountain [cf. John 4.14], that is to say, as Christ's representative, hear these words: "Behold the lion of the tribe of Judah, the root of David, hath prevailed" [Apoc 5.5]. The meaning of this is as follows: The Son, the brightness of holy divinity, is like a root. For He roars like a lion, when He hurls the followers of that first fallen angel into hell, so that, with mighty jaws, He casts down all injustice, and so He is the root of fortitude. But He draws to himself all those who confess Him in faith and reach out to Him with good works, and thus, like a lion, He prevails over all things. This is my admonition—heed it.

Altwick
50
Abbess Sophia to Hildegard
1164–70

An abbess who wishes to lay aside the burden of administrative duties seeks Hildegard's advice about the advisability of such a course of action.

Sophia, abbess of Altwick in the diocese of Utrecht—abbess in name only—sends greetings to the blessed Hildegard of St. Rupert, with a prayer that she may enter that choir which is illumined by the light of lights.

Because no one is able to renounce the lust of the flesh and pant after the heavenly country with whole heart without Christ's help, I desire to impart to you, devout lady, the idea I have conceived in my heart by the prompting of God and the grace of his Spirit. Our Lord does not wish any of His sheep to go astray, but like a good shepherd desires to call them all back to the way of eternal salvation. This same Lord has inspired me, I believe, to lay down the heavy burden of administration which I bear, and to seek the seclusion of some little cell. I would be happy to follow this way of life, but whether I can successfully fulfill it or not lies in our Lord's power.

Therefore, because you have such merit in God's eyes, I know that you can discern a person's proper course of action through the revelation of the

Holy Spirit, and so with humble prayers I beseech you, pious lady, to ask the Lord if my contemplated change pleases Him. For I do not want to be among those singled out by Gregory's famous dictum: "It would have been better for them never to have known the way of truth than to have fallen away once having known it."[1]

Finally, farewell in the Lord, and please do not fail to address these matters of concern to me, returning your answer by way of the present messenger, along with whatever else the grace of God is pleased to reveal to you through the Holy Spirit.

Note

1. *Regula pastoralis* 3.34. Cf. 2 Peter 2.21.

50r

Hildegard to the Abbess Sophia

1164–70

Hildegard advises against the abbess's plan and warns her against the dangers of instability.

In a true vision of the mysteries of God, hear these words: O daughter born from man's side and formed by God as the type of the building up of His kingdom, why are you languishing, so that your mind is like the shifting clouds that the storms blow about, at times bright in the sunlight, at times dark in the shadows. This is true because of the cacophony of the morals of those who do not shine before God.

You say, I long to rest, to seek out a nesting place for my heart, where my soul may find peace. But, O daughter, it is not serving God to cast off your burden and to abandon God's sheepfold, when you have that light through which you may illuminate it, so that you may lead the sheep to pasture. Now then, rein yourself in, lest your mind become inflamed with the sweetness which is very harmful to you in the instability of secular life. But be true to your calling, because this is what the grace of God wishes. Beware, therefore, lest you lose that grace through the instability of your mind. May God help you to stay alert through pure knowledge.

Amorbach
51
Certain Monks to Hildegard
After 1159

The monks of Amorbach, gravely concerned about the schism and the general state of the times, since "almost the whole world is overwhelmed by the darkness of error," write Hildegard asking her to preach to the laity.

O., C., and V.,[1] sinners and (in name only) priests, on behalf of the whole congregation of the monastery of St. N. in Amorbach, send greetings to Hildegard, superior of St. Rupert in Bingen, with a prayer that she go into the eternal wedding feast with her lamp brightly shining [cf. Matt 25.1ff].

The Living Light is the worker of all good things, and every spirit, vibrantly alive [cf. Ecclus 16.31] and preordained to the tenth order,[2] is its coworker. Although unchanging in its purity, this light is shared in by the blessed to different degrees according to the capacity of the recipient. For the highest orders[3] of the royal hall are inflamed the more brilliantly the nearer they are to the fountain of light, and the more directly they contemplate it. The lower ranks of angels, on the other hand, reflect that primary light the more weakly the further they are from the source. So it is, too, with those earthly, embodied spirits: although they are predestined to eternal life, they acquire their luminescence from the power of the brightness ever radiating from Majesty, some more abundantly, some less, and they are elevated from their extreme remoteness to seek after that beatific source. There are certain souls so absorbed in that ocean of brightness that they seem to see nothing, to sense nothing, except the presence of that light which vivifies all things. And by their brightness, all other souls, while still weighed down by mortal darkness and buffeted about, are brought into harmony with the receptacle of that brightness, and from that light they gain a more certain self-knowledge.[a]

Therefore, most reverend mother, because you have ascended close to that brightness, may the refulgence bursting forth from your heart enlighten our minds so that our darkness may be dispelled by the rays of admonition, of exhortation, of chastisement. For because iniquity has abounded and love has grown cold, we suffer the darkness of error brought about by the schism in the Church, and because the sun of justice [cf. Mal 4.2] is darkened by obtruding iniquity, the moon (that is, the Church) has gone astray from her original principles in many ways. Yet Christ's words do not pass away, but remain forever, as He himself testifies: "Behold, I am with you always, even to the end of the world" [Matt 28.20]. And so even though almost the whole world is overwhelmed by the darkness of error, that ray of ancient grace has shone in you, lest all the people perish. For the order of monks is going around in circles, the clerical order is limping about lamely, the order of nuns is teetering, and when the clergy abandons its calling in this way, then the laity completely neglects the law that the Lord has established for them.[b] Besides other abominations, they cast God into oblivion: they abandon their lawful spouses, they delight in adultery to satisfy their lust, they commit murder; and by all these means they think to achieve importance. And any one of them who is discovered to be free from these perversions seeks to excuse himself by his own laziness.[4] Therefore, the priests who ought to be speaking the truth and crying out against such wickedness now are forced to remain silent.

Now, O venerable mother, since you have frequently directed your admonitions to the clergy, as we know from your own writings, we ask as sincerely as we can that you direct them also to the laity, for it is necessary to rail with harsh and frequent chastisement against those who are not willing to endure any chastisement at all. Indeed, since they believe and, in fact, know that you speak on the authority of divine visions and commands, we hope that they will incline their hearts more attentively to your words than they have to ours, since they see that we too are unstable through our manifold sins. Farewell.

Notes

1. Presumably, the initials of the monks who are writing this letter to Hildegard. Similarly, the initial *N* is used, just below, for the name of the saint to whom the monastery is dedicated.

2. That is, the elect of humankind. The reference is to the commonly held belief that mankind was created to become this tenth order of angels, that is, to assume the place vacated by the fallen Satan and his followers. See *Scivias* (III.ii.19), "Thus in height of blessedness he [mankind] was to augment the praise of those heavenly spirits who praise God with constant devotion, and so in that same blessedness fill up the place left empty by that lost angel who fell through his pride. And so man is the full number ten, and he brings all these things to perfection by God's power. But in this proposition the number ten is multiplied to a hundred. For although man fell away from God through the temptation of the devil, yet admonished by divine mercy and inspiration, he strenuously began to acknowledge God through the law and prophecy of the Old Testament, and at last even more keenly through the sanctity and all the various means of virtuous constancy given by the Church." See also Newman, *Sister of Wisdom*, pp. 102–3.

3. The actual expression here is *suprema organa*. Clearly, the monks have in mind the heavenly choirs of angels, but the general context and the specific references that follow also make it clear that they are referring to the (with starting point at the living light) descending orders of the angels.

4. *ac quisque uelut inertem se esse dicit, si his maculis immunis inuenitur.* This passage is very messy. Perhaps heavy irony is being employed here to lay stress on the great sinfulness of the times.

Andernach
52
Mistress Tengswich to Hildegard
1148–50

> This letter from the superior of a foundation of canonesses is quite remarkable for the heavy irony and innuendo that lies just beneath the surface of its all-too-polite exterior. Tengswich keeps assuring the reader that she is merely seeking the grounds—in Scripture or the patristic tradition—for certain of Hildegard's outlandish practices, but the hostile tone comes through quite clearly. For an illuminating discussion of the sharply contrasting views of the proper monastic life in the twelfth century as revealed by this correspondence between Hildegard and Tengswich, see Haverkamp, "Tenxwind."

To Hildegard, mistress of the brides of Christ, Tengswich, unworthy superior of the sisters at Andernach, with a prayer that she eventually be joined to the highest order of spirits in heaven.

The report of your saintliness has flown far and wide and has brought to our attention things wondrous and remarkable. And, insignificant as we are, these reports have highly commended the loftiness of your outstanding and extraordinary mode of religious life to us. We have learned from a number of people that an angel from above reveals many secrets of heaven for you to record, difficult as they are for mortal minds to grasp, as well as some things that you are to do, not in accordance with human wisdom, but as God himself instructs them to be done.[a]

We have, however, also heard about certain strange and irregular practices that you countenance. They say that on feast days your virgins stand in the church with unbound hair when singing the psalms and that as part of their dress they wear white, silk veils, so long that they touch the floor. Moreover, it is said that they wear crowns of gold filigree, into which are inserted crosses on both sides and the back, with a figure of the Lamb on the front, and that they adorn their fingers with golden rings.[b] And all this despite the express prohibition of the great shepherd of the Church, who writes in admonition: Let women comport themselves with modesty "not with plaited hair, or gold, or pearls, or costly attire" [I Tim 2.9]. Moreover, that which seems no less strange to us is the fact that you admit into your community only those women from noble, well-established families and absolutely reject others who are of lower birth and of less wealth.[c] Thus we are struck with wonder and are reeling in confusion when we ponder quietly in our heart that the Lord himself brought into the primitive Church humble fishermen and poor people, and that, later, at the conversion of the gentiles, the blessed Peter said: "In truth, I perceive that God is no respecter of persons" [Acts 10.34; cf. Rom 2.11]. Nor should you be unmindful of the words of the Apostle in Corinthians: "Not many mighty, not many noble, but God hath chosen the contemptible and the ignoble things of this world" [I Cor 1.26–28]. We have examined as accurately as possible all the precedents laid down by the fathers of the Church, to which all spiritual people must conform, and we have found nothing in them comparable to your actions.

O worthy bride of Christ, such unheard-of practices far exceed the capacity of our weak understanding, and strike us with no little wonder. And although we feeble little women wholeheartedly rejoice with all the esteem due your spiritual success, we still wish you to inform us on some points relative to this matter. Therefore, we have decided to send this humble little letter to you, saintly lady, asking by whose authority you can defend such practices, and we devoutly and meekly beseech, worthy lady, that you not disdain to write back to us as soon as possible. Farewell, and remember us in your prayers.

52r
Hildegard to the Congregation of Nuns

1148–50

Hildegard answers Tengswich's criticism at length, especially concerning herself with the restrictions on dress (to which virgins are not subject) and with the criterion of nobility for entrance into her community (one does not plow with an ox and an ass). For illuminating discussions, see Haverkamp, "Tenxwind," and Dronke, *Women Writers*, pp. 165–67.

The Living Fountain says: Let a woman remain within her chamber[1] so that she may preserve her modesty, for the serpent breathed the fiery danger of horrible lust into her. Why should she do this? Because the beauty of woman radiated and blazed forth in the primordial root, and in her was formed that chamber in which every creature lies hidden. Why is she so resplendent? For two reasons: on the one hand, because she was created by the finger of God and, on the other, because she was endowed with wondrous beauty. O, woman, what a splendid being you are! For you have set your foundation in the sun, and have conquered the world.[a]

Paul the apostle, who flew to the heights but kept silent on earth so as not to reveal that which was hidden [cf. II Cor 12.2ff.], observed that a woman who is subject to the power of her husband [cf. Ephes 5.22ff; Col 3.18], joined to him through the first rib, ought to preserve great modesty, by no means giving or displaying her vessel to another man who has no business with her, for that vessel belongs to her husband [cf. I Thess 4.4]. And let her do this in accordance with the word spoken by the master of the earth in scorn of the devil: "What God hath joined together, let no man put asunder" [Matt 19.6].

Listen: The earth keeps the grass green and vital, until winter conquers it.[2] Then winter takes away the beauty of that flower, and the earth covers over its vital force so that it is unable to manifest itself as if it had never withered up, because winter has ravaged it. In a similar manner, a woman, once married, ought not to indulge herself in prideful adornment of hair or person, nor ought she to lift herself up to vanity, wearing a crown and other golden ornaments, except at her husband's pleasure, and even then with moderation.[b]

But these strictures do not apply to a virgin, for she stands in the unsullied purity of paradise, lovely and unwithering, and she always remains in the full vitality of the budding rod.[c] A virgin is not commanded to cover up her hair,[3] but she willingly does so out of her great humility, for a person will naturally hide the beauty of her soul, lest, on account of her pride, the hawk carry it off.

Virgins are married with holiness in the Holy Spirit and in the bright dawn of virginity, and so it is proper that they come before the great High Priest as an oblation presented to God. Thus through the permission granted her and the revelation of the mystic inspiration of the finger of God, it is appropriate for a virgin to wear a white vestment, the lucent symbol of her betrothal to Christ, considering that her mind is made one with the interwoven whole, and keeping in mind the One to whom she is joined, as it is written: "Having his name, and the name of his Father, written on their foreheads" [Apoc 14.1] and also "These follow the Lamb whithersoever he goeth" [Apoc 14.4].

God also keeps a watchful eye on every person, so that a lower order will not gain ascendancy over a higher one, as Satan and the first man did, who wanted to fly higher than they had been placed. And who would gather all his livestock indiscriminately into one barn—the cattle, the asses, the sheep, the kids? Thus it is clear that differentiation must be maintained in these matters, lest people of varying status, herded all together, be dispersed through the pride of their elevation, on the one hand, or the disgrace of their decline, on the other, and especially lest the nobility of their character be torn asunder when they slaughter one another out of hatred. Such destruction naturally results when the higher order falls upon the lower, and the lower rises above the higher. For God establishes ranks on earth, just as in heaven[d] with angels, archangels, thrones, dominions, cherubim, and seraphim. And they are all loved by God, although they are not equal in rank. Pride loves princes and nobles because of their illusions of grandeur, but hates them when they destroy that illusion. And it is written that "God does not cast off the mighty, since He himself is mighty" [Job 36.5]. He does not love people for their rank but for their works which derive their savor from Him, just as the Son of God says: "My food is to do the will" of my Father [John 4.34]. Where humility is found, there Christ always prepares a banquet. Thus when individuals seek after empty honor rather than humility, because they believe that one is preferable to the other, it is necessary that they be assigned to their proper place. Let the sick sheep be cast out of the fold, lest it infect the entire flock.[4]

God has infused human beings with good understanding so that their name will not be destroyed. It is not good for people to grab hold of a mountain which they cannot possibly move. Rather, they should stand in the valley, gradually learning what they are capable of.

These words do not come from a human being but from the Living Light.[e] Let the one who hears see and believe where these words come from.

Notes

1. Note the repeated use of the word *chamber* here, and see Introduction for remarks on Hildegard's wordplay.

2. This passage, which, one might note, is nothing if not Hildegardian, does not readily lend itself to translation. A literal rendering would give something like: "The earth sweats forth *[sudat]* the vital force *[viriditatem]* of the grass."

3. Literally, the *viriditas* of her hair. Hildegard deliberately echoes the passage above about the earth and grass ("The earth sweats forth the vital force *[viriditatem graminis]* of the grass"), for the hair in the little world of man has its counterpart in the grass of the macrocosmic universe. See *Causae et curae* 8a–8b: "For the firmament of heaven is like the head of a human being; the sun, the moon, and the stars are the eyes; the air is the auditory sense; the wind, the olfactory sense; dew is taste; the sides of the world are the arms and the sense of touch; other creatures in the world are the belly; and the earth is the heart . . ." As edited by P. Dronke, *Women Writers*, p. 242.

4. Cf. *Regula Sancti Benedicti* 28.8. It should perhaps be noted also that Hildegard wrote a commentary on the *Rule*.

Augsburg
53
Canon Udalric to Hildegard

Before 1170

A letter from a very humble canon, reminding Hildegard of the time when he came to see her, and beseeching her prayers.

To the Lady Hildegard, steeped in religious discipline, wisdom, good morals, and in every human virtue, from Udalric, her servant in all things, with prayers that she labor with Martha in the sixth hour, be renewed in the seventh, and rejoice with Mary in the eighth [cf. Luke 10.38ff].

How I could have withdrawn myself, beloved lady, for so long a time from your sight and your sweet conversation, more delightful to me indeed than honey, or why I have postponed visiting you in the meantime even with a short letter, I am completely unable to understand, though I must attribute it all, I suppose, to the sloth that results from my insignificance. I am terrified of offending you, pious lady, with such a lack of grace—God forbid!—and rightly so since earlier, though I was yet unknown to you in voice, dress, face, or even reputation, you welcomed me very graciously and kindly when I first came to you (a difficult task for me, to be sure), and immediately deigned to refresh me by allowing me to partake in conversation with you—something which I consider a very great favor.

But because I am penitent, you will forgive me. For my mind has never been unwilling, but the ability was lacking. Therefore, if I am able to make a true promise, I vow to change my ways as quickly as possible, if God grants me the means. In the meantime, however, please deign to be mindful of me, a poor sinner, in your prayers before God.

53r
Hildegard to Canon Udalric

Before 1170

Hildegard writes very general reflections back to the canon.

He who is life has revealed these words to me, saying: O man, you are like the water which the storm makes turbulent, but which then settles down tranquilly. Victory says to you: I would gladly come to you, but you withdraw from me when you hide the face of your mind and thus are filled with doubt, having neither the soaring wings of security nor contempt for the world.

O knight, resurrection will come to you quickly if you will shake off the dust of your ashes, saying: If I cannot stand in the sun, at least I will drag myself out of the mud and wash my garments clean of the unstable morals of this age. Then the dove will anoint you and will wash your wounds. Arise now, and live forever.

Averbode
54
Hildegard to Provost Andrew

Before 1166

A letter of general admonition and criticism, ending on a note of hope.

The Secret Light says: You are terrified as if by the wind, and the green tree of your mind is dormant.[1] But one who has vitality in his inner heart builds on the height of the wall. Yet a shepherd who feeds his flock but who still lacks the inner fortitude to come to its aid in peril and indeed runs away weary of his duty [cf. John 10.12f]—that one is not suited for pastoral office. Therefore, let him act the sheep, and not the shepherd.

You, O man, are like someone struggling in the water, scarcely able to rescue himself before he drowns. Thus although you see prudence all around you, you lack strength—but not will, and, therefore, the grace of God shines for you.

Note

1. Hildegard's phrase is *in ligno viriditatis mentis tue*, literally "in the wood of the viridity of your mind." *Viridity* appears again in the very next sentence, where we translate "vitality."

55

An Abbot to Hildegard

Before 1166

This letter asking for Hildegard's prayers certainly attests to Hildegard's high reputation. Is this from a Cistercian monastery in Averbode? The writer has clearly been influenced in his choice of language and style by St. Bernard.

N.,[1] humble and unworthy superior of the brothers in Averbode, sends greetings to Hildegard of Bingen, the glorious handmaiden of Christ, who has been crowned with the flowers of holy virtue, with a prayer that she may be rewarded with the penny of the gospel's day laborer [cf. Matt 20.2] because of her zeal for the life of purity.

I will not cease pouring out my great thanks to God, who has set the loftiness of your person like a brilliantly blazing lamp, not under a bushel, but on a candlestick [cf. Matt 5.15; Luke 8.16, 11.33]. For He has not left off watching over and consoling you, reverend and saintly lady, with the visitation of his angels and the grace of his spirit. And He has diffused your good name far and wide like a delicious fragrance, not only throughout Germany but also in our region and other parts of the world, so that you may justly say with the Apostle: "We are the good odour of Christ unto God in" every place [II Cor 2.15].

And rejoicing because you have advanced far in faith, we are compelled to say: How beautiful you have become in delights, daughter of the prince; We will be glad and rejoice in thee, remembering thy breasts more than wine [cf. Cant 7.1ff; 1.3]. For in them, we, weak though we are, have put our weakness to flight, and each of us, having become strong and robust according to the wisdom God has given to you, takes solid food [cf. I Cor 3.1–2; Heb 5.12ff], and is able to say without fear of censure: Thy "lips distill choice myrrh" [Cant 5.13] and "thy lips are like a dripping honeycomb" [Cant 4.11], O beloved bride of God. For like a city set on a mountain [cf. Matt 5.14] of virtues, you cannot be concealed, because the Lord has established you as an unmovable and unshaken column in the middle of his Church, so that among the lamentable crises of this world, his people, redeemed with the price of his blood, may learn through you what they ought to seek and what they ought to avoid. And instructed by the example of your great virtue, they may advance day by day and ascend vigorously from virtue unto virtue to see the God of gods on Zion [cf. Ps 83.8].

Confident, therefore, in the protection of your prayers, although I am not worthy to receive the crown for my labors, may I be granted at least to escape punishment. I commend myself wholeheartedly to your prayers, because I have often offended God by my great sins. Farewell, beloved lady, and pray to the Lord for me, unworthy though I am, and call upon Him with the words God himself gives you.

Note

1. N. has not been identified, although his monastery, as the first sentence of the letter makes clear, was in Averbode in Brabant.

55r
Hildegard to the Abbot

Before 1166

This answer directed against malicious gossip seems a little beside the point of the letter sent to Hildegard. Is this one of those instances where the messenger delivered additional information?

The spears of malicious words hurled by the faithless and the slanderous are like a dangerous wind, suddenly assailing a person's heart. And this is the storm aroused by the first angel when he despised God. As I frequently observe, these onslaughts often afflict even a person in felicity whom God cherishes highly, because the Enemy has learned of his bliss and seeks to oppress him with that storm so that he, too, may fall. But he is not powerful enough to snatch him from God's bosom. Although difficulties and tribulations from the elements befall him, he retains his self-restraint, because God is watching over him. Yet just as the Church received a new birth in the blood of Christ, so it was proper and fitting that water, the dowry of the Holy Spirit [cf. John 3.5], be mingled with the blood of Christ, because the blood of every human being is tainted.[1]

Note

1. Some MSS give the following addition to the letter: "But, O head of the household on Mt. Zion, I admonish you to become a trumpet sounding aloud among the

spiritual people of your flock so that they may not lag in love and obedience. Then you will live forever. Furthermore, keep your eyes upon justice and truth with your mind ever vigilant, so that you are not hampered by the cacophony of this age."

Bamberg (St. Michael)
56
Hildegard to an Abbot
1169–70

Although the letter to Hildegard has not come down to us, her response to the abbot sounds as if he had written her seeking advice about giving up his administrative responsibilities for a quieter monastic life. Van Acker believes that the letter—as well as the following one—was addressed to Helmrich, abbot of St. Michael in Bamberg, who resigned his office in 1170.

In fiery admonition it has been foreordained what the people will hear from my lips, for they will drink deep of the flood gushing from the rock in the obscure mysteries of God [cf. Ex 17.6]. Sometimes I see you glowing like the dawn in your aspiration, but still the labor and difficulties which you experience, both in yourself and in others, wear you out so completely that you become blinded to your own ability.

Now listen to the great Father of the household admonishing you: Strive to keep awake and rise up in the light, so that you may bear His staff honorably while it is day. For if the outer man sometimes is worn down by God's chastisement, the inner man rises all the stronger by that mighty power which will sustain you on the turning wheel of His grace.[a]

57
Hildegard to an Abbot
1169–70

Hildegard reinforces her advice to the abbot to continue to fulfill his duty by means of an allegorical vision from the Serene Light.

I heard these things in the Serene Light: Wisdom and Discernment spoke to each other, asking, Whom shall we get to help us? And they responded with one voice, Temperance. But let us do our duty, and have Mercy announce salvation to the people. And so they sat down. Then Wisdom said: What are we to do, for there are wars and more wars among the sons of men? And Discernment answered: When the sons of men rush at each other in the streets, seeking to kill each other, blind them with sunlight, and I, for my part, will darken their eyes with a cloud. And let us teach them that, first and foremost, God imbued them with angelic principles, and, then, gave them bodies, like His own. And so why should they strangle their spirits when they have such great merit? You, therefore, should give them a shield formed from the sun, and I will give them armor and iron armbands from the cloud, so heavy that they will not be able to move. Then, Temperance said: And I will spread a net before their feet which will ensnare them if they seek to tread the paths of unrighteousness. And Mercy said: I declare that Wisdom has established heaven and earth in great glory, and that Discernment has made all things beautiful for the eyes to behold, and that Temperance has changed all bitter and cloyingly sweet things into nutritious food, so that they can be eaten and digested. But I have a flashing sword, and with it I destroy all things dangerous and injurious to mankind, and I flatten out all the impassable mountains so that both the meek and the mighty, the strong and the weak, are able to pass through them without harm.

Now, you, O diligent and solicitous father, understand this parable, and with energy, mercy, and great reverence, show your sons the lofty justice and judgments of God, because when they begin the wars of evil deeds and seek to fight it out to the bitter end in the streets of their will, then blind their eyes with the sun of justice [cf. Mal 4.2] and with the cloud of chastisement. For they are celestial by spirit, and they have their bodies in the image of Christ. And so prevent them from snuffing out their spirits, which have many merits in heaven. And show them the shield of defense from the sun of justice, and from the cloud of discipline load them down with the armor and armbands of obedience, from which they can scarcely extricate themselves, because of the weight of their sins. Stretch out the net of chastisement before them and compel them to walk on the straight path, because God has established heaven and earth in great glory, and has tempered all things, both pleasant and difficult, and made them bearable. Imitate Mercy, who levels all things so that they may be overcome. But do all things in the proper time, keeping in mind the weakness of your sons' bodies, in accordance with God's words: "I will have mercy, not sacrifice" [Matt 9.13; 12.7; cf. Hosea 6.6], and as the Apostle also says: "Who need milk, and not solid food" [Heb 5.12ff; cf. I Cor 3.2]. And anoint them with oil so that they may not grow weak out of bitterness, or stray out of ignorance.

Now, therefore, O dear son of God, make your temple bright with benevolence, and do not let your mind be blown about like shifting clouds, as if by the unrest of war. Set your heart in the pure fountain, and embrace Him in sweet love.

58
Hildegard to Prior Dimo

1169–70

A general admonition couched in allegorical terms.

I saw and heard these words in a true vision: Life sees death and overcomes it, just as David, a mere boy, conquered Goliath. A mountain is visible because it is lofty, and a valley lies beneath it, sometimes causing flowers to bud in their vitality, but more often producing useless weeds, nettles, and thorns.

Now, understand, O man. Two men were sitting in a house, one of whom was a knight; the other, a serf.[a] And two wise and beautiful girls came to that house, knocked on the door, and said to them: You have become notorious even in far distant lands, for many people allege that you have slandered the king, and the king has asked, Who are these miscreants to be saying such things about me? Therefore, you two, hear our advice, for it will bring you victory. I am Humility: I have seen life in the incarnation of the Son of God, and I have crushed Death under my heel. The works of obedience are a mountain, and benevolence is a valley lush with flowers, though frequently choked off by nettles and thorns watered by the storms of sins.

Listen, therefore, O man, for it is the house of your heart that the knight and the serf—that is, Obedience and Pride—are sitting in, and it is at the door of your mind that the two girls—that is, Divine Love and Humility[1]—are knocking, to prevent you committing all the sins that you are capable of. Now, therefore, observe that the knight defeats the serf, lest he trample the beauty of obedience beneath his feet, for Pride says, Those chains with which I bind mankind cannot be broken. But respond to him in the words of Love: I sat unsullied in heaven, and I kissed the earth. Pride swore against me and wanted to fly higher than the stars, but I threw him into the abyss. Now, therefore, join me in trampling the serf underfoot, my son, and take your stand with me, Divine Love, and embrace Humility as your lady. Thus you will escape condemnation and eternal death.

Note

1. The texts of both Van Acker and Pitra (and, therefore, presumably, the MSS) give *obedientia* here as the name of the allegorical character. But since the name Obedience is already assigned the soldier sitting inside and since the allegorical figure speaking above identifies herself as *humilitas*, it seems reasonable to assume that the repeated *obedientia* here is simply the result of scribal dittography. It might be argued further that Humility is the proper virtue to stand in opposition to Pride *(superbia)*. Observe below, too, that *caritas* refers to *humilitas* as the lady that mankind should embrace.

59
Hildegard to the Congregation of Monks

1169–70

Hildegard exhorts the congregation of monks to be obedient to their superior. The interest of the letter, however, lies in Hildegard's explication of biblical verses.

I looked into the purest fountain, and I heard these words: A certain man went into his garden to see if the flowers were blooming and if the herbs were growing. And he said: "I went down into the garden of nuts, to see the fruits of the valleys, and to look if the vineyard had flourished, and the pomegranates budded" [Cant 6.10]. "Return, return, O Sunamite[1]: return, return that we may behold thee" [Cant 6.12].

Here is the meaning of this passage: the Son of God descended from the heart of the Father and clothed Himself in flesh in the bitterness of human nature,[a] and in that bitterness he endured many sorrows without any sin, and so he saw the fruits of the valley when prophecy was fulfilled in Him. After the dew descended from heaven, the apostles also budded when they heard the precept of God and fulfilled it, just as it is written: Go into the whole world and preach [cf. Mark 16.15]. And there He looked to see if the vineyard had flourished. Then also the burning sun poured into some of them, and they, in turn, poured out their blood on account of their love for God, so that they became martyrs, and thus in them the pomegranates budded. And in this way, through a life different from that which they received in the first Adam, they returned, and another, new, race of men appeared, which did not exist before the nativity of that Man, when it was said to humankind: "Return, return, O Sunamite." And so all the ornaments, the praise of angels, have been lifted up in the Church, as if into celestial harmony, when it is said again, "Return, return that we may behold thee." For all the celestial virtues gazed in wonder at the face of the Church, which saw clearly in its virginity and heard keenly among the publicans and sinners, and spoke in true widowhood. What does this mean? When God was born, the eyes of the Church were opened in virginal nature, and it heard clearly the summons of the sinners and penitents, and in true widowhood[2] exclaimed with a shout, just as it is written: "Many waters cannot quench charity, neither can the floods drown it" [Cant 8.7], because the virginal flowers left the blazing wheel of carnal nature, and, following the example of the Lamb, walked in the pathway of virginity, abandoning the pomp, riches, and secular concerns of this world.[b] And none of those worldly allurements, no more than the multitude of waters, could destroy the divine love in them. Thus it is also written: "Thy heart shall be enlarged, when the multitude of the sea shall be converted to thee, the strength of the gentiles shall come to thee. The multitude of camels shall cover thee, the dromedaries of Madian and Epha" [Is 60.5–6].

O Jerusalem, your spirit will be greatly enlarged with innumerable ornaments when the mighty power in the sun of virginity will be spread abroad in you (just as the sea is greater than all other waters) and when the common people, pruned by the righteous sword of God's word and loaded like a camel, will give up this world sullied by great crimes, violations, and all the lascivious habits and vices of dromedaries.[c]

Now, therefore, hear and understand, O beloved sons of Jerusalem, for you have been called and sit in the recesses of the garden wall like doves [cf. Cant 2.14]. You are dressed in Christ's robe,[d] Christ who put on that unaccustomed robe when he clothed Himself in humanity, while still remaining whole in his deity. Therefore, walk after that one who said, "Not as I will, but as thou wilt" [Matt 26.39], Father. And so being bound by the golden bond of obedience, follow His example in the mirror of your superior, for just as a man sees his face in a mirror, so you see the face of God in your superior. And bless him, saying, lord and master, we will follow the example that you have set before us.

You ought to keep firmly in your mind's eye the fate of that first lost angel, who haughtily refused to submit to his proper master, but in his own conceit raised himself over Him. And yet he was cast into the abyss by the hand of that master. Now, therefore, beware lest you be censured in that same way for your blindness and for your slander of your master. Even if your master threatens to beat you with the rod of rebuke, humble yourselves before him in meek devotion, saying: Father, father, we cannot endure this, and we beseech you to spare us. And then with bowed head, humbly seek out the advice of other masters, and carry it out with due discretion and discipline, lest you be accused before your master in heaven.

O beloved sons, observe now with what zeal you were first planted, and beware lest you lead each other astray. May God count you in the Golden Number,[3] and may the blazing sun of the Holy Spirit plant you among all good things.

Notes

1. All MSS of this letter (followed by both Pitra and Van Acker) read *Sunamitis*, rather than the Vulgate's *Sulamitis*.

2. For Hildegard on the relative virtues of widowhood and virginity, see *Scivias* I.ii.595ff.

3. In the *Liber divinorum operum* Hildegard identifies the Golden Number as those martyrs of the primitive Church who shone like gold in the redness of their blood. And although she specifies the primitive Church, she hastens to add that the number is not yet full. See III.x.12, III.x.33.

60

An Abbot to Hildegard

1158–61(?)

The abbot of St. Michael in Bamberg requests the prayers of Hildegard.

To the Lady Hildegard, the betrothed of the High King, and mistress of the sisters of St. Rupert, B., unworthy abbot of St. Michael in Bamberg, sends whatever he can in the way of prayer and devotion.

We hear that you are aflame with love for the One who has redeemed us with his own blood, and, to the best of our ability, we earnestly beseech Him to preserve eternally the gifts He has bestowed upon you. With our whole heart we long for your presence, but because we have been ensnared by our own sins, we have been unable to gain our desire. In the name of the One you love, sweet lady, I beseech you as earnestly as I can to implore the Lord to be merciful to me, and that you pray Him to temper the lash of His mercy, with which He has scourged me, and scourges me daily. Thus may I find salvation in this world, and compassion and grace in the world to come.

But if, as I hope, divine predestination has determined to call me forth from this darkness soon, I wish to commend my soul to your hands and prayers. Please send a letter of consolation to us by the present messenger.

Bamberg (St. Theodore and St. Maria)
61

An Abbess to Hildegard

After 1157

The abbess requests to be received into Hildegard's community. Here is another instance of an administrator who wishes to be relieved of her responsibilities, this time, apparently, in order to join Hildegard's own community. Hildegard's answer is predictable.

To the beloved lady and mother, Hildegard, worthy of respect for her piety and dignity, L., abbess in name only in Bamberg, although unworthy, along with all the sisters entrusted to her by God, sends whatever the devout and frequent prayers of the humble can accomplish.

With all our hearts, we rejoice in Christ, blessed lady, that the Lord, who foreknew you and made you His elect, has illuminated you and filled you with the spirit of prophecy in our time. Christ has gladdened us especially in this:

that He not only foresaw and predestined you, a woman, for this purpose, but also His grace has illumined many through your teaching. Therefore, we offer the most devout thanks to Him for you, and we humbly pray that He mercifully finish that which He began in you, until He brings you to eternal life.

Therefore, we earnestly beseech you to consider receiving us into your fellowship, commending us heartily to your holy community. Please strengthen us with letters of encouragement. Farewell, beloved lady.

61r
Hildegard to the Abbess
After 1157

Hildegard urges the abbess to remain in her administrative position, and impose obedience upon her subordinates.

O mother, a person who does not till a fertile field and make it fruitful is letting it run to seed, because he is not working for the good of the master. Who appointed the ox and the ass to their proper functions? God, of course, created them to serve mankind. Why then should a person not toil to fulfill his proper, useful function, since he is God's own work, and God did not establish him as a useless being? For God made man like the firmament, which bears the sun and the moon and the stars so that they may give light to all creation, and mark the times and the seasons. But if a black cloud should obscure all these things, creation would fear that its end is near.

O daughter of God, be aware that you are this field, because you hold the people in the embrace of your good will, and thus they can accept your words and works.[a] Therefore, do not refuse to toil with the people, and do not abandon them merely because you long for leisure, for frequently harmful weeds grow in idleness. Set before yourself the vision of the firmament, lest, deceived by the devil, you obscure the light of your reason with a black cloud of sin, as if you were scarcely alive. Therefore, use discipline to keep your daughters in check, for just as a child fears to be beaten with a rod, so also the master must be feared by everyone. Do not be afraid to punish them, but rather through your will to order increase your reward in the life everlasting, so that the breath of the Holy Spirit may flow into you.

62

Gertrude,[1] a Nun, to Hildegard

After 1161

> This Gertrude is Gertrude von Stahleck, former countess. See Letter 30. A tender letter expressing her love for Hildegard and her longing to see her.

To Hildegard, her beloved mother in Christ, from her own Gertrude, with sincere prayers that God grant you what "eye hath not seen, nor ear heard, neither hath it entered into the heart of man" [I Cor 2.9].

I have absolutely no idea what I should write or say to you, for there is no one like you nor anyone so beloved in Christ, and indeed the very strength of my love has destroyed my ability to speak. Indeed, I have become drunk on the wine of the sorrow of your absence, blessed lady, and this has afflicted me so grievously that I have lost all desire to speak or even to see. I could almost believe that it would have been better for me never to have seen you at all, never to have known your kindness and maternal feeling toward me, for now separated from you by so great a distance, I grieve over you without ceasing as if you were lost to me forever.

But I hope in my God—*mine* I say, because I hold nothing dearer than Him—that He will not allow me to lay aside this besmirched body of mine until He has granted me the happiness of seeing you once again and enjoying conversation with you face to face. But if this cannot be because of the weight of my sins, He will not fail (I am assured by His goodness) to fulfill my hope of seeing you there where we will never be separated from His sight.

What more can I say? I ask you, beloved mother, to please pray for me to Him, in whose embrace you remain secure and in whose shadow you rest, like a young hart, from the heat of temptation and sin. Pray that He reveal himself to me, as I wander in search of Him, but, alas, without success. May He grant me to sit forever in the shadow of the one I desire [cf. Cant 2.3]. Farewell.

Note

1. See Letter 30, Headnote. Also see Van Acker, "Der Briefwechsel der heiligen Hildegard von Bingen," *Revue bénédictine* 98 (1988), 148ff.

62r

Hildegard to the Nun Gertrude

After 1161

Hildegard rejoices with Gertrude over her religious calling, for she is like the turtledove which remains alone once it has lost its mate.

O daughter of God, in pure knowledge of faith, hear the words directed to you: "The voice of the turtledove is heard in our land" [Cant 2.12]. This passage speaks of the Son of God, who, contrary to the law of nature, was born of the untilled earth of the flesh of the Virgin Mary. At that time, the flowers of all the virtues burgeoned forth in all their colorful glory, sweet with the fragrance of virtues. The garden of these virtues sprang up in the prodigal son, for when he came to his senses he ran to his father, that is, to the almighty Father, to confess his sins, and the father received him with the kiss of the humanity[1] of his Son.

The voice of the turtle dove is heard when, of our own free will, we give up the world for the love of God, for more than any other bird the turtle dove remains alone after it has lost its mate.[2] This is what you did, O beloved daughter, when you gave up the pomp of this world. O how beautiful were your shoes, O daughter of the king [cf. Cant 7.1], when, for the love of God, you entered the strait and narrow way of spiritual life. Therefore, rejoice, O daughter of Zion [cf. Zach 2.10], because the Holy Spirit dwells at the center of your heart. Reflect that your consoler set you "as a lily among thorns" [Cant 2.2] when you chose the spiritual life, although you possessed the pomp and riches of this world, which the Son of God called thorns. And in your passion at your entry into the order, you glowed like the rosebush of Jericho [cf. Ecclus 24.18].

Now, I rejoice over you, for all the things which I have heard and desired have been fulfilled in you. So, you should rejoice with me, too. I hope with true faith that you will be a wall adorned with precious stones and pearls in the sight of God, and that you will be praised by all the heavenly host. Therefore, rejoice and be glad [cf. Lam 4.21] in your God, because you will live forever.

Notes

1. Cf. Bernard of Clairvaux on the opening words of Canticles ("Let him kiss me with the kiss of his mouth") in his *Sermons on the Song of Songs:* "Take note: The Word becoming incarnate is the mouth which gives the kiss, and it is the flesh assumed which receives it. The kiss itself, brought to perfection equally by Him who gives and Him who receives, is that very Person, compact of each nature, the Mediator between God and men, that is, the man Christ Jesus" (II.3).

2. The turtle dove of the bestiaries.

63

Hildegard to the Congregation of Nuns

1157–70

A general letter of spiritual encouragement.

God had foreknowledge not only of good and evil, but also of disobedience. He perfected the good, crushed the evil, and rebuked disobedience. But may God bless you with every blessing, for you have trampled secular pomp under foot. Yet avoid the sin of being unmindful of God. But let that summer be in you which causes the roses and lilies and other spices[1] of the Holy Spirit to grow, so that foul weeds may not spring up in you, those perverse morals which permit pride and vanity to flourish.

Now, however, remain in that embrace which goes from virtue to virtue [cf. Ps 83.8], so that when you knock at the bridegroom's door [cf. Luke 12.36], He will receive you joyfully.

Note

1. Cf. *Scivias* III.x.309: "I will plant roses and lilies and fine spices of virtues in that field, and I will constantly water it with the inspiration of the Holy Spirit, and, rooting out harmful weeds, I will cut off the evil in it."

Bassum
64

Hildegard to Abbess Richardis

1151–52

Hildegard writes to her favorite nun and cherished friend, who has deserted her. See Letter 4, Headnote and, especially, Letter 12, Headnote. For a sensitive and insightful discussion of this letter, see P. Dronke, *Women Writers*, pp. 157–58.

Daughter, listen to me, your mother, speaking to you in the spirit: my grief flies up to heaven. My sorrow is destroying the great confidence and consolation that I once had in mankind. From now on I will say: "It is good to trust in the Lord, rather than to trust in princes" [Ps 117.9]. The point of this Scripture is that a person ought to look to the living height, with vision unobstructed by earthly love and feeble faith, which the airy humor of earth renders transient and short-lived. Thus a person looking at God directs his sight to the sun like an eagle. And for this reason one should not depend on a person of high birth, for such a one inevitably withers like a flower. This was the very transgression I myself committed because of my love for a certain noble individual.

Now I say to you: As often as I sinned in this way, God revealed that sin to me, either through some sort of difficulty or some kind of grief, just as He has now done regarding you, as you well know.

Now, again I say: Woe is me, mother, woe is me, daughter, "Why have you forsaken me" [Ps 21.2; Matt 27.46; Mark 15.34] like an orphan? I so loved the nobility of your character, your wisdom, your chastity, your spirit, and indeed every aspect of your life that many people have said to me: What are you doing?

Now, let all who have grief like mine mourn with me,[1] all who, in the love of God, have had such great love in their hearts and minds for a person—as I had for you—but who was snatched away from them in an instant, as you were from me. But, all the same, may the angel of God go before you, may the Son of God protect you, and may his mother watch over you. Be mindful of your poor desolate mother, Hildegard, so that your happiness may not fade.

Note

1. Cf. Lamentations 1.12. As with the "Why have you forsaken me" passage above, the allusion is startling and audacious, for this text was used in the Good Friday liturgy as the words, in figure, of the crucified Christ.

Bishopsberg
65
Hildegard to a Certain Monk

Before 1170

A short letter of general admonition and encouragement.

The One from whom no secret is hid says: Your mind is like a breath of wind in the turbulence of your heart, like the sun that sometimes shines and sometimes vanishes in the storm. Do not take the burnt offering by theft [cf. Is 61.8], for God himself will supply it at his own pleasure.

Do not be a fugitive from God's grace, which does not want you to be lost.

Bonn
66

A Certain Superior to Hildegard

Before 1173

A brief general letter reciting the writer's praise and love for Hildegard.

H., superior in Bonn, though unworthy, offers his service and complete devotion to Hildegard, the bride of Christ and most worthy mistress of the sisters of St. Rupert in Bingen.

If the Lord (who alone is mighty, good, faithful, and merciful) deigns to incline the ear of His majesty to the voice of any sinner, as I firmly believe, then His ear will resound with the tireless cries of my mouth and heart in praise of you. For, truly, I bear witness that there are no secrets before God: Ever since I first heard of your goodness, through the reports that reached us, and which I myself afterward discovered to be true, I have felt the most profound esteem for you. Ever since then, I have made you a full participant of everything I have said well or done well. Therefore, I hope for the same treatment from you; indeed I require it as if in payment of a debt, though more out of your goodness and your love for God.

Finally, neither fire nor sword nor flood nor the menace of any fear or danger, not even death itself can threaten the genuine love of my soul for you, or remove it in any way. Farewell.

66r

Hildegard to the Superior

Before 1173

A letter of admonition to the superior, who, as Hildegard remarks, is only limping along in good works.

O man, you who love the world and are secular in your disposition, you are like a storm in your moral character, which is seldom calm but rarely dangerous.

That is to say, you frequently refuse consolation in your daily life, and in all your affairs you are oppressed, sometimes by weariness, sometimes by sorrow, sometimes by doubt. Therefore, rise up and call on the God of Israel, saying: "Prove me, O Lord, and try me; burn my reins and my heart" [Ps 25.2].

The meaning of the passage is this: Prove me, Lord, through faith and hope, so that my faith may be an eye to see, and my hope, a mirror of life. And try me in righteous obedience like Abraham, so that I may work not according to my own will, but may abandon it for your sake and enter into your precepts, and thus become your loving friend. And in this way, burn my reins, which overflow from the sins in which I was conceived, and see that they do not lead me astray (since I am not working in accordance with my own will) but cause me to be always aflame with the fire of the Holy Spirit, so that I may desire your justice day after day, and ascend from virtue unto virtue [cf. Ps 83.8].

But your mind, O man, is like a cloud, bearing neither hail nor rain, but a cloud which the sun breaks up. For resting secure in shallow words and morals, you do not realize that anger is like a cloud full of hail, or that quarreling is like a storm. Instead, although you desire things supernal, you limp along in your good works.[a] Therefore, purify your desire through good works in the fear of God, and, in this way, kiss God, saying, "Incline thy ear, O Lord, and hear me: for I am needy and poor" [Ps 85.1]. When by the kiss of God's love, you do good works in order to touch God—for good works are like a word sounding in God's ear—immediately He inclines his ear to your desire and prayer, and fulfills them, since you are needy, and helpless, and exceedingly poor, and since you are insufficient in yourself to bring any good work to completion. But may God fulfill this in you.

67
Hildegard to the Priest Berthold

Before 1170

Berthold had, apparently, written Hildegard for advice about his friend, and Hildegard responds with some little harshness toward the friend.

God foresaw all the works of his finger, living and complete, and He established them for his glory. And may God in some measure pour their light into you, so that you may flee the darkness of the shifting whirlwind.

That person whom you count as a friend is exhausted in his foolish spirit, like an ignorant infant, at one moment heeding your admonition, at the next, refusing to listen. You, therefore, who are Christ's representative, admonish him and do not spare chastisement, because his days are arid, with no animating hope of security. Now live forever and be a mirror of truth in your spirit.

Brauweiler
68
Abbot Gedolphus to Hildegard[1]
About 1169

> Abbot Gedolphus of Brauweiler writes to Hildegard to seek help for a woman possessed of a demon.

Gedolphus, abbot, although unworthy, of the monastery at Brauweiler, and his brothers in this vale of tears, offer their prayers and devoted service as best they can to the lady and mother Hildegard, bride of Christ and daughter of the most high King.

Although we have never met face to face, beloved lady, the fame of your virtues is exceedingly well known among us, and although we are distant from you in body, we are nevertheless present in spirit, and the Lord of knowledge knows how great is our affection for you. In our country indeed it is on everyone's lips what the Lord has done for you, because "he that is mighty, hath done great things" for you, and "holy is his name" [Luke 1.49]. Both the clergy and the laity know how great are the miracles that the Fountain of Living Light manifests in you, and the outcome of events testifies to their truth. For not human but divine accomplishments shine forth in you, and grace goes before you, that mighty gift which comes not from human reason but proceeds from the bright Fountain.

But why do we delay? "It is better to weep than to speak."[2] Therefore, pious lady, may your sweet sanctity not impute it to effrontery that we have, in the simplicity of our hearts, presumed to bring this matter to your attention, for indeed we are compelled by extreme necessity. And we have no doubt whatsoever that we will receive good advice from you.

A certain noble lady has been besieged for many years now by an evil spirit,[3] and she was brought to us by her friends to be freed from the menacing enemy through the aid of the blessed Nicholas, our patron. But the insidious evil of this most shrewd and wicked enemy has brought so many thousands into error and doubt that we greatly fear harm to Holy Church. For all of us, along with the host of the people, have striven for three months in every conceivable way to free that woman, but it grieves us to report that, because of our own sins, we have made no progress whatsoever.

Now all our hope, next to God, rests on you. For that demon, when he was conjured one day, finally revealed to us that this possessed woman could be freed only through the strength of your contemplation and the magnitude of divine revelation.[4] Does not God intend great things in her liberation? Surely, He does. Thus, through you, the abundant benevolence of our Redeemer will deign to consummate the labor of our efforts and grief, but also of our joy and exultation, when He wipes away every error and infidelity of mankind and frees the possessed handmaiden of God. Then, we will be able to say with the prophet: "This is the Lord's doing: and it is wonderful in our eyes" [Ps 117.23]; and "the snare is broken, and we are delivered" [Ps 123.7].

Therefore, saintly lady, whatever inspiration or revelation God grants you please impart to us as soon as possible in a letter. This is our earnest and humble prayer. Farewell.

Notes

1. This and the following two letters are very important documents with respect to Hildegard's life and activity, dealing as they do with demonic possession and Hildegard's efforts at exorcism. The text of the correspondence between Gedolphus and Hildegard is from Monika Klaes's critical edition of the *Vita S. Hildegardis*, in *Corpus Christianorum: continuatio medievalis*, vol. 126 (Turnholt: Brepols, 1993), pp. 58–63. We are greatly indebted to Professor Klaes for sharing her text with us before the publication of her edition.

2. Gregory, *Dialogues* 3.1.

3. The woman's name was Sigewize, and according to the *Vita* (III.ii.46, 47), she had been demon-possessed for a full seven years.

4. In the third book of the *Vita* (ii.46), Hildegard herself is quoted with respect to this scene: "And when that woman had been led to a large number of saints' shrines, the possessing demon, overcome by the merits of the saints and the prayers of the people, cried out, saying that on the upper reaches of the Rhine there was a certain old woman, through whose counsel he could be expelled." And Theodoric, author of the third book, added the interesting (however questionable) detail that the demon played with Hildegard's name, derisively calling her *Scrumpilgardis*, "Wrinklegard" (ii.47).

68r
Hildegard to Abbot Gedolphus
About 1169

In response, Hildegard sends a ritual ceremony to be used in the exorcism of the evil spirit.

Hildegard to Gedolphus, abbot of Brauweiler.

Although I have been confined with a long and serious illness through the scourges of God, I have just enough strength to answer your request. What I am about to say does not come from myself, but from the One Who Is.

There are various kinds of evil spirits.[1] The demon you are inquiring about has those powers which resemble the moral vices of human beings. For this reason, he gladly dwells among people, and is not bothered by the Lord's cross, the relics of saints, or all the other things pertaining to service of God. Rather, he mocks them, and stands in no awe of them. Those things certainly he does not love, but he pretends to run away from them, just as a heedless fool discounts the threatening words directed at him by the wise. It is for such reasons that he is more difficult to cast out than other demons, for he will not be exorcised except by fasting, scourging, prayer, alms, and the very command of God himself [cf. Matt 17.20; Mark 9.28].

Hear, then, the answer, not of a human being but of the One Who Lives. Choose seven priests of good repute, recommended by the quality of their life, in the name and order of Abel, Noah, Abraham, Melchisedech, Jacob, and Aaron, for these offered sacrifice to the living God. The seventh priest will represent Christ, who offered his very self on the cross to God the Father. And with fasting, scourges, prayers, and oblations, let them celebrate Mass, and, then, clad in their priestly vestments and stoles, let them approach the suffering woman with their eyes averted. They are to stand around her, each one holding a rod in his hand in figure of that rod with which Moses struck Egypt, the Red Sea, and the rock at God's command [Ex 7.8–10.23; 14.16–29; 17.6–7; Num 20.11], so that, just as, there, God revealed his miracles through the rod, so also, here, He may glorify Himself when that foul enemy has been cast out through these rods.[a] These seven priests will represent the seven gifts of the Holy Spirit, so that the Spirit of God which in the beginning "moved over the waters" [Gen 1.2] and "breathed into his face the breath of life" [Gen 2.7] may blow away the unclean spirit from that wearied person.

And let the first one, who represents Abel, hold his rod in his hand and say, "Hear, O evil and foolish spirit, whoever you are that inhabit this person, hear these words which do not come from man but from Him Who is and Who lives, and[2] flee, driven out at His command. Hear Him Who Is saying: I Who am without beginning but from Whom all beginnings come forth, and I Who am the Ancient of Days, I say: I through Myself am the day, Who never came forth from the sun, but from Whom the sun itself was enkindled. I am also Reason, which did not sound forth from another, but from which every rationality breathes forth. Therefore, I made mirrors for the contemplation of my face, in which I gaze upon all the miracles[3] of my antiquity, which never fade, and I prepared those mirrors to ring forth in praise, for I have a voice like thunder, with which I move all the world in the living sound of all creatures."[b]

And let that same priest and the other six standing around strike her lightly with their rods upon the head and upon the back, upon the breast and upon the navel and upon the reins, upon the knees, and upon the feet, and let them say: "Now, you, O satanic and evil spirit, you who oppress and torment this person, this form of a woman, depart! Through Him Who lives and Who has revealed these words through a simple person untaught in human learning, leave this person who is here present and whom you have oppressed for a long time, and in whom you still remain. For you have been commanded, and He Himself now commands you to begone. And so by this rod at the command of the True Beginning, that is, the Beginning Itself, you are commanded to harm her no further.[4] Conjured and condemned also by the sacrifice and prayers and aid of Abel, in whose name we strike you."[c]

And again let them strike her as above: "Conjured and condemned also by the sacrifice and prayers and aid of Noah, in whose name we strike you."

And again let them strike: "Conjured and condemned also by the sacrifice and prayers and aid of Abraham, in whose name we strike you."

And let them strike her as above: "Conjured and condemned also by the sacrifice and prayers and aid of Melchisedech, in whose name we strike you."

And again let them strike her as above: "Conjured and condemned also by the sacrifice and prayers and aid of Jacob, in whose name we strike you."

And let them strike her as above: "Conjured and condemned also by the sacrifice and prayers and aid of Aaron, in whose name we strike you."

And let them strike her as above: "Conjured and condemned also by the sacrifice and prayers and aid of the High Priest, the Son of God, to Whom all true priests have offered sacrifice and offer sacrifice still, in whose name and power we strike you."

And let them strike her again: "You, go out of this person confounded in that same confusion which was yours when you first fell from heaven like lead—and do not harm her further.

"And let the height which height never touched, and the depth which depth never plumbed, and the breadth which breadth never encompassed free her from your power and foolish iniquity and from all your arts. So, confounded, flee from her, and let her neither feel nor know you further. And just as you are cut off from heaven, may the Holy Spirit cut you off from her, and just as you are estranged from every felicity, so may you be estranged from her. And just as you never desire God, so may you never desire to return to her. Flee, therefore, flee, flee from her, devil, flee with all the evil, airy spirits, adjured through the power of eternity, which created all things and which made mankind, and through the benevolence of the Savior of humanity, which freed that same mankind, and through the fiery love that made mankind eternal. Also, condemned through the Passion, which He endured on the wood of the holy cross, and through the resurrection of life, and through that power which cast the devil from heaven into hell and freed mankind from his power, go out from this person confounded in that same confusion which was yours when you first fell from heaven like lead, and harm her no further, neither in the soul nor in any of the members of her body, as commanded by the Omnipotent, who made and created her. Amen."

If the demon has not yet been cast out, let the second priest with all the other priests standing about follow that same order, until God helps her.[5]

Notes

1. The *Vita* (III.ii.45) quotes Hildegard specifically about demonic possession: "And thinking about these matters and wishing to know how a diabolic form could enter a person, I saw—and heard a response—that a devil in his own form could not enter human beings, but he covers and overshadows them with the shadow and smoke of his blackness. For if his actual form should enter a person, that person's members would be dissolved more quickly than a straw is dispersed by the wind. Therefore, God does

not permit him to enter a person in his own form. But hovering over, he brings on ill health and discomfort, and he cries out through the person as through a window. And he moves that person's members from the outside although he may not be within them in his own form, the soul all the while, as if asleep, being ignorant of what the flesh of the body is doing."

2. The remainder of the exorcism is written in the margin of the MS, and in her appendix, Klaes prints it, as edited by Dronke, "Problemata Hildegardiana," pp. 127–29.

3. The entire sentence up to this point is Klaes's restoration of the text, for where Dronke has only *abissos* (with a question mark), Klaes reads *intuitum igitur faciei mee specula feci, in quibus omnia miracula*.

4. There is a problem in the MS text at this point, but Dronke observes, quite correctly, that the formulaic quality of the ritual "allows one to reconstruct with some safety here."

5. The *Vita* (III.ii.48) apparently supplies the end of this letter, introduced by the words *Cumque venisset lector ad locum illum, ubi in finem scriptum est* ("And when the reader had come to that place where it is written at the end"): "O blaspheming and scornful spirit, I, an untaught and poor little feminine form, say to you in that truth by which I, a poor and untaught form, saw and heard these things from the light of wisdom, and through that same wisdom I command you by the true stability and not by the whirlwind of your instability to go out of this person." The repetition of the humility formula here is not, as one might think, owing merely to scribal dittography, for the two Latin phrases are quite dissimilar: (1) *ego indocta et paupercula feminea forma*, (2) *ego paupercula et indocta forma*.

69
Gedolphus to Hildegard
About 1169

Gedolphus writes to inform Hildegard that the demon came forth from the woman once they had performed the ritual she had sent them, but returned almost immediately, and attacked her even more grievously than before. And upon a second performance of the ceremony, the demon informed them that he could be exorcised only in the presence of the seer on the upper Rhine. Thus the abbot notifies Hildegard that he is sending the woman along to her.

Gedolphus, unworthy abbot, along with his brothers, to the venerable Hildegard with all due gratitude, with a prayer that she live, prosper, tread the world under foot, and whatever else more excellent that can be hoped for the handmaid of Christ.

The whole world now knows that the Lord has looked well upon you and filled you with His grace. Up until now, saintly lady, we have corresponded with you on behalf of the woman possessed by an evil spirit only through letters and messengers. Now, however, we pursue the matter through the person of that same woman, for we have sent her to you with great hope, and we devoutly add prayer to prayer that the closer she is to you in body, the more propitious you will be to her in spirit.

For conjured in accordance with the letter you sent us through the inspiration of the Holy Spirit, the demon abandoned the vessel he had possessed—but only for a brief time. Alas, he has returned, we know not through what judgment of God, and he has invaded that abandoned vessel again and now oppresses her more grievously than ever before [cf. Matt 12.43ff].[1] Then, when we conjured him again, mightily assailing him, at length he answered that he would not abandon his possessed vessel unless you were present in person.[2] We are informing you of this for her sake, saintly lady, so that the Lord may accomplish what we, because of our sins, have not merited, and so that He Who rules over all may be glorified in you when the ancient enemy has been cast out. Farewell, beloved mother.

Notes

1. The scene at the departure of the demon is described in meticulous detail in the *Vita* (III.ii.48): "That vile spirit howled and wailed so horribly that he struck great fear into all those present. Then, finally, in accordance with God's will, after he had raged so violently for about half an hour, he abandoned the vessel he had long possessed." Later, on being asked how he dared to return to the creature of God, the demon answered, "I fled terrified at the sign of the crucifix. But when I did not know where to go, I returned to my empty vessel since it had not been sealed *[signatum]*."

2. Once again the *Vita* (III.ii.49) gives the scene: "And when we conjured him once more in accordance with the instructions of that pious virgin, he cried out, with gnashing of teeth, that he would go out only in the presence of that old woman."

Burgundy (Bellevaux, Cherlieu, Clairefontaine, La Charité, Bethany)

70

Five Abbots to Hildegard

Before 1157

The bearer of this letter is a woman that the abbots have sent with the request that, through Hildegard's prayers and sanctity, she might be made fertile again.

B. of Bellevaux, G. of Cherlieu, A. of Clairefontaine, R. of La-Charité, and G. of Bethany,[1] abbots in name only, to Hildegard, the foreordained bride of Christ, with a prayer that she flourish in grace and join the canticle of praise [cf. Ecclus 39.19].

In the joy of our hearts we have rendered thanks to God, Who bestows every spiritual gift, and Who does not disdain to repeat the miracles of old in our time. Therefore, we readily assert that we have not been cheated at all of those promises with which He once comforted his followers when He said: "And behold I am with you even to the consummation of the world" [Matt 28.20]. Although we ourselves may be found unworthy of those promises, we are nevertheless aware that your heart has been greatly inspired by them through the aid of the Holy Spirit. Thus although you are inexperienced at composing books and doing many other unheard-of things to the amazement of those who witness them, still, through you, celestial harmony resounds wondrously, and things previously unknown to mortal man are revealed.[a]

And is it any wonder? Now, I say, even now, you are truly the unstained bride of Christ, leaning upon your beloved [cf. Cant 8.5]; His left hand is under your head, and His right embraces you [cf. Cant 2.6, 8.3]. He has brought you into His chamber and has graciously revealed his secrets to you [cf. Cant 2.6, 3.4, 8.3ff]. It is our hope that the Lord strengthen you in these mysteries, and we humbly beseech you to pray for some revelation concerning our condition, so that you may make it known to us.

The woman who brings this letter to you is a noble lady, the wife of a man who loves her very much. With great devotion she comes to you, humble and afoot, although she could have come on horseback with a large company. And she has come to you for the following reason: although she bore children early in her marriage, for a long time now she has been sterile. Those first children have died, and she has been able to bear no others, for which she and her husband are consumed with grief. That is the reason she has flown to you, the handmaiden and friend of Christ, in the firm belief that through your merits with God, and your prayers, she may become fertile and, having borne a child, present the blessed fruit of her womb to Christ. Therefore, because we have been petitioned by both her and her husband, we ask that you stand in prayer for them before God. May God grant them the desire of their hearts.

Note

1. Van Acker, "Der Briefwechsel" (1989), identifies four of these as Burchard of Bellevaux, Guido of Cherlieu, Aliprand of Clairfontaine, and Guillelmus of Bethany. These are all Cistercian monasteries.

70r
Hildegard to the Five Abbots

Before 1157

Hildegard replies to the abbots with a mini-sermon on penitence and mercy. Then at the end of the letter she addresses the subject of the infertile woman, pointing out that such matters are in the hands of God, though she will indeed pray for her.

O you who by the grace of God have been called by the Lord to pastoral office, reflect upon God's first calling to Adam, when He said "Where art thou?" [Gen 3.9] when he went astray through disobedience.[1] Then his name was like the darkened earth, and God gave him a garment, knowing that He himself would eventually put on the robe of humanity on account of him—and for his sake.[a] And it was in this robe that He called him back again with the clear voice of mercy, when the prodigal son came to himself, saying: "How many hired servants in my father's house abound with bread, and here I perish with hunger" [Luke 15.17], and his father received him joyfully.

Now, it is fitting that you abbots understand clearly that God called Adam back by another way, that is, through the kiss of humanity shown in the fatted calf, saying: Through disobedience man had perished, but through penitence I will bring him back.

Climb up the high mountain, but build your tabernacles in the valley,[2] and stay in them for a long time. For when you look up to seek God, you are climbing the mountain. Then you may reflect on profound humility, for the Son of God became totally human in his humanity. Thus in all your works—that is to say, in yourselves and in others—observe humility, and persevere in it always.

Beware lest your mind be like a mountain blackened by the fires of the smithies where bronze is made. Here, filthy morals become a matter of bad habit, sometimes by thinking unwholesome things, sometimes by coveting them, sometimes by actually doing them, those things which do not move one to holiness but indeed inflict the wound of licentiousness. O knights of God, flee from those things and look to that light which you have tasted a little and rise quickly to sanctity, because you do not know when your end will come.

God endowed man with reason. For man is rational through God's word, whereas a non-rational creature is like a mere sound. Thus God established it that man embodies all creation.[b] But He gave two wings to reason: the right wing signifies good knowledge; the left, bad. And man, with these two wings, is like a bird. Man also is like the day and the night. For when day overcomes night in a person, he is called a good knight, because he conquers evil with military might. Therefore, O sons of God, serve in Christ's army day after day, and in tranquility of mind flee the cloud that overshadows the day. Moreover, turn away from nocturnal treachery, which willfully and arrogantly exhorts one to excess, but be the day which is cool and dewy in the early morning but later becomes more moderate in temperature, so that with discernment you may judge all things, and provide all good things in moderation for yourselves and others.

Therefore, dwell in the dovecotes [cf. Cant 2.14, Jer 48.28] with pure simplicity, so that you may have the "voice of rejoicing and of salvation in the tabernacles of the just" [Ps 117.15]. For God has implanted the living voice of the breath of life in reason, that is, the voice of rejoicing, which by good knowledge sees and knows God by faith. That same voice is a well-sounding trumpet resonating with works of kindness, for it enjoys the embrace of divine love, and, therefore, by means of humility gathers the meek and, with mercy, anoints their wounds. Moreover, divine love flows with the gushing water of the Holy Spirit, that is, with the peace of the goodness of God. Humility also plants a garden with every fruit-bearing tree of God's grace, which encompasses all the invigorating power of God's gifts. And mercy exudes a balm to soothe all the troubles which assail mankind. This voice of divine love resounds in the symphony of all praises of salvation. It resounds through humility on high where it sees God, and where, with victory, it fights against pride. And through mercy it cries with a voice, at once both lamentable and joyous, because it gathers unto itself the poor and the lame, and seeks the aid of the Spirit so that it may fill all these things with good works. It resounds in the tabernacles where the saints blaze throughout those structures which, while they were alive in this world, they have prepared for themselves.

As for you, O sons of God, join with the voice of the good where the just are found, and God will receive you, because He wants you, and you will live forever.

With regard to your request that I petition God to restore that woman to fertility, I am compelled to reply that that is in the will and the power of God, because He alone knows when He will grant children and when He will refuse to do so, because, unlike man, God judges by the interior state not by outward appearance. Yet because you ask, I will indeed pray to God for her. The rest is in His merciful and steadfast hands.

Notes

1. The *Glossa ordinaria* (I.iii) interprets the verse as, *Dum vocat, significat quia ad poenitentiam revocat.*
2. The image of the mountains and valleys here is very pointed since Hildegard is writing to Cistercians. The older Benedictine monasteries were usually built on mountaintops, symbolizing the contemplative ascent to God, while the Cistercians perferred to build in isolated valleys, symbolizing humility. See Newman, *Symphonia*, pp. 50–51, 290–91.

Busendorf
71
Hildegard to an Abbot

About 1150(?)

A letter of encouragement to an abbot.

The Light in the Light says to you: Be a good servant in your mind, and keep watch in good desire, and be like the eagle that had rather look directly into the sun than in the shadow of shadow. And also do not grow weary of doing good works, but with firmness of mind keep your hand on the plow, and, with God's help, feed your flock as well as you can. And with all your might fly with the eagle that looks ever at the light, lest you be carried off by weariness. Also, flee the blackness of impiety, since God makes distinctions in the matter of good will. For God wants you to be dead to the things of this world. Now, live forever.

72

The Abbot to Hildegard

About 1150(?)

The abbot writes Hildegard as one seeking refuge, since, as he says, he stands in midst of danger. The letter itself is not really explicit, but, clearly, the abbot is greatly troubled about the state of things in his monastery.

W., by the grace of God abbot of Busendorf, though unworthy, to his beloved Hildegard, virgin dedicated to God, with a prayer that she receive that which is most blissful in the life to come.

The grace of God has made you a safe harbor for all who seek you out, battered by the storms of tribulation. Therefore, because we ourselves are in danger, we do not hesitate to stretch our hands in supplication to you. We are writing you with a certain sense of caution to inform you that our church, which through God's mercy was held in high esteem for many years, has, through our own sins, been besmirched by the vilest kind of rumor. For through the instigation of the devil (who always seeks the destruction of good men), certain of our number, fomenters of evil, never cease from stirring up whatever trouble they can for us and our whole monastery. Here is the gist of the matter: their unbridled pride has brought matters to such a pitch that, now, everybody is saying that this is the result of our own secret sins.

In the hope of relief we are bringing this oppressive burden to you, and we humbly beseech you to reply with some word of consolation.[1] And, above all, we earnestly ask you to reconcile us to God and men through your prayers. Farewell.

Note

1. One wonders what kind of help the abbot expects from such a vague recitation of troubles. Perhaps the bearer of the letter was more specific about the matter. The "oppressive burden" does seem to be more substantial than merely the sin of pride among the monks, since the abbot notes that he writes with some little caution.

72r
Hildegard to the Abbot

About 1150(?)

Hildegard addresses the troubles in the abbot's monastery, which, as she says, are like a hurricane, shaking it to the foundation. A part of the problem she locates in the abbot himself. But God will preserve the monastery for the sake of a few good souls within the community.

In the vision by which my spirit is frequently enlightened while I myself remain fully awake, I see a whirlwind in your monastery, a hurricane, as it were, filled with lightning, all black and murky, and the monastery itself is shaken to the foundations. But I see three colors in your soul: first of all, the blackness of malice and wrath; second, the smoke of the appetite for perverse things; third, the red dawn of good will and the sigh breathed to God. But I also see a glorious light rising to God from some of your congregation, and for their sake God sustains the whole place through His grace.

You, however, O worthy shepherd, look to that field which has been blessed by God with fruitfulness. Over this field a dark storm cloud comes, wounding the field and damaging the fruit. I speak of the lethargy and the malice in the heart of one who knows the good and is able to bring it to pass, but who prefers to dwell in lethargy and malice, and is thus prevented from good works.

Son of God, flee from these things, and, inspired by the fire of the Holy Spirit, work in the fruitful field, before that day comes when you can work no longer.

Clusin (St. George)
73
Hildegard to the Congregation of Nuns

1161–63(?)

This letter is apparently not in answer to one sent to Hildegard, but was provoked by her concern for this community of nuns. She writes that she was commanded by God to admonish and correct the nuns.

God's will, His dwelling place, and His greatness, I found in the sacrifices of this people. Indeed, they once had the wings of felicity and blessedness. But, now, the incurable venom of adders has infected them [cf. Deut 32.33]. And I heard the admonition of the Spirit of God, calling on me to admonish and correct them, just as it is written: "Go ye into the village that is over against you, and immediately you shall find an ass tied, and a colt with her: Loose them and bring them to me. And if any man shall say anything to you, say ye that the Lord hath need of them: and forthwith he will let them go" [Matt 21.2–3]. And again in a different way it is said: "Amen I say to you, I know you not" [Matt 25.12].

O woe to the derision and error of those who long in their hearts to say that contentious disobedience is not evil, that disruptive force that raised itself up against heaven and fell into hell, and threw all creation into utter confusion. O you flowers of the rod,[1] hear what is written: "Rejoice, thou barren, that beareth not: break forth and cry, thou that travailest not: for many are children of the desolate, more than of her that hath a husband" [Gal 4.27; cf. Isa 54.1]. And hear again what is said: "Arise and be enlightened, O Jerusalem: for thy light is come, and the glory of the Lord is risen upon thee" [Isa 60.1].

And so flee the incurable poison of adders, because walking in vanity and wallowing in poison is not proper to your chosen way of life, by which you have embraced God. Now, may you find salvation in that horn of salvation through which David ascended to the humanity of the Savior [cf. II Sam 22.3; Ps 17.3]. For through that humanity he was admonished, so that he repented of his sins. Now, run to me quickly, and bring the sacrificial calf to me.

Note

1. *O floriditates uirge.* I.e., virgins, as in the flowering of Jesse's rod, a figure of the Holy Virgin.

St. Disibod
74
Abbot Kuno[1] to Hildegard

Before 1155

Abbot Kuno, who was the source of great distress to Hildegard after she left St. Disibod and founded her community at Mount St. Rupert, writes a seemingly repentent letter to Hildegard, asking her to impart to him any revelations she has had about the patron of his monastery, St. Disibod.

Kuno, abbot of Mount St. Disibod, though unworthy, sends such paltry blessing as he is capable of by God's grace to the lady Hildegard, his beloved mother, in Mount St. Rupert.

Because I have been impeded by the various things that I have to do, I have neglected for some time to visit with you. But now that I have the opportunity, I will say: the more aware I am that I am growing old in the increase of my sins rather than in the advancement of justice, woe is me, the more earnestly I commend myself to your prayers.

But, saintly lady, since you see through the aid of the Spirit many secrets from Him who does not deceive nor is deceived, I ask that you impart to me any revelation God has granted you concerning our patron, the blessed Disibod, so that my brothers and I may not fail to render him our devout praise.

But because I am totally unable to shake off the sloth which lies in me, I seek with all my heart your prayers and those of the other daughters of God who dwell with you. And I commend to the prayers of all of you not only my own insignificant self but also those brothers who have been entrusted to my care and indeed our entire monastery, for such is my regular custom when I am in your presence.

Note

1. Kuno, Abbot of Disibod, was the first high official of the Church to become aware of Hildegard's gift. Seeking confirmation of his own affirmative view of this remarkable matter, he consulted with Heinrich, Archbishop of Mainz, who then took the matter to the pope at the Synod of Trier. Later, at Hildegard's break with Kuno over her removal to Mount St. Rupert, Heinrich supported Hildegard in opposition to Kuno.

74r
Hildegard to Abbot Kuno

Before 1155

Hildegard responds to Kuno's request for her to send anything she has written about St. Disibod by sending three musical compositions. At the same time, she cannot refrain from admonishing him about the evils of his life.

O how foolish is the man who does not amend his own life, and yet delves into other people's private affairs and, with a torrent of words like rushing waters, noises abroad all the vices that he finds hidden there. Let the man who does this hear the words of the Lord: O man, once having tasted of good works, why are you deaf to their music, for they resound before God like a symphony? Why do you not examine your own heart and reject your unabashed lasciviousness? I am the One who brings the lost sheep back to the fold, the One to whom you should always turn, but you fail to do so, and thereby slap me in the face, rejecting my wounded hands and feet. And so you will answer to me concerning the house of your own heart and concerning the city which I made and washed in the blood of the Lamb. Why are you not afraid to break the man that you did not create? You fail to anoint him and, therefore, neither cover nor protect him, but, rather, you afflict him too grievously with the heavy rod of correction. Now the period of your decline is at hand, but God, who created you, does not wish to lose you. Therefore, take these things to heart.

But, father, because you have asked me to send you anything that I have seen or learned about the blessed Disibod, your patron, I am writing to say that I heard some things about him in a vision of the spirit, and I saw and understood them in the following way:[1]

O mirum admirandum

O Wondrous Wonder
That a hidden form prevails
and climbs the heights of integrity
where the Living Eminence
pronounces His mysteries.
And so you, O Disibod,
with the help of that flower
on all the boughs of all the world,[a]
you will rise at last,
as you rose in the beginning.

O viriditas digiti Dei

O invigorating power of the finger of God,[b]
in which God planted a garden
which shimmers on the heights
like a steadfast column:

You are glorious in the eternal garden of God.

And you, O lofty mountain,
you will never be brought low
by God's judgment.
And yet you stand afar like an exile;
still, you stand not in the power
of the armed man
who would carry you off.[c]

You are glorious in the eternal garden of God.

Glory to the Father and the Son
and the Holy Spirit.

You are glorious in the eternal garden of God.

O presul vere civitatis

O prelate of the true city,
you who ascend to heaven
in the temple of the Cornerstone;
you were laid low on earth
through God's will.

You, O pilgrim, set apart from worldly seed,[d]
you desired to be an exile
for the love of Christ.
O mountain of the cloister of the mind,[e]
you diligently disclosed your beautiful face
in the mirror of the dove.[f]

You hid yourself in a secret place,
inebriated by the fragrance of flowers,
shining for God
through a lattice of saints.[g]

O pinnacle in the cloisters of heaven,
you sold this world
for the resplendent life:
this prize, O sustaining confessor,
you have always in the Lord.

In your mind
the living fountain poured forth
the purest rivers in blazing light
through the way to salvation.

You are a mighty tower
before the altar of the most high God,
and you have covered the summit of the tower
with the smoke of aromatic herbs.[h]

O Disibod,
through your light
with patterns of pure sound
you have built a body of wondrous praise
in two choirs
through the Son of man.

You stand on the heights,
unashamed before the living God,
and with life-sustaining dew you protect
those who glorify God in this song.[i]

O sweet life
and O blessed perseverance,
which brought forth, ever,
in celestial Jerusalem
the glorious light in this blessed Disibod.

Now, praise be to God
for the manly work
in the form of a beautiful tonsure.

And let the heavenly citizens rejoice
over those who emulate them
in this manner.

And you, O father, who have asked these things of me, make your own self a poor wretched creature in the sight of God, like me, so that when the time of your death comes in this world, your felicity may be lengthened out to all eternity, and you may receive the salvation of the just.

Note

1. The following texts are translated from Newman, *Symphonia* (pp. 180, 182, 186–88), since Van Acker does not include the hymns, but refers the reader to Newman instead.

75
Hildegard to the Abbot

About 1155(?)

It is impossible to determine whether this letter was addressed to Abbot Kuno of Disibod or his successor Helengerus. The letter details the treatment she received when she returned to negotiate over the question of property that Hildegard felt belonged properly to her own newly established institution, but that matter dragged on for a long time and was dealt with by both abbots. For the sake of simplicity, Van Acker assumes Kuno as recipient, hence his dating, "before 1155," the year of Kuno's death. One can see how embittered the monks of her former monastery were toward Hildegard by her depiction (however exaggerated) of her reception during her visit. Note, too, her apparent need still to justify her departure.

O you who are a father in your office—and how happy I am to say it—I pray that now you may be father to me in deed. I returned to the place[1] where God has bequeathed to you the rod of his authority. But a mob of some of your monks rose up and gnashed their teeth at me, as if I were a bird of gloom or a horrid beast, and they bent their bows against me in order to drive me away. But I know for a fact that God moved me from that place for His own inscrutable purposes, for my soul was so agitated by His words and miracles that I believe I would have died before my time if I had remained there.[a]

Now, salvation and blessing upon those who received me there with devotion; as for those others who wagged their heads at me [Lam 2.15; Ps 21.8; 108.25], may God extend His grace to them, as He sees fit in His mercy.

Alas, O my mother,[2] with what sorrow and grief you have received me.

Notes

1. That is, to St. Disibod
2. That is, the monastery at St. Disibod.

76
Abbot Helengerus[1] to Hildegard
About 1170

Helengerus confesses his sinfulness in this time when monastic life has fallen off, and asks Hildegard to send a letter to console him in his wretchedness.

To Hildegard, his beloved mother and more worthy to be embraced than any other precious thing, Helengerus, her son and overseer of the flock of the blessed Disibod, overseer not in deed but only in name, alas, sends whatever is better than temporal good.

Although the whole world rightly proclaims that you are enriched with the joy of the Holy Spirit, I (who should have been the first to invite others to come to you, blessed lady) have remained hidden in my sloth. But now, seized by fear and love, I have found it necessary to address you in this letter.

For I have been too concerned to establish my superiority over those I should be serving, seeking my own advantage more than theirs.[a] But I have endured the oppressive heat of the day while working in the Lord's vineyard—although halfheartedly—and I have resolved to persevere, with God's help, until I eventually receive my penny [cf. Matt 20.1–16]. But now, O my mother, the spiritual wine at the Lord's wedding feast has completely run out [cf. John 2.2–3], because the enthusiasm for monastic life is all but dead, since the mother of Jesus is not there, nor Jesus himself, and indeed not even his disciples are invited. And, therefore, all manner of hostile forces come out against us.

There is no need for me to detain you with my prolixity, especially since I am unskilled in speech and knowledge. I know, my mother, I know that there is no goodness in me, none from head to toe. Therefore, please send a letter to console me in my wretchedness, for then your name will be inscribed in the book of eternal life on Zion. Farewell.

Note

1. Helengerus succeeded Kuno as abbot of Disibod in 1155 and remained in office until 1179.

76r
Hildegard to Abbot Helengerus
About 1170

Hildegard writes a harsh letter to Helengerus, whom she finds useless and unstable.

In a spiritual vision which I received from God, I heard these words: If, amidst his desires, a man wishes to find his soul, he must abandon the wicked works of the flesh and affirm that God-given knowledge of the way to conduct his life. And so let his soul be the lady[1] and his flesh his handmaiden, as the Psalmist says: "Blessed is the man whom thou shalt instruct, O Lord: and shalt teach him out of thy law" [Ps 93.12]. And who is this man? Why, he is the one who keeps his body under control like his handmaiden, and cherishes his soul as the lady he loves and serves. For the person who is impiously ferocious like a bear, but then renounces that ferocity and sighs in his soul for the loyal and merciful Sun of justice [cf. Mal 4.2]—that one pleases God. And God gives him charge over His precepts, placing in his hands an iron rod [cf. Ps 2.9] to teach his sheep the way to the mountain of myrrh [cf. Cant 4.6].

Now, listen and learn so that in the inwardness of your soul you will be ashamed. Sometimes you are like a bear which growls under its breath; but sometimes like an ass, not prudent in your duties, but, rather, worn down. Indeed, in some matters you are altogether useless, so that, in your impiety, you do not even put the malice of the bear into practice. You are also like certain kinds of birds, which do not fly on the heights and yet do not hug the earth, neither excelling nor being subject to harm.[2a]

The great Father of the household responds to character of this kind: Ah, I do not like the shiftiness of your character, with your mind growling at my justice and failing to seek the proper solution from it, nursing instead a kind of growling inside yourself, like the growling of a bear. But when you do get a flash of insight, you pray for a little while, and then you grow weary again, and you do not even bother to finish your prayer, but you take the road which your body knows well, and you never fully renounce it. But sometimes your desires rise up to me concerning some aspect which is not wholly sanctified by works, but resting only on your general acceptance of the faith. I sometimes have chosen people of unstable disposition like you so that I might hear the sound of their intellect, that is, what they were thinking to themselves. But when they were found to be of no use, they also fell. Therefore, do not let your mind despise the work which God does, for you do not know when He will strike you with His sword.

Poor little woman that I am, I see a black fire in you kindled against us,[3] but use your good knowledge to consign it to oblivion, lest the grace and blessing of God depart from you during your time in office. Therefore, love the justice of God so that you may be loved by God, and faithfully trust in His miracles so that you may receive the eternal rewards.

Notes

1. *domina*. Note the play with secular and divine love in this letter.
2. Although there are problems in these first two paragraphs of this letter, the inner logic of the passage seems to demand the rendering we have given. A large part of the problem stems from the extreme grammatical looseness of the passage. See Introduction. A further problem, of course, is why she would have him bring the "malice" of the bear to fruition, unless heavy sarcasm is intended: he does not even have enough character—and note that it is that word she employs in her comparisons with bear and ass—to perfect his bear-like malice. That is, he is lukewarm, a characteristic deadly sin in Hildegard's register of sins.
3. The problems that they are having stem from Hildegard's attempt to secure property rights consequent upon her move to Mount St. Rupert.

77
Abbot Helengerus to Hildegard
About 1170

Helengerus seeks to make peace between Mount St. Disibod and Mount St. Rupert. He again asks Hildegard for any writing she will produce about his patron, St. Disibod.

Helengerus, by the grace of God servant on Mount St. Disibod and overseer, though unworthy, of the Lord's flock there, along with the whole congregation of brothers, sends greetings to the venerable mother, Lady Hildegard of St. Rupert, who is fully illumined by the ray of divine splendor beyond all human understanding, as we know very well. May you abound in the gifts of the septiform Holy Spirit [cf. Apoc 1.4, 3.1], and may you offer the cup of the holy fountain to the thirsty, so that you may receive your reward in heaven.

We know, beloved mother, that you recently came to us at the prompting, and indeed at the command, of the Paraclete, the holy spirit of Almighty God, "who wishes all men to be saved and to come to the knowledge of the truth" [I Tim 2.4]. And thus we offer our ceaseless, though unworthy, thanks to that Paraclete as best we can, because, to confess the truth, we have become fully aware of the burning power and strength of His illumination among us and indeed within us. At the same time we have, with one accord, cast off the inveterate hostility and animosity that we have nurtured for many years now, and we have come together fully into the unity of genuine divine love, as with one body and one spirit.[a]

With earnest prayers we knock at the gate of your love, saintly lady, beseeching that you look to that brightness conferred upon you by divine grace and reveal to us whether, in fact, we are united in true love, which is the beginning of all good things, or if some root of dissension still lies unseen between us.[b] For it is through this brightness that things concealed are disclosed to your love and things hidden from all other mortals are opened up to the eyes of your heart. Indeed, this is something you owe us as a debt, because you (along with your sisters) are the one who left us, admittedly not in spirit but only in body as we hope, and, indeed, know in truth. But with these minor matters out of the way—which, after all, we have already confessed—may we now request that you reveal to us in writing all the other, more important matters which you know to be contrary to the eyes of divine majesty.

In this regard, all of us in full unanimity pound upon the gate of your love, beseeching you earnestly, fervently, for a written account of the deeds, virtues, and life of our patron, the blessed Disibod[1]—and not only ours, of course, but yours, for you were nourished under his roof from your earliest years. And we earnestly urge you, pious lady, and, with unwearying prayers poured forth, desire that you make known to us whatever God reveals to you about him, so that the memory of your own blessedness may be preserved through this record in praise of this our father.

May the almighty Father of eternal compassion inflame your devout mind with His radiant light, and may He offer to those who so sincerely desire it the cup that rekindles to life.

Note

1. This request was fulfilled by Hildegard's life of the saint.

77r
Hildegard to Abbot Helengerus
About 1170

Originally published (by Pitra) as "Proem to the life of St. Disibod," this piece is more "sermon" than "letter," but a sermon with direct application to Mount

St. Disibod since, as she makes clear in the sermon itself, it was delivered there. Hildegard is at her most eloquent here in her disquisition on salvation history and the creation, on the active and contemplative life, et cetera.

When all of creation came forth at God's command, many stars, which were at that time innumerable in the light, fell with that one who was called Lucifer, and the night of death was prepared for those who fell. But the planets, that is, the angels of justice who are flames of fire, remained firm by God, and they served the inextinguishable fire, which is life. But the fire has a flame which the wind quickens, so that the flame becomes a blazing fire. Thus the word is in the voice and the word is heard, and the fire has a flame and it is praise to God, and the wind moves the flame and it is praise to God, and the word is in the voice and it is praise to God, and the word is heard and it is praise to God. Therefore, all of creation is praise to God.[a]

He who does not fear does not love, and he who does not praise does not work.[1] And fear is a fire, and divine love spreads out like a flame. Thus creation is praise, and man is work. If there were no created thing, however, man would not know how to work. But creation came forth at God's command, and this was God's plan, because He made man to His image and likeness.

For when the falling stars did not praise God, nor recount His works, the night of death was written for them, because they disregarded life and had contempt for God's works, and thus they were reduced to nothing. For it was God's great plan that those fallen angels could by no means prevail against His might, and He foresaw that through a feminine nature He would make such a work that neither angels nor man nor any other creature could themselves accomplish.[b] Yet after God formed man, the fallen angels came at him with false delusions—because they themselves are false—and so man became subject to death.

But God foresaw in Abel those planets who had stood firm by Him, because He is the praise of angels and of men, and He established in Abel the foundation of the sacerdotal office and of His temple, for which reason he suffered death in the body. From the time of Abel to the time of Noah, all the sons of mankind were, as it were, asleep to proper knowledge, like infants at the breast.[c] But at God's command Noah built the ark, through which God prefigured that He had preserved mankind, like the angels, for the purpose of praising Him. And Abraham performed a great work of obedience, which, through circumcision, wounded the head of the ancient serpent, and thus God confounded him because he had filled mankind with lust, and it was that sensuality which the Virgin ground underfoot when she gathered the unicorn into her lap.[2] For it was the unicorn which, in accordance with the ancient plan, put on the robe of flesh in the Virgin's womb. Moreover, Moses wrote the Law, which obedience made clear through the mortification of the flesh. Through this law, the seducer who had wounded mankind's flesh was confounded, and the craftiness that he used to deceive mankind through pride was brought to an end through the mortification of the flesh by the faithful.

Both Abraham and Moses were like two planets heralding the incarnation of the Son of God, just as the planets are like a flame of fire. Abraham foresaw

Christ [cf. Gen 14.18ff; Heb 7.1ff], but Moses performed His deeds through animals. That is, by offering up bulls and sheep and goats—through the sacrifice of the flesh of animals—he prefigured the sacrifice of the Son of God. This came to fruition when the Virgin captured the unicorn and when God, as was fitting, made the ivory tower [cf. Cant 7.4], which is a pure virginal work. And in this, the work of the great plan was perfected, that is, because God is man.[d] For because the woman, who obeyed the word of the serpent, cast the whole world into darkness, death entered into her, and she became a weak infant, and every creature, although once strong and noble, became debilitated because of her weakness.

But God ordained his great plan in her, something so miraculous that neither angels nor humankind nor any creature can grasp it, a design through which a virgin in the sunlight of the ancient plan reversed the fall of woman, transforming it into good. And God did this to confound the devil, who had deceived the woman, himself totally unaware of what was to be accomplished through her, just as he did not truly know God, and, therefore, was buried in hell, deprived of all felicity.[3]

For God by his command made all created things to fulfill their proper function, and these preceded man in order to serve him. Then, He created mankind and bestowed all His works upon him, so that if he chooses the good, God will help him, but if he gives in to evil, the devil lays ambushes for him from the north, because man has the two wings of reason, that is to say, the knowledge of good and evil. After all, a word does not exist apart from the voice, and a voice cannot be understood without words. Sometimes one may hear a voice, and yet be unable to make sense of it, but word and voice working together declare all things—both the useful and the useless. Thus knowledge is as indispensable to reason as internal organs are to a human being.

Now it is necessary to speak about the way a man begins to do his work. First, he sucks his mother's milk. Then, he takes soft, mushy food, babbling with childish contentment. Afterward, in the third age he masticates with his teeth, and, with full awareness, chooses what he wishes and casts aside that which he does not want. Then, he is a young man. Finally, he enters the state of mature age, so that his brain is filled with all knowledge, with the result that he forgets the age of milk and all the other states, and his new state completely fulfills him, and he knows truth.

Thus the age of milk was before the flood, the age of pablum in the time of Noah, and the age of mastication and choice of food was the time of Abraham. But in the age of Moses all childish works came to an end, when through the offering of a sacrificial animal, he foreshadowed the truth and touched the Son of God. And in him all previous ages were completed and changed to the better, when he in the fullness of his years taught wisdom and truth.

But a girl's youth is sometimes lustful, when, that is, she runs after vanity in her wantonness, but if she is really a virgin, she shows it in many ways by her physical and moral deportment, just as, if she is not a virgin, there will be many clear signs of it. For if a virgin directs her gaze to heaven so that she truly abandons the world, she imitates the Son of God and waits upon God, the one who told the serpent that his head would be bruised by woman [cf. Gen 3.15], because his beginnings were evil, so that the Virgin was destined to trample him underfoot, that is to say, she who bore the Son of God.

For a new age began with the Son of God through the water of redemption, and He gathered unto himself those two planets which adorned his incarnation, that is, virgins and monks. These planets had not appeared before His nativity, but arose with it, heralding Him, just as the morning star heralds the sun. Thus signs and miracles blazed forth more abundantly than ever before, since He touched the earth through his humanity. Therefore, that which had been declared by the voices of the prophets before, the Son of God now worked out fully in his own person, just as it is written: "Thou art beautiful above the sons of men" [Ps 44.3]. And just as the secret Son of God came secretly into the world, so, too, He gathered to Himself a foreign nature, that is, those who give up the world and the pomp of the world.[4] But just as the star revealed Him to devout people, who, in turn, illumined the whole world, so, too, virgins and monks once adorned the Church, and all people spoke of them as if they were angels, just as the prophet had exclaimed about them, "Who are these, that fly as clouds, and as doves to their windows?" [Isa 60.8]. And the same spirit that declared that also said, "Behold a virgin shall conceive, and bear a son, and his name shall be called Emmanuel" [Isa 7.14].

Thus through various signs the Son of God was gradually revealed to all creation, since wisdom does not act in haste, but looks ahead diligently to see that there is no flaw in all its arrangements. A foolish man does not act in this way, but he hastily puts into action whatever he hastily dreams up. And so frequently his work is not well thought out, as was true of the first angel, who, in the impetuous estimation of his own honor, fell into the black lake in the twinkling of an eye, where, as a result, he lost all his ornaments and gave himself up to the black and inextinguishable fire.

The aforementioned planets, however, kept running through their various signs with great honor and the reverence appropriate to their religious calling, until the time of a certain tyrant who began to embrace the counsel of the ancient serpent.[5] And then a womanish time came, a time almost as grievous as the first fall, so that all justice was debilitated like to the infirmity of woman.[e] And in such a manner, the time will rush along past its midpoint, but amid great calamities an elephant[6] will call forth justice, causing a new time to arise, and thus a fruitful time of just wars and righteousness will come.

Now, however, all these things are spoken as a warning to the people of this place, that is, how their way of religious life began, what its status is now, and how it will be in the future. For this monastery was born in the blazing sun with such great strength of the spiritual people (as if it were dead to the things of this world) and also in such great simplicity that out of their love for the abundance lavished on them by God their guardian, they felt no compulsion to receive worldly people among them, refusing to cater to anyone because of his high station, but rather remaining steadfast in the rigor of their monastic way of life. At first, they were like a fire, but they did not spread their flame abroad, being completely indifferent to other people, because, like eagles, they were directing their gaze to heaven. Afterward, like a hart to the fountains of waters [cf. Ps 41.2], they ran to the better part [cf. Luke 10.42], ascending from virtue to virtue [cf. Ps 83.8], and in the light of divine love they shone for God and for men. And since they were inflamed with their love of God, they were therefore the praise of God among the people, just as a planet is a flame of fire.

Then many praised those people like precious stones—topaz, emerald, sapphire, and jacinth—because they had prepared themselves for the better part and arose from virtue unto virtue [cf. Ps 83.8] and spread themselves abroad in divine love for the people. For through the active life, they looked to all people with hospitality and acts of mercy and at the same time they kept their gaze fixed on Mount Zion, and for this reason everyone called them the daughters of Zion.[7] For in obedience—with Abraham—they worked for the mortification of the flesh, and in the sweet odor of the Rule—with Moses—they cast aside the pomp of the world, and on account of the humility of the incarnation of Jesus Christ, they made themselves vile in the eyes of the world.

But, later, a pale cloud of vainglory and pride came over the fire of their good works, like a cloud that obscures the sun so that it is barely seen, and storms came upon them and cast them down, although they, later, did manage to struggle haltingly to their feet. But only a little, for the pale cloud of vainglory and pride rendered their fire virtually invisible, that fire which is discipline and the good conduct which is prescribed by the Rule.[8] And so while attempting to maintain spiritual values, they also stooped to embrace secular mores, and have continued to do so almost to the present day. And now they are all bent over, because they have a defect in their understanding of the two sides of the disposition of wisdom. For heaven is properly ordained for praise, and earth is properly established for dispensing justice.[9] Heaven and earth are like the soul and the body, and earth desires what heaven refuses to praise, so that the two of them are at continual war with one another, and yet they are both instruments of God. For because of the lust of the flesh, the body hungers after sin, while the soul, for its part, stands always in opposition to such fleshly longings, and yet they are one instrument of God.

But those to whom this sermon is directed hold that the pomp of the world and the point of their monastic life are one. But this, in all wisdom, cannot be. They wish it to be so, but it can never be. Therefore, they are bent down to the knees like the Samaritans, who refused the rule of law and worshipped a foreign god [cf. Hosea 10.5]. Thus they are darkened in their works as by a pale cloud, so that the burning sun of the high principles of the Rule is obscured in them. And so great storms of harm befall them, because they become the servants of those whom, rightly (because of their own true service to God), they should rule.[10] And yet they are their servants, servants of those who do not see the blazing sun in them. For man was made, and he has works, but his virtues are praise, and those that he performs with his right hand are done in the Holy Spirit, but those performed with the left turn, with the devilish host, to the north.

Hear, therefore: Shame, which is the enemy of virtue, walks among you on one foot, like the foot of a ram, since you are all bent over. But look to the honorable knight and imitate him, who defended himself with his sword although he had fallen on his knees before his enemies, and with strength renewed again and again, he, happily, stood up and continued the battle. Stand ready, therefore, and kill your enemies with your sword. For your sword is obedience and the precepts of the Rule, but your enemies are disobedience and failure to abide by the precepts of the Rule, as well as pride and neglect of your true calling. For by such lapses you have been beaten down so that you can scarcely rise to your knees.

But the time of great strain and destruction has not yet arrived, that time of immense pressure which squeezes the juice from the grape in the winepress.[f] Nevertheless, the present age is still a time most vile. Therefore, look to times past, consider how honorable they were, and, in this way, defend yourself from your enemies, for God will not refuse you his aid. Indeed, a time of righteousness and morality will come soon, a time which will look back to the first dawn,[g] and those who abandon the world out of their love of God will sigh to God and thus will persevere in good. And then the people will raise a loud cry about them in the Holy Spirit: "The voice of the turtle dove is heard in our land" [Cant 2.12], that is, the voice of the hermits and pilgrims of this world who look so assiduously to heaven that they yearn to take the strait path which leads to heaven. These look at all things past, both favorable and unfavorable, so that they may take thought how to escape the ravenous hawk, like a dove which flies away at the hawk's reflection in the water.

Listen to me once more: There is still some bright and fiery light among you, although it flickers unsteadily: bright with your good intentions, fiery with your fear of the Lord, although still flickering foolishly. Guard yourselves against that black putrescence which opposes God and men, and which indeed is the heart of the devil, because the devil, in the might of his full will, throws his spear at those who are caught in their sins.

And so, poor, wretched little woman that I am, I saw and heard these words in the mystic vision which God has used to instruct me from my infancy, and I was ordered from my sickbed to proclaim these things in person to your monastery.[h] Therefore, do not despise them or reject them, lest you die on earth. But may the Holy Spirit build his tabernacle in you, and bring you to a good end, for your monastery has been blessed because the Lord gathered it from the common people for His service, just as He has done from the beginning, for He has always preserved some people as His heritage. Keep yourselves from shame, lest it walk among you on two feet,[11] for if that happens God will strike you with His terrible vengeance, although this has not yet befallen you. And so He has defended you in all your dangers. But when you work your own will to the exclusion of all else, as if you were not to look to God, then harm will befall you, and you will fall into those misfortunes which I have heretofore proclaimed.

Notes

1. See John 5.17 "But Jesus answered them: My Father worketh until now; and I work." This concept of work, divine and human, has evident significance—although

Van Acker neglects to cite the reference—for this entire passage, as is made clear by the ending phrase "because He made man to His image and likeness." *Fearing* and *loving*, *praising* and *working*—these are her images for the active and contemplative lives.

2. See Letter 15r, note 22.
3. See Letter 15r, note 23.
4. See Introduction for a discussion of this passage.
5. This "certain tyrant," who marks the beginning of the "womanish age," is probably Henry IV, as Barbara Newman (*Sister of Wisdom*, p. 239) notes. The time frame is certainly correct, since Henry reigned as emperor of the Holy Roman Empire until 1106. In the *Vita*, Hildegard marks the beginning of this age at around 1100, near the date of her own birth.
6. For such beast prophecies, cf. *Scivias*, especially Book III.
7. The nuances of this clause—*unde et ab omnibus filie Sion nominati sunt*—are impossible to render into English. The subject—*filie*—is clearly feminine, while the past participle—*nominati*—is just as clearly masculine. The use of the feminine form is dictated by theological concerns, an allusion to Cant 3.11.
8. I.e., the *Rule* of St. Benedict.
9. Further images of the active and contemplative lives.
10. Hildegard is speaking of the relationship between the monks and their patrons.
11. For at present Shame walks among them only on one foot, as she says earlier.

78
Prior Adelbert to Hildegard
1150–55

Adelbert wonders why Hildegard, who was nurtured among them, has left Mount St. Disibod, and now ministers to other people more than to her former friends at Mount St. Disibod.

To Hildegard, truly filled with the grace of the Holy Spirit, Adelbert, monk (though unworthy) and prior at Mount St. Disibod, along with the brothers of that same monastery, sends our prayers that you may ascend from virtue unto virtue and may see the God of gods in Zion [cf. Ps 83.8].

Since you send the words of your admonition into foreign regions and cause large numbers of people to desire the paths of righteousness, we (who have known you almost from the cradle and with whom you lived for many years) wonder why you have withdrawn the words of your celestial visions from us who thirst for them.

We remember how you were educated among us, how you were taught, how you were established in the religious life. For your instruction was that appropriate only to a woman,[1] and a simple psalter was your only schoolbook. Yet without complaint you embraced the good and holy religious life. But the will of God filled you with celestial dew [cf. Gen 27.28] and opened up to you the magnitude of its secrets. And just as we were set to rejoice in these things with you, God took you away from us against our will, and gave you to other people. We cannot fathom why God did this, but, willy-nilly, we are suffering great distress from the deed. For we had hoped that the salvation of our monastery rested with you, but God disposed matters differently than we wished. Now, however, since we cannot stand against the will of God, we have yielded to it and rejoice with you, for through divine revelation you make many things clear that were, before, unseen and unheard, and you open doors that were closed before. Indeed, filled, as you are, with the Holy Spirit, you write many things which you never learned from man, things that holy and learned men[2] marvel at.

Wherefore, although we are far from holy (because we remain sinners), we beseech you, both for the glory of God and for old and true fellowship, to remember us and to offer us some words of consolation. We ask also that you seek God's help for us, so that that which is least in us God may deign to supplement through the merits of your prayers. Farewell.

Notes

1. Her first instruction was also only *by* a woman, the nun Jutta, in whose care Hildegard was placed when she was dedicated to the religious life at the age of eight.

2. The writer makes a distinction here between *mankind* and *men:* Hildegard has not learned from *homines* "mankind" those things that holy and learned *viri* "men" marvel at.

78r
Hildegard to the Congregation of Monks

1150–55

A sermon to the monks of St. Disibod.

In a true vision I heard a voice saying these things against the injuries done to justice by both spiritual and secular people: O Justice, you are a pilgrim and stranger in the city of those people who make up fables to justify their own misguided will, and although you are the purple-clad friend of the king, they long neither to learn your mysteries nor to obtain your friendship. Thus you cry out against that fate, against which no real justice can keep quiet, and you say in grief: I am so terribly ashamed that I hide my face in my cloak, lest my betrayers see me. They, however, say: Whatever we devise is good for everyone. And, therefore, O Justice, you are zealous to see to it that whoever resists you is liable to judgment.

And again, O Justice, you say in your grief: Where did I come from? From the bosom of the Father. And all the regions of the earth were my kingdom. And when all the statutes of the nations and all the institutes of the generations were laid down, there I was present. And so the pillars of a cloud were erected upon me.[1] Now, however, I have become a tedium to those who were born of my domain in the first root.[2] Yet as much as I grieve for them, I sigh even more over the ignorance of the people, and, like pouring waters, so is my shrill roar like the sound of many waters [cf. Apoc 1.15; Ezech 43.2] on account of the excessiveness of foolish men in the bombast of their morals and the screeching of their dishonesty. Alas, O eagles, with my help you passed through the fire of the Holy Spirit and through the water of salvation, which is red like the dawn and flashing like a gem, but now you are asleep, and you act like dumb beasts, sometimes going forward, sometimes going backward, and sometimes mingling aimlessly with one another.

But about the mountain of the sons of God, I saw these things by mystic inspiration: I saw a lofty mountain, on whose peak a large man sat, and in both hands, like Moses, he held the law of God like a document. And under this man's feet a crowd gathered, people who had received spiritual circumcision, and they all received the documents of his law with joy and sighs, saying: O our Lord God, when will we come to thee? We will gladly obey thee. But sometimes they were tossed about by a whirlwind, and sometimes great sins were found amongst them, sins which, with many tears, they washed away in the sprinkling of the blood of Jesus Christ [cf. I Pet 1.2]. For when mankind wallowed in such great sins, because, lacking vital force, he was unable to raise himself from them by his own power, God said: I want to raise mankind up by My own power, and to plant him anew with a heart of compassion, so that he may abide in the mirror of confession. For by his own strength, he has not been able to extricate himself from the bowels of the devil.[3] But, poor little woman that I am, although I saw many sins in these people, I did not see in them that pride which obstinately condemns sinners to death by stoning.

And under their feet, in turn, I saw another crowd of men with beautiful faces, enveloped in a white cloud. They gazed at heaven, but like fat bulls they sometimes grew perverse because of their meddling in all sorts of useless things. Although they directed their gaze to heaven, they stretched their bows and fired arrows into heaven and beat against it with leaden clubs [cf. Matt 11.12], and thus "They have set their mouth against heaven: and their tongue hath passed through the earth" [Ps 72.9]. And therefore it thundered over them and hail fell upon them, and thick clouds concealed them. And they murmured in wonder why they were mired in such squalor.

And the grace of God responded to them: I chose you to be highly blessed, but you rashly reject me when you ask who is able to reach up to you or what word can overcome you or what hills or trees can strike you. You are acting just like the children of Israel who rejected God even though, through the blessing of Abraham, He lifted the horn of blessings over them and raised them up into His bosom. Still, they murmured against the Lord and rashly opposed God, and they gave up their sanctity through the shedding of Christ's blood. Then their blessing departed from them and vanished completely, for they turned away and rushed headlong to death. And God has built a new city, the Church, from their sacrifices and burnt offerings, while all the waters of the wells are drawn out into the valley of the black clouds. And then all the eagles will be gathered together into one flock on the turning wheel, because, earlier, they were included in the blessing.

And under their feet I saw a third crowd of men, before whose eyes a ram hung on golden thorns, redolent with myrrh and incense, and its face was like flashing lightning. And from the hands of that large man who sat on the peak of the mountain, rivulets flowed into their hearts. And with a clear tone they shouted to the bosom of wisdom: God once gathered us together with many sacrifices, but we have fallen away in many of our obligations. And thus we have been placed on the winepress, saying with the prophet: "I have trodden the winepress alone, and of the gentiles there is not a man with me" [Isa 63.3]. And again: When they cast the net into the sea and all kinds of fish were gathered in, they chose the good ones and put them in vessels [cf. Matt 13.47–48]. Just so the grace of God chose out for glory those who were humble of heart and devout in the fear of the Lord, not trusting to violence [see Matt 11.12].

Now may the first voice who gathered you to praise God establish you in the root of goodness, just as he did those first ones who were consecrated within the temple. But you, O mountain, hear the admonition of God: God established you like Mt. Sinai to offer unto Him the sacrifice of praise [cf. Ps 115.17]. But now turn to your God and be the king's candelabrum, so that you may not be ashamed in your first root, for the right hand of God has planted you there.

Notes

1. See Ex 33.9, where Moses, the lawgiver, speaks with God in a pillar of cloud at the door of the tabernacle.

2. Hildegard's frequently used metaphor for the generation of Adam and Eve.

3. The wordplay is difficult to render in English: *"Volo hominem per memetipsum erigere ac denuo in uisceribus misericordie plantare, ita ut in speculo confessionis resideat qui se de uisceribus diaboli per se ipsum eripere non potuit."*

79
Hildegard to a Certain Monk
Before 1170

A brief admonition to a monk of St. Disibod.

Your mouth is heavenly and your mind flowers forth like a cloud. Therefore, may your roots flourish. So worship your Lord God, and, putting on the breastplate of God [cf. Ephes 6.14], fight against bacchanalian vices, fleeing lust and refusing to embrace avarice. Then God, whom you pray to in secret, will receive you in His love.

80
Morard, Monk, to Hildegard[1]
Before 1173

The monk Morard reminds Hildegard of his visit to Mount St. Rupert and asks to be remembered to the sisters, whose prayers he seeks.

To Hildegard, most beloved and honorable mother and lady in Christ, Morard, monk and priest (though unworthy), sends that little that he has.

If it were fitting to boast—and indeed it is proper to boast in the Lord—I should congratulate myself, not in myself, of course, but in the Lord [cf. II Cor 11.30; 12.1], Who granted the grace of friendship with one of your sanctity to a person of such unworthiness as myself, a boon which my humility neither merited nor presumed to hope for. I give thanks from the bottom of my heart first to divine compassion and then to you, worthy lady, because you treated me well when I was in your presence and considered me worthy of your greetings in my absence. Therefore, kindly lady, I ask that you deign to greet for me all your fellow sisters, my cherished ladies, and advise them not to let the consolation of their society and their prayers (which they promised me) vanish from their memory. For my part, I, as far as the Lord has allowed me, have fully done and continue to do all those things which I promised them, as God knows. Indeed, I am confident that as long as I have life I will not cease praying for all of you, so that the grace of God, which aids you so abundantly, may follow you closely and crush Satan under your feet [cf. Rom 16.20]. Thus may I, puny as I am, be able to obtain, with your prayers, the salvation I do not deserve.

Concerning the other things which I conferred with you about in secret, you will, I know, inform me in writing when the time is ripe. Fare you well in the Lord, always.

Note

1. Three MSS give only the initial *M.* to designate this correspondent—both here and in Hildegard's response. Only one MS gives the full name Morard of Disibod, which Van Acker accepts, but has not been able to confirm.

80r
Hildegard to the Monk Morard

Before 1173

Hildegard gives advice to Morard in allegorical form.

Dear son, hear this parable which I saw in a true vision.

A certain noble and beautiful lady had a room ornamented all in gold, and frequently she chose two girls with lovely faces to live with her. And great multitudes saw this lady, praised her beauty, and desired to live with her. But she said to them: I will give you gifts which please you, but it would be profitable, neither to me nor to you, for us to be together. For I am unwilling to give my nobility and my beauty to wolves and dogs to be derided. But a certain wrinkled old woman, with blotched and ruddy complexion, wanted to make herself like this noble lady, and was jealous of her nobility and beauty. This wrinkled woman walks over the mountains, and runs in all sorts of regions and countries, seeking praise and honor. And nobody gives anything to her, but they all say: This disturbed and undisciplined creature is of the devil, and everybody ought to drive her away.

Also, a woman merchant collected all sorts of beautiful, eye-catching things, and she gave thought to how she could bring all kinds of unknown and marvellous things to the attention of mankind. But, later, she placed a very beautiful, pure crystal in the blazing light of the sun, and it caught fire from the sun and gave light to all people. Thenceforth, as a result, she exercised all her arts in moderation.

Now, my son, pay heed to that first woman and her virgins, but flee that wrinkled, old woman with all your might. Put your whole heart, however, with the merchant woman. For the first woman is Divine Love, with her virgins who are Benevolence and Generosity. But the wrinkled, old woman with the blotched complexion is Love of the World, that shameful longing through which lustful people become entangled with one another. But the merchant woman is Philosophy, who created every art and who found the crystal, faith, by which one comes to God.

I believe in God that you will partake of the better part, for, through the fiery crystal, you have offered up the gifts of the passion and the resurrection of the Lord to God.

Eberbach
81
Hildegard to the Abbot Ruthard
1153–54

General advice offered through a host of (rather mixed) metaphors. Ruthard is abbot of a Cistercian monastery.

He Who Is says: The Serene Light sees the abode and the appointed meal of each congregation, the members of which have the duty to distribute nourishment in proper moderation, lest the faithful fail to receive joy of the soul. A pastoral overseer is obliged to offer the sword in the sheath to the strong-minded, and to display the arrows in the quiver to those of high moral character, and to offer medicinal herbs to those filled with benevolence.[a] Yet evil tyrants bear the scourges of death. The brave knight fights, unwearied by derision. And Good Understanding labors to achieve sufficiency for the common good, and Morals feasting on righteousness are girt with all the virtues, and thus they hunger to bring justice to perfection. But savage men, strangers to the noble mother Mercy, slaughter the simple sheep in the king's hall. Alas, alas, such people who rage for murder will be exiled from the house of the king unless they repent, because they scatter the Lord's sheep.

But you, O shepherd, look kindly upon the miseries of those who are too weak in spirit to hold on to the plow of discipline. But surround yourself with good, benevolent people in the harmony of the Holy Spirit. Do not become torpid in the light, but let your intellect be watchful. And do not be duplicitous, so that you say one thing inwardly and quite another outwardly, for those who do this cover their faces in darkness. If, later, however, they become fearful because they do not hold in their hearts what they show in their faces, they are chastened and thus are snatched away from infidelity.

As for you, O man, your nourishment will come when you gird your loins, for in so doing you have your true desire in your possession, since then you are not neglecting the treasure of the true money. Worldly things are asleep for you, since the shipwreck of this world has not injured you.[b] At the end of your days, God will bring you back to life. For He has placed you in great honor. O good servant, you will praise Him, and He will save you in eternity.

82

Abbot Eberhard to Hildegard

Before 1166(?)

Eberhard requests Hildegard to intercede for him with the Almighty. One can clearly discern the influence of St. Bernard on this Cistercian abbot.

To the venerable lady and mother Hildegard in Bingen, beloved of God and of men, Brother Eberhard, abbot (although unworthy) of Eberbach, sends what little he has.

    Because of you, we magnify and glorify our Savior, Christ, who looks with favor on those who fear Him, and, although He is mighty, exalts the humble, and Who has done great things for you, because He is powerful. As we have heard and seen, He has chosen the shrine of your heart for His habitation. He has made divine knowledge, the unknown and hidden things of His wisdom manifest to you [cf. Ps 50.8], bringing you into His chamber, to the flowers of the rosebush and the lilies of the valley, to the flowery fields of the eternal mountains. His left hand is under your head and his right embraces you [cf. Cant 2.6; 8.3], so that you can truly say: "My beloved is mine, and I am his" [Cant 2.16]. In all these things your name is oil poured out [cf. Cant 1.2]. And so young women have esteemed you, and we run in the odor of your perfume [cf. Cant 1.3], and we pray God that He design to preserve the gifts of nature and the gifts of His grace for you—as a glory to Himself, as a crown for you, as a joy for us, as an example to many.

    We pray also, and we claim it with a humble prayer, that you design to be mindful of us, and, when your bridegroom comes, that you commend us, lowly as we are, to Him, so that, just as we rejoice and are glad at the fame of your sanctity, so through your intercession we may merit the joy and receive the exultation. If you design to require any service of us, we gladly embrace it. We will continue just as we have done, and we are prepared to faithfully serve all your holy will.

83

The Congregation of Monks to Hildegard

About 1165–66

A general request for admonition and consolation.

To Hildegard, whom the Lord chose as His handmaid and made partaker of His multitudinous secrets, a poor flock of brothers in Eberbach sends greetings with wishes that you be in that number of the wise virgins with the true lamp and the burning wedding torch, and that you may enter happily into the wedding feast with the Bridegroom of the faithful souls and the citizens of heaven [cf. Matt 25.1–13].

The Spirit of the Lord has never forsaken those whom He has predestined and chosen for Himself, but rather He has nourished their thoughts with His paternal gentleness. So He chose you, happy and blessed soul, as His instrument and the vessel of His election [cf. Acts 9.15].[a]

Beloved in the Lord, we are bound to obey your maternal admonition, for the truth of the Lord speaks through you. We have gladly received your admonitions, and we humbly pray you not to hide anything from us which we should amend in ourselves. And since it has pleased the Lord to reveal many secrets to you, please hasten to reveal to us that which we ought to correct. May the angel of counsel and of fortitude [cf. Isa 11.2], who is always near you, preserve you and keep you healthy and unharmed.

83r

Hildegard to the Congregation of Monks

About 1165–66

A letter of general admonition and consolation.

The mysteries of God command me to say these things in the shadow of the vision of God: You have climbed up a very high mountain and wish to look down into the valley. Meanwhile, a fierce storm has come upon you. Alas, for the languor that is in your loins, as David, the proven servant, says: "I walked sorrowful all the day long. For my loins are filled with illusions; and there is no health in my flesh" [Ps 37.7–8]. And so because of your neediness, your eyes are weak.

Beware, therefore, lest you cast aside that happiness which appears in you through God's predestination; do not cast it away on account of your excessive heedlessness in spiritual battles. For when God had made the face of the first angel like an exceedingly beautiful and blazing gem, that angel became heedless, and so his glory perished, because he desired nothing good. Then God planted his brightness in another vineyard. And since God will have nothing to do with evil, see to it that the special grace of God in you be not changed by the activity of the ancient serpent, because he rejoices in himself and says: I am delighted when I find discord among spiritual people, and I walk among them with a stiff neck.

Resist the devil, therefore, and let not the light of brightness fail in you, as it was taken from him because of his pride. For those who falter sometimes, but then rise up again, will not lose their heritage of God's grace. They will be bowed in the whirlwind of God's vengeance, and yet, afterward, God will rebuild in them the root of the first inception, the sacrifice made by God.

And I say to you, you who have been planted by God: The mysteries of God say about your monastery: I will never destroy you since you do not resist me in the evil heedlessness which refuses to be washed clean, like the heedlessness of diabolic craftiness, as I said before. But the Living Light blesses you with the blessing of Abraham.

84
A Prior to Hildegard[1]

About 1169

The prior asks Hildegard to send him her treatise on lay-brotherhood, a well-known problem within his Order. Soon after being founded—in the very year of Hildegard's birth—the Cistercian Order began making use of lay-brothers to help with the manual labor, to deal with secular affairs, et cetera. Rather than hiring day laborers or simply renting out their land (as the Benedictines regularly did), the Cistercians brought these laymen into the Order, making them, in effect, bona fide members of the monastic community, different from the choir-monks only with respect to liturgical functions and certain legal matters. Although this system of lay-brotherhood was not created by the Cistercians, it certainly became a distinctive characteristic of the Order, and it unquestionably led to the rapid and unparalleled expansion of the Order throughout Europe. Already by the mid-twelfth century, however, the lay-brothers were becoming the Order's most difficult problem. They were notorious for their unruliness and disorder, fighting among themselves (and with the monks), and by their force of numbers beginning to influence abbatial elections, etc. The problems might well have been foreseen, because in most Cistercian monasteries at this time the lay-brothers far outnumbered the regular monks. At Eberbach in the twelfth century, for example, there were only sixty monks but some two hundred lay-brothers.

To the venerable lady Hildegard, the beloved and the elect of God, A., prior, and the whole congregation of the brothers, with a prayer that you enjoy the eternal delights in the bridechamber of the high King.

O lady most acceptable to God, we have often heard of your fragrant and delightful reputation, and, sluggish and unworthy as we are, we have rejoiced with an inexpressible happiness of spirit that the grace and mercy of almighty God has bestowed such marvellous gifts of His generosity upon you. It is clearer than light to people who love God that the Lord loves you, for you are so worthy, so pleasing, so lovable, so venerable to all those in whom He dwells that there is no question that He dwells in you. Indeed, when such great benefits of virtue have been bestowed upon one, we cannot doubt that the gifts of sacred piety are yours also and that you do not lack a heart of divine love and compassion.

Therefore, we humbly pray for the largess of your piety, that you have mercy on us and that you deign to pray for us—for the Lord was born of the flesh of the blessed Mary (ever virgin) to redeem and to save sinners, and so we ask this in the love of that same Lord omnipotent, our Creator and most loving Redeemer. Moreover, we earnestly beseech you also to send us the treatise which we have heard that, inspired by the Holy Spirit, you wrote concerning those secular and unlearned people who have taken up the spiritual way of life, those that we call *conversi*.[2] Please send it so that we may see the marvellous works of God and His will, and, as far as we are able, follow those things and fulfill them with the happy result of good works. Farewell.

Notes

1. The various MSS assign various names to this and the following letter, and so Van Acker has decided to stay with the ubiquitous anonymous.

2. This is the technical term for lay-brothers. In the middle of the twelfth century the book entitled *Usus conversorum* was produced regulating the brothers' daily routine of work and prayer. The *conversi* were bearded laymen, and they were assigned a distinctive dress, a habit of brown or gray darker than the customary white or light gray of the regular Cistercian monk. Their duties consisted of domestic chores or labor in the various workshops. Most, however, were sent out to work as farmers or herdsmen in the monastery's granges, where they spent most of their time, coming back to the monastery proper only on Sundays and great feast days. Those who did stay in the monastery had living quarters similar to those of the choir-monks, but separate and distinct.

84r
Hildegard to the Prior

About 1169

This letter is actually an exegetical treatise interpreting the four beasts of Ezechiel in contemporary terms. The lion prefigures monks and nuns; the calf, priests. And both these first two creatures, as Hildegard says, draw to themselves another group called lay-brothers. The creature with the face of a man signifies the righteous laity; and the eagle, penitent sinners.

I, a poor little woman lying in a sickbed more than two years, saw these things and heard a voice from heaven saying to me:

Write what you see and hear to the spiritual people [cf. Apoc 1.11, 19], whom God in His prescience foreknew and endowed with the miracles of prophecy, as it pleased Him. And begin in this way: Through the four living creatures that represent the secrets of God, the Lord foreshadowed many mighty works which He accomplished in the saints and the elect. Through those living creatures and other miracles, He reveals to mankind His hidden mysteries, just as He revealed them through those creatures to the prophet Ezechiel and John, His beloved disciple [cf. Apoc 4; Ezech 1], because it was His wish that the spiritual people be segregated from the common people and gathered together into one body. Indeed, John says: "In the midst of the throne, and round about the throne, were four living creatures, full of eyes before and behind" [Apoc 4.6]. The meaning of the passage is this: In the mighty power of God, who is both God and man, and in every place—for His power extends everywhere—the faithful must be empowered by the four evangelists,[1] pondering God's precepts and filled with virtuous prudence, so that they may see whence they came and what they will become. For God is fire [cf. Deut 4.24; Heb 12.29], and His angels, from time to time, announce to mankind His miracles and the wonders of His throne. They are burning spirits, who shine before His face and who are so on fire in their love for Him that they desire nothing other than what He wishes.

About these angels it has been written: "Who makest thy angels spirits; and thy ministers a burning fire" [Ps 103.4; cf. Heb 1.7]. The meaning is this: O Almighty God, You are the One who make your messengers (that is, those who are directed by You for the salvation of mankind) to be spirits, for, their task completed, they stand before Your face in life eternal. And, again, You make spirits Your messengers, since they become messengers for the fulfilling of Your precepts. For angels are messengers, since they report back to God every breath of that breath that God sent into mankind. In this way they perform their function toward mankind, because they collect human works and evaluate them, and it is on account of the works of men, which are done through the Spirit, that they are called spirits and angels, for, over and over again, the Ruler of heaven sends them to fulfill His judgments. But You make Your ministers, who carry out Your will unfailingly, a burning fire, because they are ablaze with love for you, and in this blazing love they serve You with ceaseless praise, and never grow weary.

These ministers of God, who gaze always on His face, blaze always like a flame, and in that blazing they see His miracles, and acknowledge them, marveling and praising. And so they are a burning fire and they derive their fire from God, who is fire, and never can they be either kindled or extinguished by any other being. But blazing unquenchably with love for Him, they marvel at His new miracles with praise, and they serve Him in these too, because clothed in the mantle of humanity,[a] He always causes them to be amazed at His miracles. For God girt Himself in the mantle of His might [cf. Ps 92.1], through which He established mankind as the mirror of His glory and of His miracles,[b] so that man could fight against the devil and overcome him, and thus would always stand firm in divine praise.

In the same way, God makes those who are His messengers spirits, those who proclaim the words of salvation to the children of the Church, when He commands them to resist the flesh and serve the spirit. And these, rendered completely spiritual in their hearts, He ordains to proclaim His commandments to His people all the more confidently. Also those who minister to Him, laboring by day and night, He makes to burn in His love, and so to become a burning fire, and those who are thus set afire sweat in His service without weariness. For in His prescience God preordained that His miracles and His mysteries (which are in the angels) should become active among men through signs, and so He caused the angels to speak to men, as happened with Abraham [cf. Gen 12.1] and Jacob [cf. Gen 26.2–5], and even Balaam through an ass [cf. Num 22.28–35].

He covers with His mysteries, as if with a garment, those angelic spirits ministering to Him, praising and honoring His presence, and thus they, too, are called a burning fire. Through those fiery ministers, who are covered by God's mysteries, as if by a garment, the hermits are designated, who deny themselves as if they were not human beings, living apart from all human society. For God through His work, which is man, effects the great wonders which He predestined in the angelic spirits and which flash like lightning with praise and wondrous adoration before His face.

But also, as was said before, "and round about the throne, were four living creatures, full of eyes before and behind," because they all are the holy works which God effects in those people who gaze upon Him and His throne. They look to the east through faith; to the south, through hope; to the west, through remembrance of the fall of the first parent; and the eyes behind are always, through God's providence, directed toward the north—lest the enemy of the north[2] overthrow them with the falling sickness of pride and the searing flame of lust. With these eyes on all sides, they ought to sigh to God, lest the fire of their faith die out, and they become separated from the light, and lest they approach the north and be choked by eternal death. This, indeed, is the meaning of "round about the throne," since the east and south and west reveal God, but the north has been completely conquered by Him and has been made His footstool [cf. Ps 109.1; Heb 1.13, 10.13].

And it is also written: "And the first living creature was like a lion: and the second living creature like a calf: and the third living creature had the face, as it were, of a man: and the fourth living creature was like an eagle flying" [Apoc 4.7]. The meaning is this: The first living creature represents those who have assumed the hood,[3] the first ones to withdraw themselves completely from the world like a mighty lion. Thus they are like those fiery spirits who have been covered by the mysteries of God like a cloak and forever gaze upon His face. For they did not receive their dress from the world, but, miraculously, from God, just as God ordained in those who first proclaimed this garment by revelation and teaching. For this hood was prefigured by those angelic spirits who gaze, unceasingly, upon the face of God, and its breadth is like a cloud, for angels have often been seen in clouds, and the garment of Adam's innocence was like a bright cloud. And so these men cover their heads with the hood, so that, swerving neither to the left nor to the right, they walk upright before Him through the inspiration of the Spirit, looking always at God, lest they turn aside from good works [cf. Ezech 1.12].

All these things must be done in the obedience which the Son of man revealed in Himself so that the commands of superiors may be obeyed in the fear of God and so that a man may fear sin as much as he fears death at the sound of thunder. For just as a lion excels all other beasts in might, so, too, these men who took the hood excel all the rest of mankind in the might of divinity, for, although they are men, they do not live like other men.

When a man has offered himself to God by rejecting the world, he condemns the world, so that it becomes useless to him in all things, and thus he elevates his mind, just as Daniel says: "I beheld in the vision of the night, and, lo, one like the son of man came with the clouds of heaven, and he came even to the Ancient of days" [Dan 7.13]. Here is the meaning of the passage: Upon contemplating the many adversities of the world, I lifted up my mind to heavenly matters, and understood that through His Son when He was among men, God prefigured all those heavenly and divine miracles that He had accomplished among angelic spirits. And it was in this way that the Son "came even to the Ancient of days," because the Son of God is both God and man, and so God and man are one God. For God is man, and this man is God. And also the good works of men and the praises of angels are joined together, and they become one in God.

Also, a host of virgins join themselves to these hooded men, and they give up the world and riches, and renounce the love of a husband. For just as a virgin ought to be cut off from the delights of this world, lest she suck the breasts of worldly delights, so also monastic orders ought to be cut off from the world, so they are free from performing secular functions. And just as a virgin is dissociated from a man, no longer under his care and power, and is free from him, so, too, a monk, cut off from the world, ought not to be subjected to it, but should remain free from it. Virginity also signifies the sun, which illumines the entire world, because God joined virginity to Himself, and virginity, without knowing a man, gave birth to Him Who, suffused by the rays of divinity, rules all things. For the king who rules all things is God, and virginity was joined to Him, when the One Who is both God and man was born from the Virgin. So "the queen stood on" his "right hand, in gilded clothing; surrounded with variety" [Ps 44.10], since in resisting the devil virginity stood by the power of divinity in a refulgent work, completely surrounded with a host of virtues. Indeed divinity betrothed itself to virginity when the first angel fell to the left, and, then, divinity chose for itself a people in Adam destined for salvation, and called them His right hand. And from this people, He joined virginity to Himself, which brought forth the greatest work of all, for, just as God created all things through his word, so, too, virginity bore the Son of God through the heat of holy divinity.[4] And virginity is not without fertility, since the Virgin gave birth to God and man, through Whom all things have their being. And in this way all the virtues of the Old and New Testament which God activated in his saints are like a vestment made of the finest gold, and a virgin will gladly gather all these to herself, because she is not bound by any obligation to a man.

The wheel which Ezechiel saw [cf. Ezech 1.15] prefigured virginity, because virginity was prefigured in the law before the incarnation of the Son of God. After His incarnation, it performed many wondrous miracles, since, through it, God purified all expiatory rites and properly set in order every institution. Virginity bears up the old and sustains the new, and is the very root and foundation of all good, because forever and ever it has been with Him Who is without beginning or end. For the nature of mankind was fallen because of sin, but through virginity gained salvation and new life, for it removed sin from man through its very nature.

The second living creature, like a calf, stands for those in clerical habit[5] who zealously perform the divine sacrifice, that is, those who dig a trench around the vineyard of the Lord of Sabaoth and plow the field of the precepts of God [cf. Isa 5.7; Matt 21.33; Mark 12.1; Luke 20.9]; they are those who are called the angels of the Lord of hosts, who, therefore, ought to gird themselves with chastity, so as not to fall into the vanity of carnal pleasure, but rather to spend every effort to plow the field of the Lord. They will also receive the circumcision of sobriety, since, through them, the sins of mankind are washed away, and they will do this with compassion because they are aware of their own sins.

These two types, symbolized by the lion and the calf, draw another type of person to themselves, whom they call *conversi*.[6] Yet many of these are not truly converted, because they prefer dissension to rectitude, and in their works they resound with rashness, speaking thus about their superiors: Who are these people, and what are they; and what were we, and what are we now? And because they do this, they are like false prophets, and they misjudge how God has established His people.[7]

You who fear God, therefore, hear what the Spirit of the Lord says to you: Rid yourselves of this wickedness, and cleanse yourselves so that henceforth you exercise more restraint than you have heretofore. Thus purify yourselves before the day of those tribulations when God's enemies, and yours, force you to flee into your proper place of humility and poverty. Thus it is that God changed the old law into the spiritual life and cleansed every earlier institution and made them all more profitable. In the beginning of creation, God granted Adam to till the earth, Abel to make sacrifice, and Noah to build. This dispensation lasted all the way up until that supreme priesthood which arose in the incarnation of Christ, and that priesthood was prefigured by Abraham through circumcision, and then by Moses through the law. The Son of God brought all these things to perfection in His humanity, and therefore they must all be understood to pertain to mankind. For after the fall of Adam, God prefigured His plan in men as well as angels.[c]

But by no means would it be proper for a priest to perform the functions of a farmer, or for a student to perform the tasks of a master, because the farmer should imitate the priest, and the pupil, the master in the fear of God and with humble patience. Almighty God is recognized in His works, just as He began to work in Adam, to whom He granted to till the earth and beget the human race, because God himself is the father of all things. And just as through the sacrifice of Abel, He prefigured His Son, who was to be sacrificed for the redemption of the world, so through Noah, the builder of the ark, He foreshadowed that masters were to be established among spiritual people.[d]

Now, masters, seize and correct those people I mentioned earlier, the laybrothers in your order, because day and night the greatest part of them refuses to work, failing to serve perfectly either God or the world. Rouse them out of their ignorance, just as an experienced perfumer eradicates rank weeds from his garden.[e] And be provident and shrewd, as befits your rank, so that you may not make unjust judgments. And so it would be unfitting that the lion, the calf, the man, and the eagle should strive against one another in their symbolic meanings. Rather, each one of them in the figure of truth should weigh out justice to the other.

In company with the moon and the stars, the sun illumines the whole world efficiently and well. Therefore, those who are sealed by the Son of man as guardians of mankind can heal, anoint, and perform the sacrament of baptism with humble obedience. For every priest who has been anointed and named a priest by God will be able to anoint and care for the wounds of sinners with proper justice, because he has received this office from God. And so let him not fail to fulfill it.

And I, a poor little woman and an untaught feminine form,[f] saw a certain beast, whose face and front legs were like a bear's, but the rest of the body was like an ox, except that its hind legs were like those of an ass, and it had no tail. And it had three horns on its head, two of which, near the ears, were like those of an ox, but the third, which was in the middle of the forehead, was like the horn of a mountain goat. The face of this beast was turned toward the east, with its hindquarters toward the west.

Here is the interpretation of the vision: This beast, whose face and front legs are like a bear's, stands for certain people who secretly have a bestial character—they utter mild words, but instead of going forward toward righteousness, they leave telling footprints behind of perverse imprudence and hardness of heart. The rest of its body is like an ox, except that its hind feet are like those of an ass, and it has no tail, since these same people pretend that like an ox they are bearing God's yoke, but in their actions they are the ass that falls under the burden. Thus, too, in keeping with the metaphor, they are lacking a tail, because they fail to obey the Lord's injunction that a beast with a tail is to be offered up in sacrifice [cf. Levit 3.9, 7.3; Ex 29.22], since the good they had begun in humility and poverty they fail to bring to full perfection.

The fact that it has three horns on its head, two of which, near the ears, are like those of an ox, stands for the three kinds of lives that men lead, according to their principal occupation. Two of these have the appearance of those who work in the field of the Lord and of those who present what they have heard from the word of the Lord. The third, in the middle of the forehead, and like the horn of a mountain goat, represents those spiritual people, in the strength of their assurance, who, in the squalor of the mountain goat, strive with might and main to ascend to that height, on which it is by no means possible to remain. On this height they spurn the other spiritual people and despise them, just as the Pharisees despised the publicans [cf. Luke 18.11]. And they take up certain secular matters of the region, so that through them they might be regarded as better and loftier than the other two horns, and appear to have scaled to a greater height of sanctity than all others. For they involve themselves with the world and undertake to multiply their wealth, so that by their labors they might overturn the whole world, and in this way acquire greater wealth than they should. In this way, they resemble that young man whom the Son of God told to sell whatever he possessed and give it to the poor; that rich young man went away sorrowful, because he wanted to possess both the riches of the world and eternal life—and this is very difficult to attain [cf. Matt 19.16ff]. These people want to possess both heaven and earth at the same time, but this is impossible, for in the acquisition and possession of wealth they are by no means able to stand apart from the pride of elation and their own will, just as it would be impossible for one on the peak of the mountain to stand and not fall when shaken by tempests and strong winds. They do not possess the love and fear that a poor man has, who extends his hand to lend aid and give alms. But they make themselves as foolish as an ass, which allows itself to be loaded with great burdens until it collapses under them, for they wish to bear both the yoke of spiritual life and the troubles that come with the secular life, but they cannot stand up under their combined weight and, therefore, they collapse like an ass. And so the face of that beast looks to the east with his posterior to the west, because although such people seem to attend to spiritual life, they also cling to the secular, imitating in this the lost angels, who, trusting in themselves, fell headlong from celestial glory.

And the third living creature, with the face of a man, represents those secular individuals[8] who perform their work with the proper concern for body and spirit, and therefore ascend with good intention to God, as if they were flying with wings, because all good desires come forth from the heart of the just man like the rays of the sun and thus those desires appear to have wings.

They also hasten to observe the commands both of the law and of the priest, and they are moved by compassion to give alms, and they observe how they were born of the earth, and in the begetting of offspring they account themselves equal to the dust of the earth, calling themselves sinners. And so in secular life, they suffer the burden of the flesh more than the joy of carnal pleasure, and thus they come to their masters, that is, the priests, weeping for the sins they have tasted, and through the grace of the Holy Spirit confessing their sins in penitence. In this way they are renewed, as it is written: "Thou shalt renew the face of the earth" [Ps 103.30]. The meaning of the verse is this: O God, in a new spirit You will renew the will of man, for he is prone to sin, and thus You will divert him from his wicked pursuits and direct him to wholesome desires. For through the penitent, You will renew the face of the earth when man becomes fully aware that he is so entangled in sin that he cannot keep himself from sinning, being able to gain renewal only through penance. For if man were not a sinner, he would not need to be renewed.

Some are renewed when they flee sin because they fear the penalty of penance, and thus they are eager to refrain from sinning. And others, out of their love for virtue, avoid their latent, but potential, sins, and thus are renewed by the Holy Spirit. Just as the earth bears fruit in the verdant season, withers away in the winter, but, then again, returns to its former fertility, so, too, God placed man so that he might be renewed in his own self through his works. For the Scripture has to be divided up properly in all the works of mankind, just as many waters are divided from the one water and just as God distributed the waters all over the earth.

Also, those secular people constantly examine themselves, pondering what they are and how they are living and how to rid themselves of their sins. Living thus in the fear of God, they are among the earthly, and yet do not let go of the heavenly [cf. John 17.15ff]. For in worshipping God, they make sacrifice in their very selves, and thus they are as radiant as the moon when they sigh to God from the bottom of their hearts. But although they wane like the moon in their sins, they rise again immediately through their penance, just as the moon, after its waning, regains its brilliance through the sun. Thus they sleep in the midst of clerics endowed with the silvered wings of the dove [cf. Ps 67.14], since sleeping in the midst of these high-flying masters, lest they sin, they maintain the simplicity of pure knowledge. And they do this when they turn aside from their nascent sins and rest from them, just as a bird tucks its head under its wing to sleep, that is, loving heavenly things and, among secular concerns, confessing their sins through penitence. Therefore, "blessed are the dead, who die in the Lord" [Apoc 14.13], because although they live a secular life according to the law, O how great a miracle is found in them, that living thus and abandoning their sins through the bitterness of penitence, they remain men! And thus they will be like the living creature with the face of a man, for when they commit earthly sins, they strive against them through penitence, and distance themselves from them, just as animal nature is distanced from human nature. And so they appear all silvered in the knowledge of good works, because they have the simple character of an infant who does not know how to sin, being unwilling either to embrace or nurture sin. And since they are eager to shine in this simplicity, then "the hinder parts of their backs" will appear "with the paleness of gold" [Ps 67.14], because their hinder parts in which they were first strong in their sins (when they were habituated to sin) now have been cast behind them, and thus they show wisdom in the fear of the Lord, since in their good deeds they are resplendent with gold.

The fourth living creature, like a flying eagle, reveals certain people who refrain from sin and, coming forth from among the aforementioned secular people, rise up to self-restraint.[9] One of these was Mary Magdalene, who, regarding her sins as filth, cast them off, and thereby choosing the best part, she sat in the dawn of holiness. But in the Old Testament, many abandoned their sins on account of the weariness of this world, and many kept themselves from sin out of their love for righteousness. Now, in the new sun, that is, Christ Jesus, however, such are called abstinent, because they have the simplicity of the infant who does not know how to sin, when they repudiate their sins and no longer will to sin. They ascend to heavenly things in two ways: since with good intention and holy desire, they esteem celestial things, and they do so far more than those people who never knew the world at all. And because like the eagle which flies higher than any other bird, they fly upward, because they are so directed to the brightness of eternal life that they cannot get their fill of it, and through the brilliance of the true sun, they trample underfoot those things they had done previously when they were enmeshed in their sins.

In the mighty power of holiness, they reflect upon what great grief and what heaviness there are in those sins which they themselves had once so fully embraced, but which now in themselves they kill as dead as a cadaver. And they bind up their bodies like a slaughtered sheep and scourge it. Thus they look into the blazing sun, casting behind them all those secular things they were caught up in before like so much worthless dust, rejecting, in their blazing love for God, all fear of hell and knowing that they are bound to persevere in faith and hope.

And in this way they follow the verse in Isaiah: "The seraphim covered their faces with two wings" [Is 6.2]. These wings stand for faith and hope, because, in faith, the faithful see God and, through hope, they desire the eternal rewards. "And with two they covered their feet" [Is 6.2]. These wings stand for the senses and the intellect, with which these men cover the nakedness of their sins, lest, from their own distorted will, they fulfill their carnal desires. But they flew with the other two [cf. Is 6.2], and these wings stand for the love of God and neighbor, for, since they love God above all else, they stand by their neighbor in his need, and thus in God's might they fly above all things. In this way, they pass beyond all earthly things and diligently inspect each and every sinful act they had committed, so that they might mortify themselves through abstinence from sin. And thus in their full desire they adorn the heavenly Jerusalem with the precious stones of good works [Apoc 21.19ff]. And so in the joyful life of God's commandments, they do not sleep, but, rather, they resound like a blaring trumpet in the renewed desire of their souls, because they are the ardent sighs raised to God by one born in the dark night of sin when they come to know Him in fear and love. Thus they say: Holy is the one who created all things, and holy is the one who has never been subject to death, and holy is the one who shattered hell and drew forth his elect. For the blessed will never in this life cease doing good works and praising God, and when they have brought their work to completion after the end of their life, they will never leave off praising their Creator.

But I, poor little woman that I am, weak and infirm from my earliest childhood, have been forced by a mystic and true vision to write this treatise, and indeed at God's command and with His help, I did write it, even though I lay seriously ill upon my bed, so that I might reveal to the prelates and masters ordained to God's service that they are to contemplate, as if in a mirror, who they are and what they are about. And, moreover, they are to show and expound this vision to those who are subject to them through obedience. And I heard a voice from heaven saying [cf. Apoc 10.4, 11.12, 14.2, 18.4]: Let nobody despise these words, lest the vengeance of God fall upon him [cf. Apoc 22.18ff].

Notes

1. The four creatures are traditionally the typological symbols of the evangelists: Matthew, the man or angel; Mark, the lion; Luke, the ox; John, the eagle. In the course of this letter, Hildegard engages in extending the boundaries of those signified by the creatures.

2. The traditional seat of Satan.

3. I.e., the monks.

4. Compare *"O Splendidissima gemma"* in the *Symphonia:* "To you the father spoke again/ but this time/ the word he uttered was a man/ in your body./ Matrix of light! through you he breathed forth/ all that is good,/ as in the primal matrix he formed/ all that has life." Newman, *Symphonia,* p. 115.

5. I.e., priests.

6. I.e., lay-brothers. Like most writers of the twelfth and thirteenth centuries, Hildegard has difficulty locating the *conversi* (who are neither laymen, nor clerics, nor monks) within her hierarchical scheme. Hence her vague "these two draw another type of person to themselves."

7. This is one of Hildegard's favorite themes: each person in his proper place in accordance with appropriate medieval hierarchy. It is a variation of this theme that she used in answer to Tengswich's criticism. See Letter 52r.

8. I.e., the righteous laity.

9. I.e., penitents. Note the reference to Mary Magdalene, the supreme image of the penitent.

Ebrach
85
Abbot Adam to Hildegard

Before 1166

Adam writes to Hildegard in concern over his monks, seeking her prayers. He also refers to a letter he wrote on her behalf to the emperor.

To his lady and mother, the beloved Hildegard, mistress of the sisters of St. Rupert in Bingen, Adam, brother and abbot (although unworthy) of Ebrach, sends what little he has.

When I first heard of your fame, I rejoiced with great joy [cf. Matt 2.10]. Then God added to my joy when, with a gracious and marvellous command, He directed you to come into our land where you might be seen and heard,[1] and, as I could not possibly have hoped, granted to me a meeting face to face with you. During this conversation, I confessed my anxiety to you (I trust that you remember), and because different people feel different things—some this, some that—I wish to know if prosperity and safety are in store for me, and if so, blessed be God. If, however, there is danger, please pray God that He grant good to me and salvation to my soul, and preserve me from all danger.[a]

Now I am sending a letter and messenger on your behalf to the lord Emperor, and I hope through the grace of God to be heard.[2] And whenever you have need of our service, we will be prepared to serve you.

We pray also that you deign to pray for us, for truly we are in a whirlwind on account of concern for our brothers. We pray that the grace of the Holy Spirit—which works many miracles in the spirit of prophecy through you—look also with favor on us and protect us. We ask also that you deign to write in order to console and fortify us.

Notes

1. Hildegard preached at Ebrach on her first preaching tour, which took place some time between 1158 and 1161.
2. It would be interesting to know the substance of this letter, but we are completely in the dark.

85r/a
Hildegard to Abbot Adam

Before 1166

Although it is not clear from his own letter to Hildegard, Adam must have expressed a desire to step down from his administrative duties, for Hildegard refers explicitly to such a wish in this letter, and advises against it. The letter is quite remarkable in its opening allegorical discourse on divine love and the creation. On this vision of Caritas as divine mother, see Newman, *Sister of Wisdom*, pp. 63–64.

In a true vision of the spirit, my body fully awake, I saw, as it were, a beautiful girl of such great brightness, with so shining a face, that I could hardly gaze upon her. She had a cloak whiter than snow and brighter than the stars, and she had on shoes of the purest gold. And she held the moon and the sun in her right hand, and she embraced them lovingly. On her breast there was an ivory tablet, and on this tablet there was an image of man colored like sapphire. Every creature called this girl sovereign lady. And to the image on her breast, she said: "With thee is the beginning in the day of thy strength: in the brightness of the saints: from the womb before the day star I begot thee" [Ps 109.3].

And I heard a voice saying to me: This girl that you see is Divine Love, and she has her dwelling place in eternity. For when God wished to create the world, He bent down in sweetest love,[1] and He provided for all necessary things, just as a father prepares the inheritance for his son. Thus it was that in great ardor He established all His works in order. Then all creation in its various kinds and forms acknowledged its Creator, for in the beginning divine love was the matrix from which He created all things, when He said, Let there be, and it was done [cf. Gen 1.3].[a] Thus every creature was formed through divine love in the twinkling of an eye.

And this figure shines with such great brightness, with so shining a face, that one can scarcely gaze upon her because she displays the fear of the Lord in such pure knowledge that mortal man will never be able to fully realize it. And she has a cloak whiter than snow and brighter than the stars because, in pure innocence and without pretense, she embraces all things with the refulgent works of the saints. And she wears shoes of the purest gold, because her paths lead through the best part of God's election. And she holds the sun and the moon in her right hand, embracing them lovingly, because God's right hand embraces all creatures and because divine love is dispersed among the good of all nations and all realms. Whence also it is written: "The Lord said to my Lord: sit thou at my right hand" [Ps 109.1]. Moreover, the ivory tablet is on her breast because, in the knowledge of God, the land of integrity flourished always in the Virgin Mary, so that, in her, the image of man appears colored like sapphire,[2] because the Son of God, in divine love, radiated forth from the ancient of days [cf. Dan 7.9, 13, 22] in divine love.

And all creatures name this girl sovereign lady because they all came forth from her—since she was the creator of all things from the beginning—just as, also, the image on her breast shows that God dressed himself in humanity for mankind's sake. For when all creation was fulfilled by God's commandment—just as He himself said: "Increase and multiply, and fill the earth" [Gen 1.28]—the heat of the true sun descended like dew into the womb of the Virgin and made man from her flesh, just as also He formed Adam's flesh and blood from the mud of the earth. And the Virgin gave birth to Him immaculately.

But it was not fitting for divine love not to have wings. For when the creature[3] began circling aimlessly about in the beginning, it wished to fly, despite its earthbound nature, and so it fell, but it was the wings of divine love that lifted it up. These wings were holy humility. For when horrible misjudgment laid Adam low, divinity kept a sharp eye on him so that he might not perish utterly in the fall but that divinity itself might redeem him in the holiness of humanity. These were wings of great power, for humility—which was the humanity of the Savior—raised up mankind who was lost, for divine love created man, but humility redeemed him.[b] Hope is, as it were, the eye of divine love; celestial love, its heart; and abstinence, the link between the two. But faith is, as it were, the eye of humility; obedience, its heart; and contempt for evil, the link between the two. Divine love was in eternity, and, in the beginning of all sanctity, she brought forth all creatures without any mixture of evil, and she brought forth Adam and Eve from the immaculate earth. And just as the two of them brought forth all the children of mankind, so, too, those two virtues bring forth all the other virtues.

Now, therefore, O man to whom I address these things, those virtues knock at your door, and say: O tabernacle of this man who remains with us in the morning but is now exhausted! And Divine Love says to you: O faithful friend, we do not wish for you to withdraw from the obligations of your office. For when God in the vault of heaven wished to spread abroad all creatures, we had all His works in our embrace, and we labored with Him. But man fell, and we wept with him, but we did not give him up, even though he rejected us. And humility speaks especially to you: Oh alas, in what great griefs I have sustained mankind. Yet you say: I wish to flee. But you have a burden to bear into the vineyard, and yet you stand still and will not walk forward. And so totally caught up in your own weariness, you look for another way. Certainly, our companion will not act like this. For since the people love you, work with them. But when the wind begins to roar with the disturbance of war and the instability of men's morals, look to me, and on the wheel of the power of my wings, I will help you.

Through a woman's folly, Samson lost his great power. Beware, therefore, lest this happen to you, if you respond merely out of your weariness. Solomon's glory was also destroyed through the folly of women.[4] Watch carefully lest your God-given viridity dry up because of the instability of your thought. But pay heed to the ornaments of gold and precious stones which Divine Love and Humility possess in you. But give glory to God because of the bracelets given to you by wisdom, that jewelry for which the people run to you. And labor for the people, and you will remain forever with the sun.

Notes

1. The word here is *amor*, a little odd, given the general context. In this letter, Hildegard shifts back and forth between *caritas* and *amor*. In order to keep the distinctions that are being made in this letter clear, we adhere rigidly to using "divine love" for *caritas* and simple "love" for *amor*. Cf. Newman, *Sister of Wisdom*, pp. 63–64. See also Peter Dronke, *Medieval Latin and the Rise of European Love-Lyric*, 2d ed., vol. I, Oxford: Clarendon Press, 1968), pp. 66ff.

2. See *Scivias* II.vi.612f: "The sapphire represents the divinity of my Son who . . . through my divine heat, miraculously became incarnate from the sweet virgin."

3. The word used here is *creatura*, but, as will become clear in the course of the letter, Hildegard clearly intends mankind.

4. The text is rendered properly: it *is* women's folly, not men's, in Hildegard's view. The Latin is quite specific: *per stultitiam mulieris* and *per stultitiam mulierum*.

85r/b
Hildegard to Adam, the Abbot

Before 1166

Hildegard continues her advice to Adam in the form of another elaborate allegory. With the representation of the vices and virtues presented here, compare the Ordo Virtutum.

He Who Is says: The sun shines and sends forth its rays. And a certain man, a friend of the sun, had a garden in which he desired to plant many herbs and flowers. And the sun, in the fire of its rays, sent heat upon those herbs and flowers, and the dew and rain gave the moisture of viridity to them. Then from the north a contorted figure with black hair and horrible face came to that garden, but at the same time from the east came a handsome young man with bright shining hair and a comely, pleasant face. And the contorted figure said to the young man: Where have you come from? And he answered: I come from the east to the garden of this wise man, for I greatly desired to come to him. And the contorted figure said: Listen to me: A destructive wind and hail and fire and pestilence will come upon that garden, and will dry it out. But the young man answered: Not so, it will not be so, because I do not wish it, and I will bring forth a pure fountain and will irrigate the garden. And the contorted figure answered: Ha! That is as possible as if locusts would eat through hard rock. And so that crafty figure brought winter into that garden and sought to dry up the herbs and flowers. And that aforementioned young man, caught up in playing his harp, did not see what was happening. But when he did take notice, he called the sun back with a loud sound, and the sun came into Taurus and brought the viridity of summer back into that garden. And taking up an ivory horn and a hart horn, with them he cast that contorted figure down to the earth. And then he said to the man who owned the garden: From now on, do not rely so fully on yourself that you fail to enclose your garden with a high wall, so that the black birds in the storms will not be able to dry it up.

Now, you, O father, understand these words spoken to you, for you have the highest of all callings as Christ's representative. Listen, therefore: The grace of God shines like the sun and sends its gifts in various ways: in wisdom, in viridity, in moisture. But wisdom can degenerate into grossness, viridity can fall under great labor, and moisture can turn into harsh bitterness.[a] But you, O friend of the grace of God, you have a garden of people, in which as the representative of Christ you seek to plant many wholesome desires and good works. And through the power of His gifts, the grace of God pours out His dynamic good will upon those desires and those works, and causes the garden to grow green through the dew and the rain of the fountain of living water [see Cant 4.15, Jer 2.13; cf. John 4.11, 7.38].

But vices come from the devil in the turmoil of vainglory and the uproar of impertinence which fights against just governance, but the virtues, planted by God, burgeon in divine love with the full benevolence of proper discipline and complete contempt for the world, springing up for the benefit of the people. And the vices ask the virtues why they have come. And they answer that they have come from God to the people of the friend of God, because they greatly desire to build a sacrifice of praise in them. And the vices respond: Great ruin and ire and insidious interrogations that cause great distress will fall upon this people, so that they will grow weary in their service to God. And the virtues respond: That will not happen, because we will not cease from doing good, but the fountain of living water will pour forth and will defend this people with its compassion. But, with scornful laughter, the devil's vices say that this is as possible as if fragile flesh were to remain unblemished and unwrinkled.[1] Then the crafty vices bring the cold cloud of ignorance upon this people, so that their wholesome desires and their good works fail, because they have faith in themselves alone. But showing obedience in their praises to God, the virtues permit this thing to be done by the just judgment of God, so that men may understand what they are.[b] And so when the people come to their senses in humility, the virtues zealously tender the grace of God to them in order to impress the passion of Christ on their minds, so that the people may be brought back to their pristine praise of God. Thus by looking to the divinity and humanity of the Son of God, they cast those vices down to contrition. And to the leader of those people, they say: Warned by these things, do not trust in your powers alone, but see to it that you flee to the grace of God, so that you may protect and admonish your people in every way, lest the treacheries of the devil turn them aside into all sorts of vices through negligence.

And you also, O father, hear us: As the morning star comes before the dawn, offer your help to us with the kiss of love which God gave to you. And God will give you that life which He looked upon on the first day.

Note

1. With this dialogue between the vices and the virtues, compare the *Ordo Virtutum*.

86
Hildegard to Adam, Abbot

Before 1166

Another allegorical presentation to Adam, in the hope of fortifying him in the faith.

The Living Light says these things in his miracles: The first root appeared in the day and flourished in all branches, and established two paths. The one path was lined with buildings, in which eagles and other birds made their homes. But the other path was very different, with giants running in it, who fought against those eagles and other birds, but could not prevail against them. Then the sun came out, with a golden shield on his outstretched arm, and he fought against those giants. For the first angel's fall from life had already taken place, and, afterward, Adam's fall diminished the light of paradise, and Adam, along with all his descendants, was walking in the way of the devil. But the sun shone in topaz and sapphire, that is, in mercy and divine love, which proclaimed the incarnate Word of God. And the sun continued to shine as it had done from the beginning, and continued so that absolutely no shadow of change fell upon it, as had happened to the first angel and to Adam through the instigation of the devil. And so it was written: "Thou art a priest for ever according to the order of Melchisedech" [Ps 109. 4]. For mercy is to be understood in the topaz, and divine love in the sapphire, the virtues which this priest put on like a priestly vestment for the sake of mankind.[a]

Now you, O father, who serve as vicar for this priest, let your soul flow like the water He made to flow from the rock struck by the rod of Moses, so that your words may give the drink of salvation to unbelieving hearts, and so that the day which shines in your spirit may grow in the multitude of virtues. I see that although you are on the way that leads to God, you are anxious in your spirit. But when your mind comes into the whirlwind on account of the instability of your labors and others', then the dove will anoint you and make you a simple tower before the face of God.

O foresightful man, on account of the concern that you had toward us, I saw and understood these things about mercy, and so may the grace of the Holy Spirit fortify you.

87

A Certain Monk to Hildegard[1]

Before 1166

A humble monk, cringing before the saintliness of Hildegard, beseeches her prayers and consolation.

To his lady and mother, Hildegard, most blessed olive branch of Christ, N., sinner of Ebrach, a worthless monk of the Cistercian order, sends wishes that she may live and die in the Lord.

I want you to know, beloved lady, that I have sent so brief a letter to you, because I thought these things scarcely worthy of your saintliness, and also because, with trembling mind, I scarcely dared to write to so high a person. Neither did I think myself worthy to write. Similarly, if I dare, saving your grace, I, trembling and on bended knee, commit myself, filthy as I am, to your prayers in the mercy of Jesus Christ, and as far as I can, with grace amending my sloth, I will gladly be mindful in Christ of you and your sisters. And if absent in body, I am with you in heart and love, as God is my witness.

Now, therefore, keep me in your memory, and, as I believe you will, commend me assiduously to Christ and St. Mary, and take care to console me with the words of your consolation in accordance with your divine vision. May the grace of the Holy Spirit be with you.

Note

1. Van Acker puts *notarius* with a question mark in the title of this letter because Hildegard's response is addressed *"ad notarium."* Some MSS make the title very specific: *"Abbatis nothario de Ebra,"* that is, "secretary of the abbot of Ebrach."

87r/a
Hildegard to the Secretary
Before 1166

Hildegard sends the secretary words of encouragement.

The Mystic Light says: The earth in its fertility brings forth abundant fruit, but tares and noxious weeds frequently flourish among them. But sometimes a temperate wind comes over the earth, and its power is such that it debilitates the useless plants and yet does not harm the good fruit.

Hear these things: Some people have very good qualities in the fertility of their nature, but they produce useless works because they let the lust of the flesh impinge on the plenitude of their knowledge. But sometimes the admonition of the grace of God warns them—through contrition of spirit or the sad infirmity of the foolish body or such like things—and causes them to shun evil and produce good fruit.

Understand these things in reference to yourself. May God let the dew of heaven fall upon you, and you will live forever.

87r/b

Hildegard to the Secretary

Before 1166

More words of encouragement. And note the almost fortune-teller-like prediction.

I see that God does not hide his face from you, but He restrains you with his scourges, as it pleases Him. Also, I see that a great light of consolation will soon come into your soul and into the joy of your body, in God's own good time. For God lives in your tabernacle, and His grace is not overshadowed there. You will live in eternity, and your soul will be praiseworthy before God (despite your doubt), for a victorious man is loved by his Lord.

88

Hildegard to a Hospitaler[1]

Before 1170

Hildegard sends words of great encouragement.

Your mind prays and your desires are blazing in thirst for the justice of God, and you say: Where am I, and where will I go? But with a lamentable voice you are also seeking medicine for your sins, and, on account of God's judgment, your soul is swollen and bloated by doubt and trepidation. And you do not say, rejoicing: God in His great mercy will receive me.

But He will. Believe, have faith, and hope, because God loves you and wishes you, and He will receive you. Wash yourself, therefore, in confession and in penitence, and you will live in eternity.

Note

1. Hildegard's word here is *eleemosynarius*, one in charge of distributing alms to the poor.

89
Hildegard to Rudeger, the Monk
About 1153

This is a quite bizarre letter, or, at least, an answer to a bizarre letter. Rudeger apparently has had strange dreams and visions which he has shared with Hildegard and from which he seeks to divine the time of his death, and perhaps the pope's also—or perhaps the pope has appeared to him in a dream. Moreover, he has apparently expressed doubts to her about the eucharist.

A clear revelation in a true vision says: O son of God, in the creating act by which you are a man, and through the faith expressed by your good works, acknowledge that you have no power except in God and through Him. God knows all things, and He gives full knowledge to no person, save as he foresees the need. For nobody—either in prophecy, or in the inspiration of God, or in his own wisdom—knows all things, or can say anything, save as far as God will show it to him through a miracle.

That light that I saw in your spirit in a true vision is this: that you are a son of salvation, but yet you live in great tribulation—sometimes in the weariness and weakness of the flesh, and in various thoughts, which at times lift you up to the heights and, at others, cause you to wander in secular concerns, and sometimes lead you into vainglory by means of a strange revelation, as it is written: "The Lord knoweth the thoughts of men, that they are vain" [Ps 93.11]. Beware, therefore, of inquiring rashly into your thoughts and dreams about how long you will remain on this earthly journey, for God has shown me no other signs concerning Pope Eugenius.[1] Yet I see you terribly bound up and hence you ought to be freed in this life. God also shows me nothing about the length (or brevity) of the days of that brother that you asked me about, neither in years nor in seasons. And yet he still has time.[a] But let him run mightily, because he is a little tepid and a little wearied in fleshly matters, and he goes astray somewhat in his thoughts. Let him show all these things to his priest in confession.

Concerning the body of Christ, I saw also that that power which descended into the womb of the Virgin (so that the Word of God became true flesh) remains up to the present day, as it is written: "Thou art my son, this day have I begotten thee" [Ps 2.7]. And that same power from the time that the Word of God became incarnate in the Virgin will remain even to the last day. I saw also that that same power appears like a red dawn in fire upon the altar. And that One Who made flesh and blood in the womb of the Virgin also makes the bread and wine on the altar flesh and blood.

Now, I also see that you, in the lifting up of your hands, are like a shifting cloud on account of your unstable thoughts, which cause you to doubt.[2] Put such things aside and recognize who He is who works His works on the altar.

And who is the one who can recount these marvels? When you think simply in this way, I see you pure like the sun, and your sacrifice is pleasing to God. And He will free your soul.

Notes

1. Has Rudeger confided to her a dream or vision of his in which the spirit of Pope Eugenius, who died in 1153, appeared to him, revealing secret and future things? Or has he had some "revelation" of the approaching death of Eugenius?

2. Rudeger, it seems, has communicated to Hildegard his concern over his doubts with respect to the Real Presence in the eucharist. See Letter 46, Headnote.

90
Hildegard to a Certain Monk

Before 1170

A brief letter of consolation about the future.

God foresaw you and foreknows you in two parts, that is, on the one hand, a little frivolous and, on the other, full of divine love. And in your levity, your pain will subside somewhat, though you will always have anxiety in this life. With respect to divine love, on the other hand, you have gained people's respect so that the people will never cast you aside, but indeed will love you. And God wishes your soul.

Endnotes

Letter 1

a. *Pater, ego sum ualde sollicita de hac uisione, que apparuit mihi in spiritu mysterii, quam numquam uidi cum exterioribus oculis carnis. Ego, misera et plus quam misera in nomine femineo, ab infantia mea uidi magna mirabilia, que lingua mea non potest proferre, nisi quod me docuit Spiritus Dei, ut credam.*

b. *Scio enim in textu interiorem intelligentiam expositionis Psalterii et Euangelii et aliorum uoluminum, que monstrantur mihi de hac uisione, que tangit pectus meum et animam sicut flamma comburens, docens me hec profunda expositionis. Sed tamen non docet me litteras in Teutonica lingua, quas nescio, sed tantum scio in simplicitate legere, non in abscisione textus. Et de hoc responde mihi, quid tibi inde uideatur, quia homo sum indocta de ulla magistratione cum exteriori materia, sed intus in anima mea sum docta. Vnde loquor quasi dubitando.*

c. *Bone pater et mitissime, posita sum in animam tuam, ut mihi reueles per hunc sermonem, si uelis ut hec dicam palam, aut habeam silentium, quia magnos labores habeo in hac uisione, quatenus dicam quod uidi et audiui.*

d. *dum transeas per foramen anime tue.*

Letter 2

a. *ego paupercula forma.*
b. *viuens lux.*
c. *quia multi prudentes de terrenis uisceribus spargunt hec in mutationem mentium suarum propter pauperem formam, que edificata est in costa et que est indocta de philosophis.*

Letter 5

a. *Oculus uiuens uidet, et dicit: Qui sapit et discernit quamque creaturam, qui et eas omnes exsuscitat, uigilat.*

b. *Montes autem transiliunt clauim uie ueritatis.*

Letter 8

a. *Et tu, o Roma, uelut in extremis iacens, conturbaberis ita, quod fortitudo pedum tuorum, super quos hactenus stetisti, languescet, quoniam filiam regis, uidelicet iustitiam, non ardente amore, sed quasi in tepore dormitionis amas, ita quod eam a te expellis. Vnde et ipsa a te fugere uult, si non reuocarueris eam. Sed tamen magni montes maxillam adiutorii tibi adhuc prebebunt, te sursum erigentes et magnis lignis magnarum arborum te fulcientes, ita quod non tota in honore tuo, uidelicet in decore desponsationis Christi omnino dissipaberis, quin aliquas alas ornamenti tui habeas, usque dum ueniat nix morum diuersarum irrisionum, multam insaniam emittentium. Caue ergo, ne ad ritum paganorum te commiscere uelis, ne cadas.*

b. *Sed ille qui sine defectione magnus est, modo paruum habitaculum tetigit, ut illud miracula uideret et ignotas litteras formaret, ac ignotam linguam sonaret. Et dictum est illi: Hoc quod in lingua desuper tibi ostensa non secundum formam humane consuetudinis protuleris, quoniam consuetudo hec tibi data non est, ille qui limam habet, ad aptum sonum hominum expolire non negligat.*

Letter 9

a. *O homo, diram duritiam leenarum et fortem fortitudinem leopardorum patiendo sustinebis et naufragium in captura predarum senties, quoniam omnibus his datus es in fatigatione ad te currentibus. Habes autem intelligibilem intellectum contra seuissimos mores hominum, in quibus estuando frenabis capillos currentium equorum, qui non desistunt currere ad semitas predarum. Sed tamen rixando contra te ipsum inclinas te interdum quasi ad probitatem quorundam hominum, ubi celas loculos aliquorum, qui mortui sunt preliari in planis uiis. Vnde patieris pugnam seuitie preliorum, sed destrues mobilia reliquiarum illorum, qui in foueam uadunt per asperitatem suam. Attamen uenam habes fortissime clauis, que non uadit libenter ad azyma in forma sardii.*

Letter 10

a. Omitting here Van Acker's *caligine confusa*, which appears to be merely a dittograph of the same phrase two lines down, where it properly belongs.

Letter 10r

a. *priorisse montis sancti Roberti in Binga.*

Letter 11

a. *Faciat etiam in te fenestras, que in celesti Ierusalem lucent, que sunt pulchra edificia in virtutibus.* An interesting variation of Hildegard's architectural imagery.

Letter 12

a. *O laudabilis persona, que necessaria est homini, habens in altissimo Deo successionem, quod est pontificale officium.*

b. *Quia Deus sciens omnia, scit ubi pastoralis cura utilis est, ideo fidelis homo non circueat querens prelationem.*

c. *Nunc audi me, non abiciens uerba mea sicut mater tua et soror tua et comes Hermannus ea abiecerunt. Non facio tibi iniuriam sine uoluntate Dei et sine salute anime sororis tue, sed rogo ut ego consoler per eam et ipsa per me. Quod Deus ordinauit, non contradico.*

Letter 13r

a. *Deus eam in hoc zelo habuit, quod uoluptas seculi illam non potuit amplecti; sed semper contra eam pugnauit, quamuis ipsa uelut flos in pulchritudine et decore et in symphonia huius seculi appareret.*

Letter 15

a. *sicuti reuera de Dei oraculo.*

Letter 15r

a. *Firmamentum cum omnibus ornamentis suis posui, nulla ui carens. Oculos enim quasi ad uidendum, aures ad audiendum, nares ad odorandum, os ad gustandum habet. Nam sol quasi lumen oculorum eius est, uentus autem auditus aurium eius, aer odoramentum eius, ros gustus eius uiriditatem sudando ut oris spiramen. Luna quoque tempora temporum dat, et sic scientiam hominibus ostendit. Stelle autem, uelut rationales sint, sic sunt, quia circulum habent, sicut etiam rationalitas multa comprehendit. Quattuor etiam angulos orbis igne, nube et aqua firmaui, et sic omnes terminos terre quasi uenas coniunxi. Lapides de igne et aqua sicut ossa fudi, et terram de humiditate et uiriditate quasi medullam constitui. Abyssos uelut pedes qui corpus sustinent in fixura extendi, circa quos sudantes aque sunt ad firmamentum eorum. Sic omnia sunt constituta, ne deficiant. Si nubes ignem et aquam non haberet, firma coagulatio non esset, et si terra humiditatem et uiriditatem non haberet, uelut cinis esset. Et si cetera luminaria lumen de igne solis non haberent, per aquas non fulgurarent, sed ceca essent.*

b. *Vos autem in unaquaque uolante seculari fama iam lassati estis, ita quod interdum milites, interdum serui, interdum etiam ludificantes cantores exsistitis, sed per fabulosa officia uestra muscas in estate aliquando abigitis.*

c. *Nam eos per precepta legis perfundere et constringere deberetis, ne ullus eorum per fragilitatem, quasi per medullam faceret quod sibi eligit, uelut terra humiditate et uiriditate perfusa et constricta est, ne cinis sit. Propter uos autem ut cinis sparguntur et in unaquaque causa que uolunt faciunt.* See Introduction for a discussion of this passage.

d. That is, on Mt. Ararat? This reading apparently gave pause to the scribes of two of the MSS, which read instead "when he fulfilled the commandments of God" (*iussa Dei compleuit*). The passage is very messy: *Noe in tremendo iudicio suffocationis creaturarum angustiatus multum sudorem emisit, cum mortem ualde timuit, ubi super nubem stetit.*

e. Hildegard's word here is the German form *wach.*

f. *unde Ecclesia nouam generationem per alienam uiam genuit, qua Eua sterilis uite fuit, Maria autem maiorem gratiam contulit quam Eua nocuisset.* See *Symphonia* 23.

Letter 18

a. *Quod si feceris, gratiam nostram deinceps plus quam hactenus experta fueris, senties; sin autem, eadem tibi iterum fortius mandabimus, nec cessabimus dum precepta nostra in hoc facto compleas.*

Letter 18r

a. *Perspicuus fons qui non est fallax, sed iustus, dicit:* He cause que de potestate huius puelle sunt allate, apud Deum inutiles sunt, quoniam ego altus et profundus ac circuiens, qui sum incidens lux, eas nec constitui nec elegi, sed facte sunt in coniuente audacia ignorantium cordium.

Letter 20r

a. *propter mystica uerba que a me non profero, sed secundum quod ea in uiuente lumine uideo, ita quod sepe illa que mens mea non desiderat et que etiam uoluntas mea non querit, mihi ostenduntur; sed illa multoties coacta uideo.*

b. *Nunc autem oculus tuus in Deo uiuat, et uiriditas anime tue non arescat.*

c. *Et quare zelum habes quasi triticum excribres, ita quod superando deicias quod tibi contrarium sit?*

Letter 23

a. *In uisione que anime mee, antequam nata procederem, a Deo opifice infixa est, coacta sum ad scribendum ista, pro ligatura qua a magistris nostris alligate sumus propter quendam mortuum, conductu sacerdotis sui apud nos sine calumnia sepultum. Quem post paucos sepelitionis sue dies cum idem a magistris nostris nos e cimiterio eicere iussisset, ex hoc non minimo terrore correpta, ad uerum lumen ut soleo aspexi, et uigilantibus oculis in anima mea uidi quod, si iuxta preceptum ipsorum corpus eiusdem mortui efferretur, eiectio illa in modum magne nigredinis ingens periculum loco nostro minaretur et in similitudine atre nubis, que ante tempestates et tonitrua apparere solet, nos circumuallaret.*

b. *Vnde et corpus eiusdem defuncti, utpote confessi, inuncti et communicati, et sine contradictione sepulti, nec efferre presumpsimus, nec consilio seu precepto istud suadentium uel iubentium acquieuimus, non consilium proborum hominum aut preceptum prelatorum nostrorum omnino pariuipendentes, sed ne sacramentis Christi, quibus ille uiuens adhuc munitus fuerat, iniuriam seuitate feminea facere uideremur. Sed ne ex toto inobedientes exsisteremus, a diuinarum laudum canticis hactenus secundum eorum interdictum cessauimus, et a participatione dominici corporis, quam per singulos fere menses ex consuetudine frequentauimus, abstinuimus.*

c. *sacramenta indumenti Verbi Dei,* i.e., of the Incarnation. One MS, perhaps rightly as Van Acker notes, has *mei* in place of *Dei*.

d. *ex humana natura homo sine contagio totius lesionis nasceretur, per quem,* but one MS has *per quam,* which would put the stress on the incarnation.

e. *Qui uero in tali ligatura se esse nec conscientia nec uoluntate cognouerit, securus ad perceptionem uiuifici sacramenti accedat, mundandus sanguine Agni immaculati, qui seipsum obediens Patri ad salutem omnibus restituendam in ara crucis immolari permisit.*

f. *In quibus uerbis per exteriora de interioribus instruimur, scilicet quomodo, secundum materialem compositionem uel qualitatem instrumentorum, interioris hominis nostri officia ad Creatoris maxime laudes conuertere et informare debeamus. Quibus cum diligenter intendimus, recolimus qualiter homo uocem uiuentis Spiritus requisiuit, quam Adam per inobedientiam perdidit, qui ante transgressionem, adhuc innocens, non minimam societatem cum angelicarum laudum uocibus habebat.*

g. *Similitudinem ergo uocis angelice, quam in paradiso habebat, Adam perdidit, et in scientia qua ante peccatum preditus erat, ita obdormiuit, sicut homo a somno euigilans de his, que in somnis uiderat, inscius et incertus redditur.*

h. *Deus uero, qui animas electorum luce ueritatis perfundens ad pristinam beatitudinem reseruat, ex suo hoc adinuenit consilio, ut quandoque corda quamplurium infusione prophetici Spiritus innouaret, cuius interiore illuminatione aliqua de scientia illa recuperarent, quam Adam ante preuaricationis sue uindictam habuerat.*

i. *et que cantabant, in iuncturis digitorum, que flexionibus inclinantur, adaptauerunt, ut et recolentes Adam digito Dei, qui Spiritus Sanctus est, formatum, in cuius uoce sonus omnis harmonie et totius musice artis, antequam delinqueret, suauitas erat. Et si in statu quo formatus fuit permansisset, infirmitas mortalis hominis uirtutem et sonoritatem uocis illius nullatenus ferre posset.*

j. *Et quoniam interdum in auditu alicuius cantionis homo sepe suspirat et gemit, naturam celestis harmonie recolens, propheta, subtiliter profundam spiritus naturam considerans, et sciens quia symphonialis est anima, hortatur in psalmo ut confiteamur Domino in cithara, et in psalterio decem chordarum psallamus ei, citharam, que inferius sonat, ad disciplinam corporis, psalterium, quod de superius sonum reddit, ad intentionem spiritus, decem chordas ad completionem legis referri cupiens.*

k. *Istud tempus tempus muliebre est, quia iustitia Dei debilis est. Sed fortitudo iustitie Dei exsudat, et bellatrix contra iniustitiam exsistit, quatenus deuicta cadat.*

Letter 24

a. *ego ad uerum lumen, ut soleo, aspexi, et in illo Deus mihi precepit ne umquam uoluntario consensu meo eiceretur, quem ipse a sinu Ecclesie in gloriam saluationis deputandum susceperit, quoniam nigredo magni periculi nobis inde proueniret, eo quod contra uoluntatem eius ueritatis esset. Si enim iste timor omnipotentis Dei mihi non obstitisset, eis humiliter obedissem, et, quemcumque in nomine tuo, qui dominus et aduocatus noster es, eundem mortuum iussissent efferre, si excommunicatus non esset, seruandum ius Ecclesie grata uoluntate concessissem.*

b. *fidelis amicus tuus, scilicet Coloniensis archiepiscopus ad ipsos in Moguntiam uenit, et quodam milite libero homine assistente, qui sufficientibus testibus probare uoluit quod ipse et predictus mortuus, adhuc in corpore uiuens, cum pariter in eodem excessu fuissent, pariter etiam a banno, eodem loco, eadem hora, ab eodem sacerdote soluti essent, eodem sacerdote etiam, qui eos absoluit, presente, ab eis cognita huius rei ueritate, idem presul de te presumens, licentiam celebrandi diuina usque ad reditum tuum secure et in pace obtinuit.*

c. *in qua numquam me aliquo uerbo turbasti.*

Letter 24r

a. *Verum quia constabat Ecclesie, sepultum apud ecclesiam uestram defunctum in uita sua excommunicationis sententiam incurrisse, dum adhuc eidem Ecclesie de absolutione ipsius incertum exstitit, uobis interim, propter statuta sanctorum Patrum non euitanda, clamorem cleri declinare et scandalum Ecclesie dissimulare periculosum nimis fuit, donec idoneo testimonio bonorum uirorum in facie Ecclesie illum absolutum fuisse comprobetur.*

Letter 25

a. *Quicquid tamen illud est quod rescribis, pone sub sigillo.*

Letter 25r

a. *ita quod in istis uirtutibus molendinum finis corporis tui complebis.*

Letter 26

a. *et contestor uiscera tua materna per sanctam caritatem, quatenus de cella illa regis uinaria, cuius uoluptatis abundantia etiam in hac uita mirabiliter debriaris, guttas aliquas ad me peccatorem per presentium latorem stillare scripto digneris.*

Letter 26r

a. *Nunc squalidum tempus muliebris forme est.* See Letter 23, note 3.

b. *Oi, oi, Adam nouum testamentum omnis iustitie et radix omnis seminis hominum fuit. Postea in genere ipsius uirilis animus surrexit qui in tres turmas exiit, uelut arbor que se in tres ramos extendit. Prima turma talis erat, quod filii Ade elegerunt quicquid possibilitas eorum habuit; secunda autem quod homines in temeritatem homicidii surrexerunt; tertia uero quod fecerunt quicquid in idolis et similibus erroribus uoluerunt. Nunc arbor hec arida est, ita quod mundus in multis periculis euersus est.*

c. *Sed tamen uir plures uires habet quam mulier perficere possit. Mulier autem est fons sapientie et fons pleni gaudii, quas partes uir ad perfectum ducit.*

Letter 27r

a. *O tu arbor es a Deo constitutus, quemadmodum Paulus dicit: Omnis potestas a Deo est, quia secundum summum magistrum per inuocationem nominis sui omnis potestas nominata est, unde in illa arbor uiriditatem honoris nominis sui habet.*

b. *Vnde decet, ut pauper pauperem diligat et diues diuitem cognoscat, quia sapientia pauperi anulum dat et diuiti inaurem negat.*

Letter 31

a. *flagrantia* according to Van Acker. But two MSS have *fraglantia*, and, surely, the biblical verse just cited requires "fragrance."

b. *In Patre manet eternitas, in Filio equalitas, in Spiritu Sancto eternitatis equalitatisque connexio.*

Letter 31r

a. *In Patre manet eternitas.*

b. *Vita autem non procedit de mortalitate, sed uita est in uita. Arbor enim non floret, nisi de uiriditate, nec lapis est sine humore, nec ulla creatura sine ui sua. Ipsa etiam uiuens eternitas non est sine floriditate.* Compare Symphonia 28: *De te nubes fluunt, ether volat,/ lapides humorem habent,/ atque riuulos educunt,/ et terra viriditatem sudat.*

c. *Caro de carne et bonum de eo quod bonum est in bona fama emittitur, et in bono exemplo in alio homine augetur.*

d. *In Filio equalitas.*

e. *Pater enim ordinat, Filius autem operatur.*

f. *Et etiam Filius tunicam de homine induit, quem de limo formauerat, que ante corporaliter non apparuit.*

g. *Hoc nihil superbia est. Illa enim opinio est, que in se respicit et que in nullum confidit. Nam ipsa uult quod Deus non uult, et semper hoc computat quod ipsa constituit, atque tenebrosa est, quia lumen ueritatis despexit et quia incepit quod perficere non potuit; unde nihil est, quia a Deo nec facta nec creata est.*

h. *Tunc Deus alio filio suo gloriam illius dedit, qui in tam robusta ui factus est quod omnes creature ipsi assunt, et qui etiam in tam forti ui constitutus est quod gloriam illam per omnia non perderet. In illa enim maledictione qua diabolus Deum noluit, stultitia in homine Deo in honore similis esse desiderauit, scilicet ut Deus est; sed tamen illum amorem, quod Deum esse sciuit, non amisit. Vnde materia diaboli omnino tenebrosa est, quia claritatem Dei esse noluit. Adam autem claritatem Dei esse uoluit, sed in societate eius esse desiderauit. Vnde perfectus in materia sua est, quoniam aliquid lucidi in eo est; sed tamen plenus multis miseriis est.*

i. *In Spiritu Sancto eternitatis equalitatisque connexio.*

j. *Sed quelibet causa, in qua nulla uis est, mortua est, sicut abscisum lignum ab arbore aridum est, quia uiriditatem non habet.*

k. *Spiritus Sanctus enim est solidamentum et uiuificatio. Nam eternitas non esset eternitas sine Spiritu Sancto. Equalitas quoque non esset equalitas sine Spiritu Sancto.*

l. *Rationalitas etiam tres uires habet, sonum scilicet, uerbum, sufflatum.*

m. *Nam de uiriditate flores, de floribus fructus sunt pomorum. Nubes etiam cursum habent. Luna quoque et stelle cum igne flagrant, ligna per uiriditatem flores educunt, aqua tenuitatem et uentum inundando et riuulos educendo habet. Terra etiam humiditatem cum sudore habet.*

n. *Hoc est rationalitas que cum uoce sonat. Vox est corpus, rationalitas anima, calor aeris ignis, et unum sunt.*

o. *Inde omnia uitia diaboli confunduntur et omnes celestes harmonie mirantur, quia quod in inutilitate lutum prius computabant, in principali utilitate columnam nubis postea uident, quia que uilia uiderunt, postea pulchriora eligunt, quoniam omnia uitia diaboli in utilitate pro nihilo computantur.*

Letter 33

a. *Iustus enim iste hec suspiria habuit, que per speculatum oculum cherubim ad thronum Dei ascenderunt.*

Letter 35r

a. *Tu uero labia tua moues per magniloquos sufflatus morum cordis tui, et ad indignationem illos reducis.*

Letter 39

a. *calamus confractus, forma mali, esca diaboli.*

Letter 40

a. *Quia tu, domina, ancillam te fecisti Christi, ipse te super te eleuauit et secreta tibi uirginalis thalami adhuc in carne posite reuelasse ex parte creditur, ut una ex his credaris de quibus canitur: Introduxit me rex in cubiculum suum.*

b. *quoniam plurimi contendunt quod paternitas et diuinitas Deus non sit.*

Letter 40r

a. There are problems here of mixed metaphor, illogical comparison, or worse. The text reads: *Sol lumine suo descendit et multas indignationes uicissitudinis locorum illustrat. Et sic, o tu magister, in magistratione multos riuulos in scripturis habes quos inter alios interdum spargis, scilicet inter magnos et paruos.*

b. *quia homo hanc potestatem non habet ut de Deo dicat sicut de humanitate hominis et sicut de colore facti operis de manu hominis.*

c. *Deus plenus est et integer et absque principio temporum, et ideo non potest diuidi sermone sicut homo diuidi potest, quoniam Deus totum est et non alius, ac idcirco illi nihil abstrahendum aut addendum est. Nam etiam paternitas et diuinitas est ille "qui est," ut dictum est: "Ego sum qui sum."*

d. *Quicumque enim dicit quod paternitas et diuinitas non sit Deus, hic nominat punctum absque circulo, et si punctum habere uult absque circulo, illum qui eternus est negat.*

e. *Et quoniam cretura initium habet, ex hoc inuenit rationalitas hominis Deum per nomina, sicut et ipsa in proprietate sua plena est nominum.*

Letter 41r

a. *Admonitionem Spiritus Sancti que in te ascendit non abscide a te per malam consuetudinem operum tuorum, quia Deus requirit in te quod olim attendit perditam ouem reducere, quando crimina hominum abstersit, ubi antiquus illusor confusus est, cum eum fortissimus bellator superauit.* There are problems in Hildegard's grammar here, but despite that fact, the general sense seems to come through rather clearly.

Letter 42

a. We have adopted Pitra's *[in] nigram* over Van Acker's *nigrum*.

Letter 43r

a. *Nouissime autem Filius Dei uenit, quem non decebat ut in uacuo tempore adesset, in quo nullam iustitiam inueniret, sicut etiam homo creatus non est, antequam eum omnis creatura ostendebat.*

b. *Nunc tu, pastor, prouide ne in puerili tempore, quod Deum nescit, sis, sed esto in tempore iustorum et sanctorum et in ostensione prophetarum.*

Letter 45

a. *Viua autem uoce per presentem latorem tibi presentialiter loquimur, et responsum admonitionis tue toto corde exflagitamus.*

Letter 45r

a. *que sunt genera uirtutum.*

b. *Homo enim edificium Dei est, in quo ipse mansionem habet, quoniam igneam animam in illum misit, que cum rationalitate in dilatatione uolat, quemadmodum murus latitudinem domus comprehendit.*

Letter 46

a. *Sed tamen dubitas cibum illum frangere, quem tu ipse comedere uis indictante mente tua. Quomodo et quare circuis diuersa cribrando et undique aspiciendo, ubi inueniatur res illa que in cerimonia sit?*

Letter 48

a. *Credo enim per Spiritum, per quem cuncta preterita, presentia et futura perspicis, etiam tibi patere secreta mei cordis.*

Letter 48r

a. *O homo, riuuli fluunt de me ad uiriditatem mentis tue.*

b. *Et occulte cogitationes tue in mente tua interdum decipiunt te, et gustus operis tui interdum tangit te.*

Letter 51

a. *sic et spiritus incorporati, licet ad uitam sint preordinati, alii abundantius, alii tenuius impetu claritatis a maiestate semper discurrentis irradiantur, et ad illud beatificum principium consequendum distantissima mobilitate eleuantur. Sunt enim quedam anime in illud pelagus claritatis sic absorpte, ut aliud nihil uidere, aliud nihil sentire quam presentiam illius luminis omnia uiuificantis sibi uideantur. Quarum fulgore et cetere anime, adhuc terrestri graues obscuritate, dum sepius reuerberantur, ad receptaculum ipsius claritatis aptificantur, quo sibi ex ea subtilius notificantur.*

b. *quamuis totus iam pene orbis tenebris erroris inuolutus sit, radius quidam antique gratie, ne tota gens pereat, in uobis resplenduit. Ordo enim monachorum orbitat, ordo clericorum claudicat, ordo quoque sanctimonialium titubat, et, cum spiritales religione hoc modo excedunt, seculares institutam sibi a Domino legem omnino negligunt.*

Letter 52

a. *Multorum namque testimonio didicimus, de secretis celestibus plurima mortalibus intellectu difficilia uobis per angelum diuinitus ad scribendum reuelari, et queque uobis agenda non deliberatione humana, sed ipso edocente ordinari.*

b. *uirgines uidelicet uestras festis diebus psallendo solutis crinibus in ecclesia stare, ipsasque pro ornamento candidis ac sericis uti uelaminibus pre longitudine superficiem terre tangentibus, coronas etiam auro contextas capitibus earum desuper impositas et his utraque parte et retro cruces insertas, in fronte autem agni figuram decenter impressam, insuper et digitos earundem aureis decorari anulis.* Most critics refer to the images of angels on the sides (see Newman, *Sister of Wisdom* 221, and Dronke, *Women Writers* 169), but such images are from the later text of the letters. See Haverkamp, "Tenxwind."

c. *Preterea, et quod his omnibus non minus mirandum nobis videtur, in consortium uestrum genere tantum spectabiles et ingenuas introducere, aliis uero ignobilibus et minus ditatis commansionem uestram penitus abnuere.*

Letter 52r

a. *O quam mira res es, que in sole fundamentum posuisti et inde terram superasti!*

b. *Audi: Terra sudat uiridiatatem graminis, usque dum eam hiems superat. Et hiems aufert pulchritudinem illius floris, et illa tegit uiriditatem sui floris, deinceps non ualens se reuelare quasi numquam aruerit, quia hiems illam abstulit. Ideo non debet mulier se in crinibus suis subleuare nec ornare, nec erigere in ulla sublimitate corone et auri ullius rei, nisi in uoluntate uiri sui, secundum quod illi in recta mensura placuerit.*

c. *Hec non pertinent ad uirginem; sed ipsa stat in simplicitate et in integritate pulchri paradisi, qui numquam aridus apparebit, sed semper permanet in plena uiriditate floris uirge.* Hildegard is playing with the words *virgo/virga*, a medieval commonplace. See Numbers 17.1–8 and Isaiah 11.1.

d. *quia Deus discernit populum in terra sicut et in celo.*

e. *Hec dicta sunt a uiuente lumine et non ab homine.*

Letter 56

a. *in circueunte rota gratie sue.*

Letter 58

a. *alter miles fuit, alter uernaculus.*

Letter 59

a. *Filius Dei de corde Patris descendit et in amaritudine nature hominis carnem induit.*

b. *quia uirginei flores circulum ardentis rote in carnea natura reliquerunt, post exempla Agni in uestigio uirginitatis ambulantes atque pompam et diuitias ac terrenas causas huius seculi relinquentes.*

c. *et cum communis populus in uera abscisione gladii uerbi Dei seculum relinquet in magnis criminibus et preuaricationibus, ut camelus oneratus atque in omni lasciuia dromedariorum morum et uitiorum.* This is very messy. Does she mean that the common people are loaded like a camel before the sword of God's word prunes them? If so the syntax is very awkward. Or does she mean that the world, which the common people give up, is loaded like a camel? If so, the grammatical case is wrong. Besides, the camels and dromedaries of the Scripture do not seem to bear this pejorative sense.

d. *tunica Christi induti.*

Letter 66r

a. *Sed et, o homo, mens tua nubi similis est, que grandinem et pluuiam non portat, sed que per solem diuiditur. Tu enim propter securitatem leuium uerborum et morum nubem cum grandine sicut iram, et litem sicut pluuiam non habes; sed per bona opera in desiderio supernorum claudicas.*

Letter 68r

a. *Eligite septem sacerdotes boni testimonii et quos uite meritum commendat, in nomine et ordine Abel, Noe, Abrahe, Melchisedech, Iacob et Aaron, qui uiuenti Deo sacrificium obtulerunt, septimum in nomine Christi, qui se ipsum Deo patri in cruce obtulit, et ieiuniis, flagellis, orationibus, elemosinis et missarum celebrationibus premissis humili intentione et habitu sacerdotali cum stolis ad patientem accedant, et eam circumstantes unusquisque eorum uirgam in manu teneat in figura uirge, qua Moyses Egyptum, mare Rubrum petramque precepto Dei percussit, ut, sicut Deus ibi per uirgam miracula ostendit, ita et hic pessimo hoste uirgis eiecto se ipsum glorificet.*

b. *Et primus, qui in nomine Abel erit, uirgam in manu tenens dicat: Audi, maligne et stulte spiritus, quicumque in homine isto habitas, audi uerba hec non per hominem premeditata, sed per illum qui est et qui uiuit manifestata et iussu illius extritus fuge. Audi ipsum qui est dicentem: Qui sine initio sum, sed a quo omnia initia procedunt, et qui antiquus dierum sum, dico: Ego per memetipsum dies sum, qui a sole numquam processi, sed de quo sol accensus est. Ego etiam ratio sum, que ab alio non sonuit, sed ex qua omnis rationalitas spirat. Ad intuitum igitur faciei mee specula feci, in quibus omnia miracula antiquitatis mee, que numquam deficient, considero ac eadem specula in laudibus concinentia paraui, quia uocem ut tonitruum habeo, cum qua totum orbem terrarum in uiuentibus sonis omnium creaturarum moueo.*

c. *Et tam idem sacerdos quam ceteri sex predicti sacerdotes astantes eam uirgis suis moderate percutiant supra caput ac supra dorsum, supra pectus et supra umbilicum et supra renes, supra genua, supra pedes et dicant: Nunc autem tu, o satanas et maligne spiritus, qui hunc hominem et formam mulieris huius fatigas et premis, per illum qui uiuit et qui hec uerba per simplicem et humana doctrina indoctum hominem protulit et dicit, tibi preceptum est, et ipse nunc tibi precipit, ut in nomine ipsius de homine isto, qui presens est et quem diu fatigasti et in quo adhuc manes, abscedas; et ideo uirga hac in precepto ueri principii, scilicet in ipso principio, quod eum ulterius ledas. Coniuratus et conuictus etiam sacrificio ac precibus et adiutorio Abel, in cuius nomine te quoque percutimus.*

Letter 70

a. *quamuis idiota condendi libros aliaque mira perplura faciendi, hisque qui impresentiarum sunt stupendi, celestis mirabiliter aspiret harmonia, et ante incognita mortalibus per uos fiant manifesta.*

Letter 70r

a. *et Deus ipsi uestitum dedit, sciens quod propter eum tunicam humanitatis sumpturus esset.*

b. *Deus enim rationalitatem homini dedit. Nam per uerbum Dei homo rationalis est. Irrationalis autem creatura uelut sonus est. Sic Deus omnem creaturam in homine constituit.* Sometimes Hildegard's connectives are quite breathtaking. Note the force of *sic* here.

Letter 74r

a. *succurrente flore*
   omnium ramorum mundi.
b. *O viriditas digiti Dei.*
c. *tu tamen stas a longe ut exul,*
   sed non est in poteste
   armati
   qui te rapiat.
d. *a semine mundi.*
e. *O mons clause mentis.*
f. *in speculo columbe.*

g. *per cancellos sanctorum*
   emicans Deo.
h. *et huius turris culmen obumbrasti*
   per fumum aromatum.
i. *et protegis viridi rore*
   laudantes Deum ista voce.

Letter 75

a. *Et quidam de turba fratrum tuorum super me sicut super nigerrimam auem et ut super horribilem bestiam fremebant, atque arcus suos contra me intendebant quatenus ab ipsis fugerem. Sed in ueritate scio quod Deus in mysteriis suis me de loco illo monuit, quoniam in uerbis et in miraculis ipsius anima mea ita commota fuisset quasi ante tempus moritura essem, si illic permansissem.*

Letter 76

a. *Nam quibus prodesse deberem, preesse magis studeo.* This *prodesse/preesse* opposition is familiar from the *Rule*, where Benedict writes that the good abbot must know *sibi oportere prodesse magis quam praeesse* [lxiv]. By Hildegard's time, it has become a kind of confessional formula.

Letter 76r

a. *Et quis est homo iste? Scilicet ille qui corpus suum habet sicut ancillam et animam suam sicut dilectissimam dominam. Nam qui etiam ferox est in impietate tamquam ursus, et ferocitatem illam recusat atque ad solem iustitie, qui pius et clemens est, anhelat, hic Deo placet, ita quod Deus illum super precepta sua constituit, dans uirgam ferream in manus ipsius ad erudiendum oues suas ad montem myrrhe. Nunc audi et disce, ut in gustu anime tue super his erubescas, qui aliquando mores ursi habes qui sepe in semetipso occulte murmurat, et etiam interdum mores asini, ita quod non es prouidus in causis tuis, sed tediosus, sed et etiam in aliis quibusdam rebus inutilis; et ideo malitiam ursi aliquando in impietate non perficis. Item mores etiam habes aliquorum uolatilium que nec de superioribus nec de infimis sunt, ita quod superiora ea uincunt et quod infima illa ledere non possunt.*

Letter 77

a. *Quia, mater dilecta, omnipotentis Dei Sancti Paracliti Spiritus instinctu necnon et iussione, "qui uult omnes homines saluos fieri et ad agnitionem ueritatis uenire," nuper uestram sanctitatem ad nos uenisse cognouimus, eidem Paraclito prout possumus, licet non condigne ualeamus, gratias incessanter referimus, quia, ut ueraciter fateamur, illustrationis eius ardorem et tactum plenissime inter nos et in nobis persensimus, dum omnis odii et inimicitiarum fomenta per plures iam annos inueterata omnes unanimi consensu abiecimus, et in uere caritatis unitatem pleniter quasi in uno corpore et anima conuenimus.* The passage is problematic, but it seems to read as we have rendered it.

b. *si ueraciter in uera caritate, que est initium omnium bonorum, conuenerimus, uel si qua radix alicuius dissensionis inter nos adhuc lateat manifestetis.*

Letter 77r

a. *Sed planete, scilicet angeli iustitie qui flamma ignis sunt, cum Deo perstiterunt et inexstinguibili igni qui uita est, ministrabant. Ignis uero flammam habet quam uentus mouet, ita quod eadem flamma flagrando apparet. Sic in uoce uerbum est et uerbum auditur, et ignis flammam habet et Deo laus est, et uentus flammam mouet et Deo laus est, atque in uoce uerbum est et Deo laus est, atque uerbum auditur et Deo laus est. Quapropter et omnis creatura laus Dei est.*

b. *Tunc Deus magnum hoc consilium habuit in semetipso, quod fortitudini sue nulla aduersitas cadentium preualeret, atque preuidit quod in feminea natura opus tale facturus esset, quod nec angeli, nec homo, nec ulla alia creatura ad finem perducere posset.*

c. *Sed de Abel usque ad Noe omnes filii hominum quasi lac sugentes in recta scientia dormitabant.*

d. *Sed et Abraham et Moyses quasi duo planete incarnationis Filii Dei erant, quemadmodum et planete uelut flamma ignis sunt. Abraham enim Christum preuidit, Moyses uero opera in creaturis fecit, scilicet boues et oues atque hircos offerendo et in oblatione carnis creature oblationem Filii Dei presignando. Hoc definitum est, quando Virgo unicornem cepit et quando Deus eburneam turrim, sicut decuit, fecit, quod purum uirginale opus est: in qua opus magni consilii perfectum est, uidelicet quod Deus homo est.*

e. *Et tunc muliebre tempus fere primo casui simile uenit, ita quod omnis iustitia secundum infirmitatem mulieris debilitata est.*

f. *Attamen tempus pressure et destructionis, uidelicet ponderis illius quo uua in torculari premitur.*

g. *Tempus enim bone intentionis atque conuersationis quandoque ueniet et ad primam auroram aspiciet.*

h. *Itaque ego, misera et paupercula forma, in mystica uisione qua ab infantia mea edocta a Deo sum, hec uerba in magnis egritudinibus uidi et audiui, et ut ea in loco uestro uiua uoce proferrem iussa sum.*

Letter 81

a. *Serena lux uidet stabulum et statutum prandium cuiusque congregationis que officium in ministerio suo habet, cibum refectionis in recta moderatione distribuens, ne fidelibus sibi adherentibus letitia anime desit. Pastoralis uillicus debet fortissimis mentibus gladium in uagina dare et suauibus moribus sagittas in pharetra ostendere, et capaci beneuolentie aromata medicinarum tribuere.*

b. *Tibi autem, o homo, refectio fiet in cinctura femorum tuorum, ubi habes uerum desiderium in manibus tuis, cum thesauros uere pecunie non negligis. Terra tibi dormit, quoniam naufragium mundi te non ledit.*

Letter 83

a. *Ita uos felicem animam et beatam elegit sibi organum et uas electionis sue.*

Letter 84r

a. *pallio humanitatis circumdatus.*

b. *per quod hominem speculum honoris sui et miraculorum suorum constituit.*

c. *In primo enim ortu Deus Ade concessit terram colere, Abel sacrificare, Noe edificare, et hoc usque ad summum sacerdotium quod in Christi incarnatione exortum est, quod prius Abra-*

ham per circumcisionem, Moyses per legislationem prefigurabat. Sed hec omnia idem Filius Dei postea in humanitate sua perfecit, unde et ad hominem intelligenda sunt. Post ruinam enim Ade Deus tam in hominibus quam in angelis ordinationem suam recte presignauit.

d. *et ut per sacrificium Abel Filium suum pro redemptione populi sacrificandum presignauit, et sicut per Noe qui arcam edificauit, quod in spirituali populo magistri constituendi essent prefigurauit.*

e. *Nunc uos, magistri, supradictos homines, scilicet conuersos, in ordine uestro corripite et corrigite, quia plurima pars eorum nec in die nec in nocte operatur quoniam nec Deo nec seculo ad perfectum seruiunt, et eos ab ignorantia ista excitate uelut bonus pigmentarius hortum suum ab inutilibus herbis purgat.* On *pigmentarius,* "perfumer," see Introduction, and compare Canticles 5.13.

f. *Et ego paupercula et indocta feminea forma.*

Letter 85

a. *Adauxit Deus gaudium meum, cum nutu benigno et mirabili direxit uos ut uideretur facies et audiretur uox uestra in terra nostra, mihique, quod uix sperare poteram, mutuam concessit collocutionem. De quibus autem uobis me dixi anxium, confido uos non immemorem esse, et quia diuersi diuersa sentiunt, alii istud, alii illud, si bonum est et salus apud Dominum, "benedictus Deus"; si periculum, orate Deum ut bonum mihi et salutem anime tribuat et omne periculum excludat.*

Letter 85r/a

a. *Tunc creatura in his speciebus ac in formis suis Creatorem suum agnouit, quoniam caritas in principio materia eiusdem creature sic fuit, ubi Deus dixit: "Fiat, et facta est."*

b. *sed quod ipsa eum in sancta humanitate redimeret. Hoc ale magne potentie fuerunt, quia hominem qui perditus fuit humilitas eleuauit, quod humanitas Saluatoris erat, quoniam caritas hominem creauit, humilitas autem eum redemit.*

Letter 85r/b

a. *Gratia enim Dei uelut sol micat et dona sua sic interdum emittit, uno uidelicet modo in sapientia, altero in uiriditate, tertio in humiditate. Sapientia autem in pinguem naturam cadit, uiriditas uero magnos labores subintrat, et humiditas in duram amaritudinem uadit.*

b. *Sed uirtutes famulatum in laudibus suis Deo exhibentes, hoc iusto Dei iudicio fieri permittunt, ita ut homines intelligant quid sint.*

Letter 86

a. *Nam in topazio misericordia, in sapphiro caritas intelligenda est, quas uirtutes sacerdos iste* [i.e., Christ] *uelut uestimentum sacerdotale propter hominem induit.*

Letter 89

a. *Caue ergo ne de cogitationibus et somniis tuis audacter requiras, quamdiu in hoc itinere uiuis in quo finieris, quoniam alia signa de papa Eugenio Deus mihi non ostendit. Attamen uideo te ualde constrictum, et inde solui debes in hac uita. Deus etiam non ostendit mihi longitudinem aut breuitatem dierum fratris illius de quo me interrogas, et neque in annis neque in temporibus, sed tamen tempus illud habet quod nondum finietur.*

Bibliography

Editions

Hildegard's Letters

Migne, J.-P. *Sanctae Hildegardis Abbatissae Opera Omnia.* In *Patrologia Latina Cursus Completus,* vol. 197. Paris, 1855. Rpt. Turnhout: Brepols, 1976.
Pitra, J.-B., ed. *Analecta S. Hildegardis.* In *Analecta Sacra,* vol. 8. Monte Cassino, 1882.
Van Acker, Lieven, ed. *Hildegardis Bingensis Epistolarium: Prima Pars.* In *Corpus Christianorum: continuatio medievalis,* vol. 91. Turnhout, Belgium, 1991.

Editions of Other Works

Derolez, Albert, and Peter Dronke, eds. *Liber divinorum operum.* In *Corpus Christianorum: continuatio mediaevalis.* Turnhout, Belgium. Forthcoming.
Führkötter, Adelgundis, and Angela Carlevaris. eds. *Hildegardis Scivias.* In *Corpus Christianorum: continuatio mediaevalis,* vols. 43 and 43a. Turnhout, Belgium, 1978.
Haug, F. "Epistolae Sanctae Hildegardis secundum codicem Stuttgartensem," *Revue bénédictine* 43 (1931), 59–71.
Klaes, Monika, ed. *Vita Hildegardis.* In *Corpus Christianorum: continuatio medievalis,* vol. 126. Turnhout, Brepols, 1993.
McCann, Justin, ed., tr. *The Rule of Saint Benedict in Latin and English.* London: Burns & Oates, 1969.
Newman, Barbara, ed. *Symphonia: A Critical Edition of the Symphonia Armonie Celestium Revelationum.* Ithaca: Cornell University Press, 1988.

Biographies

Flanagan, S. *Hildegard of Bingen: A Visionary Life.* London: Routledge, 1989.
Führkötter, Adelgundis. *Hildegard von Bingen.* Salzburg: Otto Müller Verlag, 1972.

Gronau, Eduard. *Hildegard von Bingen 1098–1179: Prophetische Lehrerin der Kirche an der Schwelle und am Ende der Neuzeit*. Stein am Rhein: Christiana Verlag, 1991.

Translations

Hildegard's Letters

Führkötter, Adelgundis, trans. *Hildegard von Bingen: Briefwechsel*. 2nd edition. Salzburg: Otto Müller Verlag, 1990.

Translations of individual letters appear in many of the sources listed in this bibliography: Bowie and Davies, *Mystical Writings*; Dronke, *Women Writers*; Newman, *Sister of Wisdom*; Gronau, *Hildegard von Bingen*; Flanagan, *Hildegard of Bingen*.

Other Works

Hart, Columba, and Jane Bishop, trans. *Hildegard of Bingen: Scivias*. New York: Paulist Press, 1990.

Secondary Literature

Bowie, F., and O. Davies. *Hildegard of Bingen: Mystical Writings*. New York: Crossroad, 1990.

Brück, Anton, ed. *Hildegard von Bingen, 1179–1979: Festschrift zum 800. Todestag der Heiligen*. Mainz: Gesellschaft für Mittelrheinische Kirchengeschichte, 1979. Collection of twenty-one essays.

Constable, Giles. *Letters and Letter-Collections*. Fasc. 17 of *Typologie des Sources du Moyen Âge Occidental*. Turnhout: Brepols, 1976.

Czarski, C. *The Prophecies of St. Hildegard of Bingen*. Ph.D. dissertation, University of Kentucky, 1983.

Dronke, Peter. *Medieval Latin and the Rise of European Love-Lyric*. 2nd ed. 2 vols. Oxford: Clarendon Press, 1968.

———. *Poetic Individuality in the Middle Ages: New Departures in Poetry 1000–1500*. Oxford: Clarendon Press, 1970.

———. "Problemata Hildegardiana," *Mitellateinisches Jahrbuch* 16 (1981), 97–131.

———. *Women Writers of the Middle Ages*. Cambridge: Cambridge University Press, 1984.

Greenaway, George William. *Arnold of Brescia*. Cambridge: Cambridge University Press, 1931.

Haverkamp, A. "Tenxwind von Andernach und Hildegard von Bingen: Zwei 'Weltanschauungen' in der Mitte des 12. Jahrhunderts," *Institutionen, Kultur und Gesellschaft im Mittelalter. Festschrift für Josef Fleckenstein*, eds. L. Fenske, W. Rösener, and T. Zotz, 515–548. Sigmaringen: J. Thorbecke, 1984.

Herwegen, Ildefons. "Les collaborateurs de Ste. Hildegarde," *Revue bénédictine* 21 (1904), 192–203; 302–15; 381–403.

Kerby-Fulton, Kathryn. *The Voice of Honest Indignation: Reformist Apocalypticism and Piers Plowman*. Cambridge: Cambridge University Press, 1989.

Kraft, Kent. *The Eye Sees More Than the Heart Knows: The Visionary Cosmology of Hildegard of Bingen*. Ph.D. dissertation, University of Wisconsin, 1977.

———. "The German Visionary: Hildegard of Bingen," *Medieval Women Writers*, ed. K. Wilson, 109–130. Athens, Georgia: University of Georgia Press, 1984.

Lekai, Louis J. *The Cistercians: Ideals and Reality*. Kent, Ohio: Kent State University Press, 1977.

Mann, Horace K. *The Lives of the Popes in the Early Middle Ages*. 18 vols. London: Kegan Paul, Trench, Trubner & Co., 1925.

Meier, Christel. "Die Bedeutung der Farben im Werk Hildegards von Bingen," *Frühmitteralterliche Studien* 6 (1972), 245–355.

Newman, Barbara. *Sister of Wisdom: St. Hildegard's Theology of the Feminine*. Berkeley: University of California Press, 1987.

Petroff, E. *Medieval Women's Visionary Literature*. Oxford: Oxford University Press, 1986.

Runciman, Steven. *The Medieval Manichee: A Study of the Christian Dualist Heresy*. New York: The Viking Press, 1961.

Schmeidler, B. "Bemerkungen zum Corpus der Briefe der hl. Hildegard von Bingen." *Corona Quernea: Festgabe K. Strecker zum 80. Geburtstage dargebracht*, 335–366. Stuttgart: Hiersemann Verlag, 1952.

Scholz, B. "Hildegard von Bingen on the Nature of Women." *American Benedictine Review* 31 (1984), 361–383.

Schrader, Marianna, and Adelgundis Führkötter. *Die Echtheit des Schrifttums der hl. Hildegard von Bingen*. Cologne and Graz: Bohlau Verlag, 1956.

Van Acker, Lieven. "Der Briefwechsel der heiligen Hildegard von Bingen. Vorbemerkungen zu einer kritischen Edition," *Revue bénédictine* 98 (1988), 141–168; 99 (1989), 118–154.

Scripture Index

Frequency of Scripture cited or alluded to is indicated in parentheses

Acts 9.15, 10.34
Amos 7.14
Apocalypse 1.4 (2), 1.11, 1.13, 1.15,
 1.19, 2.7, 3.1, 3.15, 4, 4.6, 4.7, 5.5,
 7.3, 10.4, 11.12, 14.1, 14.2, 14.4
 (3), 14.13, 18.4, 21.18ff, 21.19ff,
 21.20, 22.18ff

Canticles 1.2, 1.3 (2), 1.14, 2.2, 2.3
 (2), 2.4, 2.6 (3), 2.12 (2), 2.14 (2),
 2.16, 3.4 (2), 3.16, 4.1, 4.6 (3), 4.7,
 4.11, 4.15, 5.2, 5.13, 6.10, 6.12,
 7.1, 7.1ff, 7.4, 8.3 (2), 8.3ff, 8.5,
 8.7
Colossians 3.18
I Corinthians 1.26–28, 1.27, 2.9 (2),
 3.1–2, 3.2, 9.24 (2), 12.11, 13.12
 (2), 13.13
II Corinthians 2.15 (3), 2.16, 7.5,
 11.30, 12.1, 12.2ff, 12.7

Daniel 4.21ff, 7.9, 7.13 (2), 7.22,
 13.23
Deuteronomy 4.24, 9.10, 32.33

Ecclesiasticus 16.31, 20.32, 24.8,
 24.18, 39.19
Ephesians 1.3, 5.22ff, 6.14, 6.14ff,
 6.16
Exodus 3.14, 7.8–10.23, 13.21,
 14.16–29, 17, 17.6, 17.6–7, 28.17,
 29.22, 31.18
Ezechiel 1, 1.12, 1.15, 1.18, 3.12,
 10.12, 22.27, 43.2

Galatians 4.22ff, 4.27
Genesis 1.2, 1.3, 1.6, 1.28, 2.7, 3.9,
 3.15, 9.20–25, 12.1, 14.18ff, 16,
 17, 21.1–21, 22.15–18 (2), 26.2–5,
 27.27–29 (2), 27.28 (3)

Hebrews 1.7, 1.13 (2), 5.6 (2), 5.12ff
 (2), 6.9, 6.20 (2), 7.1ff, 10.13 (2),
 12.22 (4), 12.29
Hosea 6.6 (4), 10.5

Isaiah 5.7, 6.2 (3), 7.14, 11.2, 24.16,
 39.2–8, 54.1, 60.1, 60.5–6, 60.8 (3),
 61.8, 63.3

James 1.17, 4.6
Jeremiah 2.13, 48.28
Job 24.8, 36.5
John 1.3 (4), 1.14, 1.27, 2.2–3, 3.5, 3.8 (2), 4.10 (2), 4.11, 4.14 (2), 4.34, 7.38, 9.4, 10.2, 10.12f, 10.34, 14.17, 15.1, 16.13, 17.15ff
I John 4.8, 16

Lamentations 1.12, 2.15, 4.21
Leviticus 3.9, 7.3
Luke 1.37, 1.49, 1.78, 5.10, 6.39, 7.16, 8.16 (2), 10.30ff (2), 10.38ff, 10.39, 10.42 (4), 11.33 (2), 12.36, 15.17, 15.18 (2), 15.20ff (2), 15.21 (2), 16.9 (2), 18.11, 20.9, 22.31

Malachi 4.2 (6)
Mark 4.21, 9.28, 12.1, 15.34, 16.15
Matthew 2.10, 5.14, 5.15 (2), 9.13 (4), 10.8, 11.12 (2), 12.7 (4), 12.43ff, 13.25, 13.45f, 13.46, 13.47–48, 15.14, 16.19 (4), 17.20, 18.7, 18.10, 19.6, 19.16ff, 20.1–16, 20.2, 21.2–3, 21.33, 22.14, 25.1ff, 25.1–13, 25.10, 25.12, 25.21 (4), 25.23 (4), 26.39, 27.46, 28.20 (2)

Numbers 20.11, 22.28ff, 22.28–35, 24.4

I Peter 1.2, 5.5
Philippians 1.6 (2), 2.8, 3.20f
Proverbs 31.30
Psalms 1.6, 2.7, 2.9 (2), 2.12, 10.7, 10.14, 13.2, 17.3, 17.12, 18.3, 18.5, 18.11, 21.2, 21.8, 21.21, 25.2, 32.2, 33.9, 37.7–8, 39.11, 41.2 (2), 43.5, 44.3, 44.8–10 (2), 44.10, 50.8, 67.6, 67.14 (2), 72.9, 72.27, 73.2, 73.3, 81.6 (3), 83.8 (7), 85.1, 91.4, 92.1, 93.11, 93.12, 103.4, 103.30 (2), 106.27, 108.25, 109.1 (3), 109.3, 109.4 (4), 113.5, 113.6, 115.17, 117.9, 117.15, 117.23, 123.7, 127.5, 139.6, 140.5, 144.1, 150.3, 150.5, 150.6 (2)

Romans 2.11, 12.8, 13.1 (2), 16.20

II Samuel 22.3

I Thessalonians 4.4
I Timothy 2.4, 2.9

Wisdom 1.7 (3), 3.9

Zachariah 2.10 (2), 9.9
Zephaniah 3.14

General Index

Aaron, 149–50, 212
Abel, 55–57, 60–61, 63 n. 4, 64 n. 20, 149, 167, 187, 212–13, 215–16
Abelard, 32
Abraham, 49, 61, 63–64, 94, 146, 149–50, 167–68, 170, 174, 181, 184, 187, 215
Abuse of Power, 65 n. 23
Adam, 4, 28, 60, 62, 76–78, 88, 97, 107, 109, 116, 137, 154, 175 n. 2, 185–87, 193–94, 197, 206–9
Adam, Abbot, 15–16, 191–92, 195–96
Adelbert, Bishop of Verdun, 117
Adelbert, Prior of Mount St. Disibod, 172
Alanus de Insulis, 63 n. 2
Albon, 119
Alexander III, Pope, 12, 45–46, 64 n. 18, 73, 80, 84
Aliprand, 153 n. 1
Alpirsbach, 120
Altena, 122
Altwick, 123
Amorbach, 125
Anastasius IV, Pope, 17, 41
Andernach, 9, 20, 127

Andrew, Provost of Averbode, 131
Andrew's, St., 46, 89, 93
Apostle, the. *See* Paul
ark, 61, 64 n. 21, 167, 187
Arnold, Archbishop of Cologne, 52–53
Arnold, Archbishop of Mainz, 71–72
Arnold, Archbishop of Trier, 89–90, 92
Arnold, Superior of St. Andrew, 25 n. 27, 93
artes dictaminis, 9
ass, 71, 140, 158, 184, 188
Augsburg, 130
Averbode, 131–33

Baal, 10, 13, 60–62
Balaam, 117, 184
Bamberg, 15, 93–95, 134, 139
Barbarossa. *See* Frederick I
Bassum, 35–36, 48–49, 69, 143
bear, 19, 34, 164, 187
Beauvais, 99–100
Bellevaux, 152–53
Benedict, St., 17, 120, 130 n. 4, 172 n. 8, 214
Benedictine, 5, 36 n. 3, 155 n. 2, 181

Bermersheim, 5
Bernard of Clairvaux, 5, 8, 13, 17, 27, 29–31, 132, 142 n. 1, 179
Bernard of St. Clement, 17, 39
Bernard Silvestris, 32
Berthold, 146
bestiary, 64 n. 22, 142 n. 2
Bethany, 152–53
Bingen, 69, 77
Bishopsberg, 144
Boethius, 76
Bonn, 145
Brabant, 133 n. 1
Brauweiler, 10, 16, 147–48
Breakspear, Nicholas. *See* Hadrian IV
Bremen, 47–51
Burchard of Bellevaux, 153 n. 1
Burgundy, 152
Busendorf, 155–56

Cain, 60
calf, 45, 154, 158, 183, 185–87
Calixtus III, 11, 64 n. 18
Canaan, 62
Cathar, 13–14, 17, 54–55, 64 n. 9, 65 n. 29
Catharism, 13
Causae et curae, 130 n. 3
Cherlieu, 152–53
Christian de Buch, Archbishop of Mainz, 12, 25 n. 27, 80, 82–83
Cicero, 7
Cistercian, 32, 93, 132, 153 n. 1, 155 n. 2, 178–79, 181–82, 197
Clairefontaine, 152–53
Clairvaux, 5, 17, 27, 31, 142 n. 1
Clement III, 10
Clusin, 157
Cologne, 25 n. 27, 46, 52–55, 63, 65–66, 68, 80–81, 93
Concordat of Worms, 11
Conrad, Archbishop of Mainz, 12, 73–75, 82 n. 1
Conrad, Bishop of Worms, 117–18
Conrad III, 17, 93
Constable, 9–10, 24 n. 7
Constance, 102–4
conversi, 182, 186, 191 n. 6. *See also* lay-brothers

Cosmographia, 32
Crusade, 13, 29 n. 3

Daniel, Bishop of Prague, 106–7
Daniel, prophet, 185
David, 77, 123, 136, 158, 180
De Musica, 76
De Natura Deorum, 7
De operatione Dei, 24 n. 3
De Planctu Naturae, 63 n. 2
devil, 10, 22, 25 n. 20, 28, 33, 39–40, 42, 45, 56, 58–62, 64, 73, 78, 89, 91, 97–98, 108, 119, 126 n. 2, 129, 140, 150, 156, 168, 171, 174, 177, 181, 184, 186, 196–97
Dialogues, 148 n. 2
Dimo, Prior of Bamberg, 15, 136
Disibod, St., 7, 159–62, 166
Disibod, St., monastery of, 5, 29 n. 6, 33 n. 1, 45–47, 49 n. 2, 158–59, 162–63, 165–67, 172–73, 176–77
Douay, 23
Dronke, Peter, 7, 25 n. 16, 29 n. 4, 32, 35–36, 39 n. 1, 76, 111 n. 5, 130 n. 3

eagle, 19, 28, 34, 105, 144, 155–56, 169, 174–75, 183, 185, 187, 190–91, 197
Eberbach, 26 n. 37, 178–80, 182
Eberhard, Abbot of Eberbach, 179
Eberhard, Archbishop of Salzburg, 14, 15, 84–85
Eberhard, Bishop of Bamberg, 93–95, 98 n. 1
Ebrach, 191–92, 197–98
Eden, 7, 30 n. 8. *See also* Paradise
Elijah, 64 n. 14
Empire, Holy Roman, 10–12, 46 n. 1, 172 n. 5
eucharist, 119, 200
Eucharius, 89, 92
Eugenius III, Pope, 5, 17–19, 30–37, 39, 41, 48, 111 n. 5, 200–201
Eve, 61, 175 n. 2, 194, 205
excommunication, 4, 10, 12, 72 n. 1, 80–81, 83, 207
exorcism, 10, 148–49, 151
Ezechiel, 40 n. 1, 183, 186

four living creatures, 183–84
Frederick I, Barbarossa, 11–12, 17, 22, 34 n. 1, 36, 39–41, 46, 54 n. 1, 64 n. 18, 72–73, 80, 82 n. 1, 84–85, 93, 102, 104, 106, 112–13, 191–92

garden, 4, 6–8, 15–16, 19, 30 n. 8, 43 n. 1, 59, 68, 104, 114, 137–38, 142, 155, 160–61, 187, 195
Gebeno of Eberbach, 18–19, 26 n. 37
Gedolphus, Abbot of Brauweiler, 10, 16, 147–48, 151
George, St., 157
Gerhoch of Reichersberg, 94
German, 12, 28–29, 84 n. 2, 205
Germany, 10, 12, 39, 132
Gero, Bishop of Halberstadt, 100
Gertrude von Stahleck, 93–94, 141–42
Gilbert of Poitiers, 32
Glossa ordinaria, 64 n. 21, 155 n. 1
gnostic, 13
goat, 91, 168, 187–88
Godfrey, Archbishop of Trier, 11
Godfrey, Bishop of Utrecht, 114, 115, 116
Godfrey, Monk at Alpirsbach, 120–21
Goliath, 136
Gottfried, 45–46
Gregory I, Pope, 124, 148 n. 2
Gregory of St. Angeli, Cardinal, 17, 39
Gregory VII, Pope, 11
Guibert of Gembloux, 17, 19, 29 n. 5, 45, 54 n. 1
Guido of Cherlieu, 153 n. 1
Guillelmus of Bethany, 153 n. 1
Gunther, Bishop of Speyer, 112–13

Hadrian IV, Pope, 20, 44
hart, 48, 114, 141, 170, 195
Hartwig, Archbishop of Bremen, 18, 47–51
Heinrich, Archbishop of Mainz, 5, 18, 33 n. 1, 35–36, 40–41, 69, 70, 71, 72 n. 1, 159 n. 1

Heinrich, Bishop of Liège, 104–5
Helengerus, Abbot of St. Disibod, 45–46, 162–66
Helmrich, Abbot of St. Michael, 134
Henneberg, Count of. *See* Gunther
Henry IV, 10–11, 13, 65 n. 25, 172 n.5
Henry, Bishop of Beauvais, 99–100
heresy, 13, 24 n. 14, 28
Hermann, Bishop of Constance, 102–4
Hermann, Dean of the Church of the Holy Apostles in Cologne, 80
Hermann von Stahleck, Count, 49, 93, 205
Hezekiah, 110
Hildebert, father of H., 5
Hillinus, Archbishop of Trier, 13, 86–88
Holy Hunt, 64 n. 22. *See also* unicorn
hortus conclusus, 4

Ingelheim, 12
Innocent III, Pope, 13
instruments, 4, 77–79, 206. *See also* music
interdict, 4, 12, 44, 76, 79 n. 1, 82, 206. *See also* excommunication
Isaac, 49
Israel, 61, 145, 174

Jacob, 49, 115, 149–50, 184
Jeremiah, 40 n. 1
Jerusalem, 14, 47–48, 101–2, 112 n. 3, 114, 118–19, 138, 158, 162, 190
Jews, 61, 62, 63
John, St., 50, 183, 191 n. 1
Jutta of Sponheim, 5–6, 173 n. 1

Klaes, Monika, 16, 148 n. 1
Kuno, Abbot of Disibod, 5, 49, 158–59, 162, 164 n. 1

Latin, 5–7, 15, 19–21, 23, 29 n. 5, 43–44, 73 n. 1, 82 n. 4, 110 n. 2, 151 n. 5, 194 n. 4
lay-brotherhood, 181

lay-brothers, 181–83, 187, 191 n. 6
lay investiture, 11
Liber divinorum operum, 19, 25 n. 20, 98 n. 2, 138 n. 3
Liber vitae meritorum, 110 n. 3
lion, 44, 123, 183, 185–87, 191 n. 1
Living Light, 4, 7, 14, 23, 29 n. 6, 32–33, 38, 51, 53, 62, 70, 72, 77, 100, 104–5, 111, 121, 125, 130, 147, 181, 197. *See also* Secret Light; Serene Light; True Light
Lucan, 7
Lucifer, 15, 76, 167
Lucius III, Pope, 24 n. 12
Luke, 191 n. 1

Magdalene, Mary, 53, 83, 122, 130, 190–91
Magdeburg, 40 n. 2
Mainz, 5, 17, 25 n. 27, 72 n. 1, 76, 79–81, 83–84, 101, 106
Mark, St., 191 n. 1
Martha, 130
Mary, the Holy Virgin, 7–8, 23, 28, 30 n. 10, 61, 64 n. 22, 68, 77, 79, 81–82, 142, 158 n. 1, 167–69, 182, 186, 193, 198, 200, 215
Mass, 76, 149
Matthew, 191 n. 1
Mechthild, mother of H., 5
Melchisedech, 49, 75, 149–50, 197, 212
Michael's, St., Bamberg, 134, 139
monastic, 127, 134, 163, 169–70, 181, 185
Morard, Monk, 176–77
Moses, 55–56, 58, 61, 63, 64 n. 7, 89, 149, 167–68, 170, 174–75, 187, 197
music, 4, 6–7, 76, 78, 110 n. 3, 159, 207
Mystic Light, 198. *See also* Living Light

Nebuchadnezzar, 71
Newman, Barbara, 15, 19, 55, 65 n. 24, 98 n. 2, 162 n. 1, 172 n. 5
Noah, 55–57, 61, 63–64, 107, 149–50, 167–68, 187

Odo of Soissons, also of Paris, 25 n. 27, 108–11
Origen, 7
ox, 128, 140, 187–88, 191 n. 1

Paradise, 3–4, 35, 60, 68, 74 n. 1, 76–79, 129, 197. *See also* Eden
Pastor Hermas, 39 n. 1
Paul, the Apostle, 36 n. 2, 66, 90, 127–28, 132, 135, 208
Peter, St., 24 n. 11, 127
Pharsalia, 7
Philip of Heinsberg, Archbishop of Cologne, 12, 25 n. 27, 53–54, 65–66, 68, 82 n. 3
Physica, 65 n. 22
Physiologus, 64 n. 22
Pitra, 16
prodigal son, 69, 98, 142, 154

Quaestiones Naturales, 7

Regula pastoralis, 124 n. 1
Rheims, 99
Rheims, Council of, 111 n. 5
Richard de Bury, 23
Richardis von Stade, 10, 18, 35, 47–51, 69–70, 143
Richardis von Stade, Margravine, 25 n. 31, 35 n. 2, 47–48
Riesencodex, 16
Romans, 24 n. 12, 44
Rome, 12, 25 n. 27, 40, 42, 79 n. 1, 81–82
Rudeger, 119, 200–201
Rule, Benedictine, 17, 35, 130 n. 4, 170–72, 214
Rupert, St., monastery of, 3, 12, 35–36, 47–50, 52–53, 69, 71, 74, 79 n. 1, 84–85, 89–90, 93–94, 99, 101–2, 104, 106, 113, 115, 117–18, 123, 125, 139, 145, 158–59, 165, 176, 192
Ruthard, Abbot of Eberbach, 178

Sadducees, 63
Salzburg, 84–85
Samson, 194
schism, 12, 13, 30 n. 7, 45–46, 54 n. 1, 64 n. 18, 84, 114, 125

Scivias, 4–5, 7, 14, 19, 24–25, 29–33, 35–36, 38–39, 43–44, 48–49, 52, 64–65, 67 n. 1, 85, 110 n. 3, 126 n. 2, 138 n. 2, 143 n. 1, 172 n. 6, 194 n. 2
Secret Light, 131. *See also* Living Light
Seneca, 7
Serene Light, 114, 119, 134, 178. *See also* Living Light
Sigewize, 90 n. 2, 148 n. 3
Simon Magus, 24 n. 11
simony, 11, 48–49, 51, 70
Solomon, 194
Sophia, Abbess of Altwick, 123–24
Speculum futurorum temporum, 26 n. 37
Symphonia, 30 n. 9, 110 n. 3, 155 n. 2, 162 n. 1, 191 n. 4, 205, 208
Synod of Trier, 5, 31, 33, 87 n. 1, 159 n. 1

Tengswich, 9, 20, 127–28, 191 n. 7
transubstantiation, 119
Trier, 5, 11, 31, 33, 86–87, 89, 159 n. 1
Trinity, 50, 61, 95
True Light, 66, 73, 75–76, 81, 89, 91, 95, 104, 106, 111. *See also* Living Light

Udalric, Canon, 130–31
unicorn, 61, 64 n. 22, 167–68, 215
University of Paris, 109–10
Usus conversorum, 182 n. 2
Utrecht, 123

Van Acker, Lieven, 9–10, 17–18, 25, 43 n. 3, 52, 64–65, 82 n. 3, 111 n. 4, 115 n. 1, 119 n. 1, 134, 136 n. 1, 138 n. 1, 153 n. 1, 162, 171 n. 1, 177 n. 1, 182 n. 1, 198 n. 1, 204, 206, 208, 210
Venice, 82 n. 1
Verdun, 117
Virgin. *See* Mary, the Holy Virgin
Vita Hildegardis, 5–6, 16, 24 n. 1, 29 n. 4, 35 n. 2, 43 n. 5, 45, 80 n. 3, 87 n. 2, 112 n. 1, 148, 150–52, 172 n. 5
Viterbo, 12
Volmar, 5–7, 19, 24 n. 3, 29 n. 6, 45

Wechterswinkel, 93
Wezelinus, 46, 90 n.1
Widukind, 40 n. 2
William of Conches, 32
winepress, 28, 94, 171, 175
Wolfard, Abbot, 119
Worms, 11, 117, 118